Gilles Deleuze's
Difference and Repetition

For Alice, Jim and Alice

Gilles Deleuze's *Difference and Repetition:* a Critical Introduction and Guide

JAMES WILLIAMS

EDINBURGH
University Press

© James Williams, 2003

Edinburgh University Press Ltd
22 George Square, Edinburgh

Typeset in ITC–New Baskerville
by TechBooks, and
printed and bound in Great Britain by
Antony Rowe Ltd, Chippenham, Wilts

A CIP record for this book is available from
the British Library

ISBN 0 7486 1817 1 (hardback)
ISBN 0 7486 1818 X (paperback)

The right of James Williams
to be identified as author of this work
has been asserted in accordance with
the Copyright, Designs and Patents Act 1988.

Contents

Abbreviations   vii
Acknowledgements   viii

Chapter 1 **Introduction**   **1**
Deleuze's masterwork   1
Deleuzian principles   4
Virtual and actual   7
Difference and repetition   11
Passive syntheses   13
Dialectics   17
Reading *Difference and Repetition*   22

Chapter 2 **Outside Repetition, Generality and Laws**   **25**
The simulacrum   25
Repetition and generality   31
Repetition and law   34
Repetition and concepts   37
Tragedy   44
Freud and masks   46
Signs and the essence of repetition   49

Chapter 3 **Difference**   **55**
Difference in itself   55
Aristotle   59
Deleuze's ontology   63
Hegel and Leibniz   69
Difference as experiment and experience   75
Plato   79

Contents

Chapter 4	**Repetition**	**84**
	Repetition for itself	84
	First synthesis of time	86
	Second synthesis of time	93
	Third synthesis of time	98
	Freud and passive syntheses	106
Chapter 5	**Against Common Sense**	**111**
	The image of thought	111
	Good will	114
	Kant, Descartes and recognition	117
	Representation	120
	Error and illusion	124
	Propositions and sense	126
	Questions	129
	Dialectics, problems and Ideas	131
	Learning	135
Chapter 6	**What is an Idea?**	**138**
	The problem of determination	138
	Ideas as multiplicities	143
	The Necessity of Ideas	150
	How to act	157
	Determination and groundlessness	161
Chapter 7	**What is Reality?**	**165**
	Science and significance	165
	Explanation	168
	Depth and space	171
	Intensity	178
	The individual	185
	Individuals and species	189
Chapter 8	**Conclusion: Beyond the Self**	**197**
	Reality	197
	The self and the subject	202
	Others	206
	Bibliography	211
	Index	215

Abbreviations

In the text, all references to passages from *Difference and Repetition* will be abbreviated as DR. Page references are given for the French original and for the English translation. The second page reference is to Gilles Deleuze's *Différence et répétition* (Paris: Presses Universitaires de France, 1968) and the first page reference is to Paul Patton's translation, *Difference and Repetition* (New York: Columbia University Press, 1994; London: Athlone, 1994). So a typical reference will be '(DR, pp. 21, 22)'. Some translations have been modified for reasons of clarity, accuracy or philosophical consistency and, where this is substantial, the changes are indicated and explained.

Acknowledgements

Many friends and colleagues have helped improve this book through generous help, debate and critical questions. I would like to thank Keith Ansell Pearson, Mike Wheeler, Aude Pichon, Robin Durie, Jenny Kermally, Livvy Williams, Michael Stewart, Rachel Jones, John Protevi, Caroline Hippisley, Andrew Benjamin, Lily Forrester, Tim Chappell and Nicholas Davey for their support and inspiration. Versions of chapters from the book were given to the Society for European Philosophy in Cork, to the British Society for Phenomenology in Oxford and to the Philosophy Research Seminar in Dundee. Graduate and undergraduate classes and supervisees gave invaluable feedback on the manuscript. My thanks goes to them for their help and patience in ironing out obscurities. Obviously, any errors that remain are nobody's fault but mine.

Claire – this book would not have happened without your love.

1

Introduction

DELEUZE'S MASTERWORK

Gilles Deleuze's *Difference and Repetition* was first published in French in 1968. It is nothing less than a revolution in philosophy and stands out as one of the great philosophical works of the twentieth century. As such, it shifts our idea of philosophy by introducing new methods and concepts and by revaluing older ones. Despite this revolution, it is still possible to situate the book's historical significance in terms of the line of other great works it adds to, reacts against and prolongs; these include, the works of Plato, Descartes, Spinoza, Leibniz, Kant, Hegel, Nietzsche, Bergson, Heidegger and Sartre.

Deleuze's outstanding achievement lies in the comprehensive and yet rigorous innovation *Difference and Repetition* implies for philosophical accounts of the structure of reality. The innovation extends to new ideas about values and action, responding to an original sense of life in terms of this new structure. The innovation is as much about how to live and how to create as it is about a philosophical view of the world. Deleuze is not working on a subsection of philosophy defined by an earlier moment, in the way, for example, some research projects can be described as Cartesian, even though they may have original discoveries of their own to impart. Instead, earlier philosophical structures and the worlds that they imply are profoundly shaken by *Difference and Repetition*.

As well as introducing the book through a systematic reading, I will show that this revolution has a philosophical legitimacy in terms of strength of methodological and conceptual invention

1

and in terms of the validity of the arguments that allow for a departure from preceding positions. I will also argue that the new arguments and methods of the philosophy call for strong critical reactions leading to a finely balanced debate on the validity of Deleuze's work. This focus on argument and validity is an invaluable tool for understanding *Difference and Repetition*. Like most works of great philosophical originality, the book is as difficult as it is important. On a first reading it can defy comprehension, to the point of appearing wilfully obstructive. Yet, powerful arguments and exciting ideas underlie the murky surface.

The appeal to arguments and to validity are essential traditional approaches to works of philosophy. It would be an error, though, to think that criteria for truth and validity are independent of Deleuze's masterwork. On the contrary, he puts forward and defends ideas about truth and thinking against the association of philosophical truth with logical validity and coherence. For him, truth is a matter of irresolvable problems. The greatest truths are those expressing those problems in all their aspects and applications, avoiding the dangerous illusions of false simple solutions. [True thinking is to respond to problems in new ways, to re-invigorate life and thought through the problems that give rise to them] 'What is essential is that there occurs at the heart of problems a genesis of truth, a production of the true in thought.' (DR, pp. 162, 210) But, in order to do justice to these demanding ideas, it is important to be able to understand the arguments that support them. This critical introduction and guide seeks to help this understanding but, in arriving at a better sense of Deleuze's text, it also seeks to invite the thought that truth and validity must now be reconsidered.

Difference and Repetition is not only significant for the development of the history of philosophy. It is also the keystone for Deleuze's work as a whole. It marks a shift from his original, offbeat and highly influential studies of other philosophers to a full account of the specifically Deleuzian ideas that gave those books their innovative flavour and sense of philosophical significance. *Difference and Repetition* brings to fruition ideas first glimpsed in *Empiricism and Subjectivity. An Essay on Human Nature According to Hume* (first published in 1953), *Nietzsche and Philosophy* (1962), *Kant's Critical Philosophy* (1963), *Bergsonism* (1966). That account is then projected forward in the concepts developed in Deleuze's more practical, interdisciplinary, works: *Anti-Œdipus* (1972), *Kafka* (1975), *A Thousand Plateaus* (1980) and, in 1991, *What is Philosophy?*

(all written with Félix Guattari). It is also important for a full understanding of the two important books on cinema, *The Image-Movement, Cinema 1* (1983) and *The Image-Time, Cinema 2* (1985) as well as for the later and even looser historical works, *The Fold (Leibniz and the Baroque)* (1988) and *Foucault* (1986).

Finally, two works are contemporaneous with *Difference and Repetition* – *Spinoza and the Problem of Expression* (1969) and *The Logic of Sense* (1969). The former lays the ground for some of the most important arguments in *Difference and Repetition* and can be seen as part of the preparatory historical works. The work done there on Spinoza's synthetic method and on the concept of expression is all important. *The Logic of Sense* develops key concepts and ideas from *Difference and Repetition* in the fields of ethics, philosophy of language, philosophy of the event and psychoanalysis. Its development of the concept of sense is essential for a full understanding of the crucial concepts of the event and of signs from *Difference and Repetition.*

Infamously, Michel Foucault, a friend and inspiration to Deleuze, once asked in jest whether the twentieth century would be called Deleuzian. Given Deleuze's opposition to the cult of the origin, to the dominance of the human self in the definition of values and to the limitation of thought to epochs, this was an ironic joke, designed to amuse and tease Deleuze and to provoke his readers. Yet Foucault's mock prediction is turning out to be accurate both in terms of applications of Deleuze's philosophy and, with greater delay, in terms of its influence on the development of philosophy as a discipline. His philosophy has already had and will continue to have a growing influence on the practical ways in which we study and react critically to the many disciplines, systems and habits of thought that dominate our lives. Researchers in as diverse subjects as literature, philosophy of science, biology, art, cinema and politics are carving out new ways of thinking that can be rightly named Deleuzian. The same is true of the philosophical reflection that guides that research, even if the line between research and practice has blurred and may blur further after his work.

Difference and Repetition is important in understanding this change in practices but no more so than Deleuze's other works, except in terms of questions concerning the claims to lasting truth of the change. In the book, we are given principles and structures that teach us to think in a new way. New methods for thought are planned carefully alongside the perspectives they imply for our most important philosophical concepts: time, space, idea, sensation, reality, individuality. Concepts are introduced to the pantheon and lesser ones are elevated: difference, repetition, synthesis, virtual. The scope of these innovations makes the work particularly difficult and dense. This has led early works on Deleuze to channel enthusiasm for the practical direction of his work into the careful explanation of these concepts. This is a necessary moment but one that must remain stunted, even on its own terms. A full understanding of philosophical revolutions lies in a grasp of the *critical* relation of the main terms of that revolution to what they stand against. What are their claims to truth? What is the validity of the arguments that these stand upon? How do these claims and arguments change and respond to our definitions of truth and validity?

DELEUZIAN PRINCIPLES

It is perhaps incautious to speak of difficulty at the outset, as when the fateful words 'the route is very complicated' are uttered to the lost tourist. So what follows is an introductory and somewhat simplified account of the main characteristics of Deleuze's methods and concepts. This simplification suspends critical impulses in favour of exposition. These return later and must form the mainstay of any deep approach to Deleuze's difficult metaphysics and to its profound resistance to common sense and to the association of reality with representations based on the empirical sciences. *Difference and Repetition* searches for new ways of understanding the meaning and significance of methods in philosophy. It also searches for new methods that respond to this understanding. In particular, his innovations apply to some of the most familiar forms of philosophical thought: creation, learning, critique and the construction of methods itself.

Like all great works of philosophy, the book moves in a positive and necessary circle where its discoveries are applied to itself. He seeks to answer the questions: 'How do we move forward best?'; 'How do we learn best?'; 'What is critique and what should be criticised?'; and 'How should we give structure to our thoughts and acts?'. The common thread to all his answers lies in a series of principles, neither laws nor rules, but ways of handling the complicated structure of things best. In this sense, principles accord with the following distinction between flexible principles, the universal claims of laws and the categorical form of rules. The *principle* 'It is best not to take important statements on trust' responds to a view of the world where the *law* 'Humans will lie where they see an advantage in it' may hold and where the *rule* 'Always trust authority' often lends to disaster.

Two principles dominate *Difference and Repetition*. They are in tension with one another. This is one of the reasons Deleuze has to deal in principles rather than laws, where a contradiction would have to be resolved. Each law should be followed but principles can be balanced against one another. The first principle of thought, or of reason, is [It is best for our actions to connect with all the things that have brought them about and that they can bring about] Later in this book I will show how, according to Deleuze, the genesis of something is in principle connected to all things that can bring about change. This means that the principle becomes Connect with everything. However, the second principle It is best to select our thoughts so that everything is left behind or, in a shorter version, Forget everything, implies a problem in following the first. It seems to counsel us to go against completeness, indeed, to move away from things in general. This is as if a philosopher encouraged us to leave behind all possessions, whilst also encouraging us to taste all things.

How can we remain pure and chaste whilst also possessing objects and currencies, in order to take pleasure in what they afford? The solution to this apparent contradiction lies in the terms 'us' and 'our' and in a link drawn between connecting and forgetting. The principles apply to individuals, where an individual is a perspective on the whole of reality, something that is connected in a singular way to the whole of reality (*You, an animal, anything capable of sensations that challenge its identity is the world but only from a perspective.*). Through thoughts, sensations and acts, individuals are irrevocably part of reality, to the point where it makes sense, from a Deleuzian point of view, to say that there is a different reality with each individual.

But that reality is ever changing and the challenge is how to live best with that change (*How will you respond to the changes in your world?*). This constant alteration means that it is a mistake to want to hold on to everything. [Individuals must find ways of connecting well but the only way of doing this is by forgetting.] To connect and to discard are joint actions – we cannot do well at one without doing well in the other. Deleuze's insight is, then, that tasting must be an ephemeral thing, at least at the level of actual possessions, whether they may be identifiable things or ideas – including our selves and our sense of acting as a free subject.

However, this simple version and explanation of his principles introduces a series of ideas that may later lead to misunderstandings because it couches Deleuze's work in a non-technical language. It makes sense to speak of individuals, things and everything when we think about principles but, in his philosophy, this does not mean that the individuals are necessarily well defined human individuals. On the contrary, the individual is a thing where thought takes place as an event but not necessarily the conscious thought of a human being. The individual is a take on the whole of reality, where reality is not restricted to actual things that we can show or identify in the world. The individual is, rather, a series of processes that connect actual things, thoughts and sensations to the pure intensities and ideas implied by them. *Why did such jealousy burst in me then? Why did it so exceed the facts? What did it signify for me (pure ideas)? Where did its power come from (pure intensities)?*

When you stand, daydreaming, looking out over your favourite land- or cityscape, or staring into another's eyes or flesh, or allowing your body to become an automaton through repeated work and exercise, allowing thought and sensation to drift through you, you are closer to Deleuze's idea of the individual than when you squeeze your head in your hand, reflect and consciously toil with a problem. An individual is not a self-conscious 'I', it is a location where thoughts may take place. It may take conscious decisions, played out in actual identifiable situations, to get you to your best daydream, to moments when you are 'sent' or 'in the zone'. You may be able to reflect back on it. But the conscious preparatory and self-analytical thoughts are not the daydream or the creative flow of thoughts and acts – think of the sense of loss when you snap out of a dream or out of creative inspiration. *I can't believe I did not turn off the phone . . .* This view of thought as independent of consciousness breaks down the difference between humans and other things. For Deleuze, the evolution of a line of animals or plants or rock formation can also be said to express ideas.

Furthermore, in the principle of connecting with everything, things must not be identified with actual physical things and fixed ideas, for they are what we have to leave behind. Individuals must connect to the changes that things may undergo. We must connect to the increases and decreases that flow through us, through our thoughts and sensations, when we are in the presence of things. For example, in order to allow children (and adults) to learn about the different consistencies of the plant world, botanical gardens allow them to touch hard, sticky, prickly, spongy plants through holes in an opaque screen. The children's ideas and sensations of these properties are heightened when they cannot see the plant and where there are elements of discovery in emerging sensual contrasts. Deleuze wants us to connect to the pure variations that ideas and sensations may connect to: becoming harder, softer, pricklier, spongier. This does not necessarily imply connecting more comprehensively to more actual cactuses and coconuts. For Deleuze, the things that operate in the processes that bring us about and make us into individuals are not actual objects and the knowledge we may gain of them but the sensual variations and the variations in ideas that take place in order for actual things to gain a living significance for us.

The view put forward with Deleuze's principles is that pure variations must not be confused with actual things. In order for these variations to enrich the way we may live with them in the future, we must leave behind the urge to identify the intensity of sensations with actual things and only those things (*Why does this collection of images and things matter so much to me?*). A pure difference is transferable through very different actual things and only depends on them for its expression and not for its essence. A pure difference has to be actualised but it is not only that which becomes actualised. This realm of pure 'becomings' is what he calls the virtual and the becomings are 'intensities' and 'ideas'. According to his principles, we must connect with these pure becomings but we can only do so through actual things that capture the variation in a particular way. When the children feel the skin of the coconut, less actual sight is more connection to a virtual becoming hard, becoming hairy, becoming grainy that apply through an unlimited range of actual things (*Your head is like a coconut but less grainy.*).

VIRTUAL AND ACTUAL

Deleuze gives us new concepts to account for what exists and for reality, in particular, in his definition of reality as both the virtual and the actual. For example, a coconut is both an actual coconut and the intensities or pure becomings it expresses in the encounter with the sensations of individuals (to become hard, to become grainy, to become hairy, to quench, to nourish). In the actual coconut, there is something of all the other things that can become hard or grainy – that something is their virtual side, the common intensities they express. Importantly, Deleuze deduces the structure of the relations that hold between the virtual and actual side of real things. This structure describes reality as a dynamic relation between the virtual and the actual.

He is, therefore, committed to the reality of things that are neither actual nor identifiable. These intensities or pure becomings are necessary for the explanation of significance and sensation in the realm of actual things. Yet, they cannot belong to that realm because, if they were identifiable – that is, measurable and comparable – then sensation and significance would be secondary to external structures of measurement and value. Deleuze wants to resist such moves because he believes that true sensation and significance are a matter of incomparable events, movements that are uniquely significant to individuals (*Well, it matters to me! How could this leave you cold?*). Many of the most important arguments of *Difference and Repetition* are developed either to show the reality and necessity of intensities as a condition for significant events or to show that there are such things as virtual intensities that cannot be accounted for in terms of actual identities. Intensities are a necessary condition for explanations of why life is significant but uniquely so for each individual. As such, intensities could not be identifiable as comparable qualities of actual experiences or objects.

Despite Deleuze and Guattari's later definition of philosophy as the creation of concepts in *What is Philosophy?*, Deleuze's philosophical arguments are not only about the invention of concepts but about thinking according to principles, in the light of a structural account of what exists. The principles loosely relate creation and structure. *Because A is in the following relation to B and vice versa, it is best to follow these principles when we think and, indeed, when we invent concepts.* So what kind of structure do the principles given above react to? It is a two-sided one, rather than one of two realms – that is, it never makes full sense to speak of the virtual without the actual or the reverse. The sides involve different things – virtual ideas and intensities on the one hand, actual things on the other. Intensities form relations where they envelop or cover one another (*My jealousy has covered my love.*). These relations of envelopment bring different virtual ideas into greater clarity and obscurity (*As jealousy covered love the idea of humanity as conflict grew clearer and the idea of humanity as trusting receded into the depths.*).

Virtual ideas are relations of all pure becomings. They differ in terms of the differences in the relations between becomings – that is, in terms of which are directly connected to most others and which are directly connected only to a few. Ideal arrangements come about when pure becomings are illuminated differently by intensities as they emphasise some pure becomings at the expense of others (*The intensity that accompanied my actual jealousy made the idea of a trusting humanity impossible for me, impossible for me to actually embody.*). So, though actual things may fall into categories such as species, Deleuze claims that, as individuals, they must also be thought of as expressions of virtual intensities and ideas, in a way that cannot be fully accounted for in terms of species. Thus, the two sides of the individual, the virtual and the actual, are said to be asymmetrical. The principles that govern the formation of ideas are not the same as the causal laws governing species. Yet, an event among individuals and species implies an event among ideas. Indeed, for Deleuze, it only really makes sense to speak of events as, at the same time, virtual and actual.

Given this definition of reality, a full explanation of an event must involve a consideration of the virtual and of the actual and, more importantly, of the ways in which actual events touch on virtual events. Deleuze describes the parallels that allow us to think in terms of this 'touch'. For example, the way in which an individual resists complete insertion into a given species is by the 'individuating factors', the relations of sensations, intensities and ideas that only that individual expresses in its particular way. According to Deleuze, you are not different from other humans because you differ in this or that actual characteristic but because your thoughts and sensations, the way you change, express a different relation of intensities and, therefore, ideas (becoming hardened, becoming receptive, becoming softer). Here, we can begin to see why the concept of difference is so important for *Difference and Repetition*. It is because he wants to distinguish actual differences, defined by characteristics that are ruled by the possibility of negation (*not-kind-hearted*), from pure differences or intensities (*Becoming hardened is not not-becoming softer and each one of us expresses becoming hardened in a different way – that is, sets it in a different relation to other becomings, including becoming softer.*).

Three pages from the end of the main body of *Difference and Repetition* (pp. 259–61, 332–4), Deleuze explains this two-sided structure in relation to death, drawing a few remarks about suicide that cannot fail to remind us of his own death by suicide at the term of a long illness (Deleuze was born in Paris in 1925 and died there in 1995). Death has two faces, an actual death, the ceasing of the heartbeat or of activity in the brain, but also a series of virtual

9

deaths, the way in which our becomings lead us to change irrevocably (*As I became more hardened, the child in me died . . . as I became
older, the adult in me died and the adolescent returned.*).

So, in terms of the two central principles of connecting and
forgetting, there is an interplay between an actual death, which
we flee and see as 'accidental' and 'violent' because it cuts our existence as an actual thing, and a series of small deaths and rebirths
that dissolve the self – that is, express pure becomings in parts of
actual minds and bodies. Both sides of death are part of dying. As
we become, we die as this particular self and we move towards a
final death. But there is something revivifying in the expression
of becomings, they make a life that must end in death one that
participates in intensities (*I just had to feel the whip of sea spray one
last time.*). So the first principle guides us to our sensations, to seek
out as greater expression of intensities as possible whilst having
to live with the restriction implied by the limitation of our actual
bodies and minds – *connect.* In order to do this, without letting our
fear of actual death restrict us, we must pay heed to the second
principle and learn to forget our attachments to any particular
self and body – *forget.*

Hence the battle cry that Deleuze borrows from Spinoza 'We do
not know what our bodies are capable of' – that is, experiment with
your body and hence your mind in order to live intensely. Forget
your attachment to this particular body and mind. Deleuze goes
on to describe suicide as the attempt to bring together both faces
of death, as if there was right time and way to die. But he knows that
this is not possible – the actual death of the self never coincides
with the small deaths of an individual because the individual is not
the self:

Every death is double, and represents the cancellation of large differences
in extension as well as the liberation and swarming of little differences in
intensity . . . Suicide is an attempt to make the two incommensurable faces
correspond. However, the two sides do not meet, and every death remains
double.

(DR, pp. 259, 333)

Suicide ends the life of an actual person and, thereby, it releases
new intensities (sensations in others as intensities envelop one another in different ways) whilst cancelling others (the sensations
of pain and suffering). But this does not mean that these intensities are different and better because they take place without the
intermediary of that actual person. Suicide may both decrease

10

connections and fail to create more intense ones. Perhaps, it can be only be said to fit with Deleuze's principles when the individual life associated with an actual person has become terribly restricted in what it can express.

DIFFERENCE AND REPETITION

Deleuze wants to give us arguments against the restriction of reality to actual identifiable things. This can be seen in the insistence on a twin but not symmetrical event: a side in pure difference and a side in actual things – a virtual death and an actual one. I have used the term pure difference, as opposed to Deleuze's preferred term 'difference in itself', in order to allow for a more simple sense of the difference between the virtual and the actual: pure difference is not actual. However, in later chapters, I will return to these terms in order to understand why pure difference is only an approximate, if useful, way of understanding him. His concern is to show how actual things alter due to their relation to pure differences or, better, to difference in itself. He also wants to show that, if we are to understand how to act in such a way as to make our lives intense and individual and to understand and react to the intensity of our environments, then we must allow our thoughts and bodies to turn to intensities, to difference in itself. But pure difference, or difference in itself, can only be thought of as well determined in relation to the actual – in Deleuze's words, there is a relation of 'reciprocal determination' between the virtual and the actual.

However, he must also explain how this interaction takes place. What processes explain change on both sides of reality, in the virtual and the actual? How do the virtual and the actual relate to one another as actual things change? This is where the inseparability of the two concepts from the book's title comes into play. Things acquire an actual identity through repetition. Intensities come into relation with each other through repetition. Repetition allows us to explain the relation of virtual events to actual events and vice versa. Put simply, this means that things acquire fixity, that is, they acquire parts and hence boundaries through repetition. These parts and boundaries then allow us to see the individual as a member of a class or species. For example, the boundaries of an animal's territory come from the repeated prowling and marking of its perimeter. Or we acquire an accent from the repetition of particular intonations. Neither the actual territory nor the accent exist prior to the repetitions. Deleuze identifies this first repetition with habit. A second repetition explains recognition and its relation to memory. We come to recognise an actual thing and assign a fixed identity to it because habitual repetitions, recorded in memory, lead us to have a fixed representation of things. I recognise my territory and its fixed limits because I have a representation of it that has emerged from repetitions stored in memory (though Deleuze has a surprising and innovative account of memory that will be studied in greater depth later in this book).

Finally, a third type of repetition, albeit a profoundly counter-intuitive one, explains how things change in relation to virtual becomings, to difference in itself. The first two repetitions are, in fact, illusory when viewed as final accounts. According to Deleuze, repetition in habit and memory are only possible on a background of virtual differences. There is not only the repetition of the prowl round the territory and the memory of that prowl but a further infinite series of other repetitions that the particular territory abstracts from: the changing cycles of weather, the repeated paths of other animals, the cycle of aging of the animal, the flux of seasons, the encroachment of civilisation that beats to human and mechanical rhythms, the ebb and flow of conflicting desires and emotions, the mutation of vegetation and species. In terms of these other series, each member of any given series is not the same as the others but different – each member is an individual. That difference, the change that runs through a repeated series, cannot be thought of in terms of a description of the actual relations between the position of two members with respect to the infinite number of other series since this cannot be grasped – hence the necessity of abstraction. Neither can it be sensed in terms of specific differences without destroying the sense of continuity in the repetition. In both cases, we can only move from a repetition of the same things to a difference with no repetition, thereby, requiring abstraction once again.

For Deleuze, the condition for what we commonly understand as repetition in habit and memory is, in fact, the continuity afforded by the variation of an intensity in an idea or sensation. The marking of the same territory takes place against the background of a variation in intensities between one parade and another (becoming hot, becoming thirsty, becoming fear, becoming impotent). It is these variations that give life, understood as the first two repetitions, intensity and value, but also risk and error. We can fight against this underlying expression of these variations and hence against life: always the same route to the end (*But doctor, I'm as fit as I've ever been!*). Or we can seek to re-intensify the patterns that give consistency to our actual lives (*How can this be done differently and better? How can a changing life be given greater significance?*). The two principles given above are Deleuze's first directions for following the second option. *Vary your life so that it expresses all deep intensities or differences in themselves (connect with everything.).* But we know that the abstractions of habit and memory militate against the emergence of new sensations and hence against the expression of virtual intensities and ideas (*After the pain of separation, she built herself a protective wall of routines and safe places.*). So do not make your variation depend on representation, habit and memory. *Leave all actual things behind (forget everything.).*

At this point, the extent of the ambitions and revolutionary aims of *Difference and Repetition* come into view. It is not only a book on 'how a life is lived best', rather, it is a book that claims that pure differences are the other face of all actual things – there is no such thing as a well-defined actual life. Deleuze claims that all our representations, senses and concepts of identities are illusions (nothing fixed is real). The book provides principles for lifting those illusions and connecting best to difference in itself.

PASSIVE SYNTHESES

Up to now, I have given descriptions of what Deleuze says, rather than a critical assessment. But how do we know that his description of reality in terms of the actual and the virtual is true? What is the claim to truth of his explanation of change in terms of difference in itself and repetition 'for itself', that is, in terms of repetition against the background of pure variations or difference in itself? What is wrong with causal explanations of events? Or theistic explanations? Or causal explanations, allied to ones in terms of human free will? The first step in answering these questions lies in a further condition for the three repetitions outlined above in their relation to difference in itself. Any given actual circuit of an animal's territory or utterance in a given accent implies a *synthesis* of prior repetitions. Deleuze's account of the structure of reality depends on arguments for the necessity and universality of synthesis.

We only acquire habits by synthesising earlier members of a series in later ones. We only acquire representations in memory and in language by synthesising earlier memories that are themselves syntheses of experiences. So the concept 'chair', or our idea of

13

a chair, depends on a synthesis of prior 'experiences' of chairs (it would be better to think of these as chair-events, in order to avoid any reliance on a well-defined 'subject of the experience' or even a phenomenological intentionality). More shockingly, with respect to causal explanations based on causal relations between well-defined things, an actual individual is only a synthesis of prior individuals. That synthesis is itself continually changing with respect to other series in which it is synthesised and with respect to the pure variations it synthesises. This fluid nature of synthesis can be understood in the same way as the third repetition outlined above: any series implies an infinity of other series, where an individual member of the series stands out due to the variations in intensity it expresses. That walk that you take everyday is different each time and significant each time because it involves variations in intensities with respect to earlier and later ones and changing relations with wider series. You change with the walk and with the sensations and their intensities (*I'm getting tired of this. Will she be at the balcony this time? Is this the last time this winter?*).

For Deleuze, well-defined things are mere abstractions. Causal explanations are, at best, convenient illusions since they hide the continuous virtual syntheses that rumble on beneath a causal chain of events. This explains why the two main chapters of *Difference and Repetition*, chapters 4 and 5, are titled 'Ideal synthesis of difference' and 'Asymmetrical synthesis of the sensible'. It is because the first explains and argues for the way in which singular variations, such as becoming fear, become synthesised with others in an idea, such as the idea 'becoming fear and becoming violent'. The chapter, therefore, explains why the virtual is not chaotic with respect to that which has a propensity to be expressed in actual things. The virtual is not an undifferentiated mass of becomings but a changing mass of relations: ideas are structures of pure becomings.

Chapter 5, on the other hand, explains and argues for the way in which individuals are syntheses of virtual ideas and intensities through a reciprocal determination of the actual and the virtual. Furthermore, both chapters argue that the virtual syntheses in ideas drive actual syntheses in habit, memory or creation – *Why have becoming fear and becoming violent become so strongly linked? Because of actual repetitions. Why have these actual repetitions happened? Because they express the relation of virtual intensities. In Deleuze's usage of 'idea', they express and deepen the becoming fear and becoming violence idea.* So, from the point of view of Deleuze's search for a

new view of thought and in terms of his principles, these chapters must be seen as difficult twins: there is a reciprocal relation
between the ideal synthesis of difference and the asymmetrical
synthesis of sensibility, between virtual and actual syntheses. So
any event implies: (i) a synthesis of virtual repetitions; (ii) the
synthesis of actual repetitions (in habit and memory); and (iii) a
synthesis of the reciprocal determinations of the virtual and actual in what Deleuze calls the third synthesis. This last synthesis
corresponds to the third repetition outlined above. It leads to the
principles of connecting and forgetting. The third synthesis and
repetition connect the actual world to the intense virtual one and
overcome the tendency of the first two repetitions to stasis (*There
is no other way. We have always done it that way. You are what we say
you are.*).

But isn't there a contradiction between the notion of synthesis
and the second principle? Do we not have to build up knowledge
and plan in order to synthesise? Isn't synthesis a conscious activity
that depends on representations? Aren't the capacity to represent and self-consciousness pre-conditions for synthesis? Therefore, aren't they things that we ought not to 'forget' according to
the second principle? No. When Deleuze uses the term synthesis
he means a *passive* synthesis, that is, one that does not require
a representation of the series to be synthesised in an active consciousness. This view is relatively uncontroversial with respect to
habit, the first repetition (*I cannot explain fully how I came to be able
to do this – it just happened with practice.*). Things are more complicated with respect to the second repetition or synthesis in memory
but, here too, Deleuze claims that the representation occurs prior
to conscious activity, that is, we acquire the idea of a chair before
we turn our conscious attention to the idea or concept chair. It
is, of course, true that our decision to investigate different types
of chairs appears to be conscious but the way in which the idea is
then organised in the presence of chairs is passive. For instance,
we have many more memories than we are conscious of at a given
time or that we have been conscious of collecting (*Haven't I been
here before?*).

The third repetition or synthesis is even more resistant. Do *we*
not choose to *seek out* intensity? Aren't Deleuze's principles dependent on freedom as a ground that denies passive synthesis since
we must choose to follow principles and represent the different
possibilities they imply? No. The senses of self and of possibilities have emerged out of prior passive syntheses in habit and

memory – they cannot represent them fully to themselves. As individuals we express pure differences and intensities, but many more and differently than we can be conscious of, or can capture in representations (*You are much more than you think you are. Your conscious choice of actual possibilities does not capture what you really are as a virtual and actual event. The future can't be caught full on.*). So the third synthesis happens irrespective of conscious choices – again, there is no reason to separate plants, animals and humans on the grounds that humans are fully conscious of their becomings. So we must be very cautious in interpreting Deleuze's principles and be aware of the great difficulties, he would say the insoluble problems, they emerge out of. *It is best for our thoughts to connect with everything, but we cannot know what we connect to, it connects to us. It is best to select our thoughts so that we forget everything, including ourselves and our sense of selecting between possibilities.*

So passive synthesis allows Deleuze to explain the necessity of the three repetitions and the relation of difference to repetition. It provides a consistent ground for the principles by cancelling the pervasive philosophical and common-sense temptation to seek a grounding in consciousness. It also cancels the presupposition that the choices implied by the principles are actual identifiable possibilities that we shall be able to divide into well-defined categories (*These things will always be bad for me.*). However, this benefit comes at the price of making the principles much more problematic. We have to seek an openness to difference in itself. We have to allow passive synthesis of the third kind to occur. Rather than selecting a pure variation, an intensity, an idea, these must happen to us and make us individuals. More seriously, we have to find ways to escape the hold of our senses of self, identities and categories in order for this happening to take place. This is why Deleuze describes the third repetition as a 'dice throw', a risky act that does not know its outcome. It is also why he describes and gives value to a 'broken self' and a 'dissolved self' that underlie the self we are conscious of: 'That is why the individual in intensity finds its psychic image neither in the organisation of the self nor in the determination of species of the I, but rather in the fractured I and the dissolved self.' (DR 259, 332)

These moves, dependent on passive synthesis, return us to the critical question concerning truth and validity. Why is this account in terms of passive syntheses true? What is the nature and validity of the argument for that truth? What evidence can Deleuze give, against common sense, science and technology, that well-defined things in causal chains are merely illusions? *Don't things have bio-chemical properties that explain actual causal reactions?*

DIALECTICS

The arguments supporting Deleuze's account of the structure of virtual and actual, of difference and repetition and of the relation between the three passive syntheses take two forms. They can already be seen in the explanations I have used in the previous sections. First, Deleuze's structure grows by asking what the conditions are for a given thing. For example: 'What is the condition for change in actual things?' or 'What is the condition for the first and second type of repetition?' Second, in asking these questions, Deleuze seeks to move towards a complete account of any structure, one where no event is left unexamined with respect to its condition. In terms of classical arguments from the history of philosophy, Deleuze provides transcendental deductions, that is, arguments that deduce the form of appearance by asking what the conditions have to be for something to be given or to appear as it is. These deductions then allow us to know more about the way a given thing must appear. He also provides synthetic arguments based on a principle of reason, that is, any event must have a reason and an event is known better the more is known of its reasons, that is, its conditions. As will be seen later in the book, Deleuze provides original twists on both these forms and together they become his full method: Deleuzian dialectics.

Transcendental deductions allow Deleuze to describe the structure of virtual and actual without having to conflate the two. We do not have to have an actual experience of the condition in order to know truths about it. So we do not have to have an experience of the virtual. The event given as the starting point for a deduction can turn out to be very different from its first appearance and our common-sense views about it. This is because many of the common-sense impressions regarding what is given are not necessary for the deduction of the condition and, once that deduction has taken place, we discover many counter-intuitive truths about the given or about how we must think about its appearance given the nature of the condition. So the common-sense view of things and causality, or the demands of scientific method regarding causality and the need to think in terms of well-defined objects, can both be avoided as necessary presuppositions for a philosophical reflection on reality. The questions asked at the end of the

17

previous section, regarding the nature of objects and the validity of syntheses are, therefore, blunted by this kind of argument, if successful.

Deleuze's strange assertions concerning difference in itself and pure variations or intensities that we cannot experience depend on transcendental deductions. But how should these arguments be deployed? What events need to be explained in terms of their conditions and, more importantly, what things can we know well enough to be sure that we can deduce their conditions? Deleuze turns to Leibniz and Spinoza in order to answer these questions. Put simply, he intends to seek completeness according to a principle of reason (Leibniz) and he intends to seek understanding by giving priority to a full understanding of the conditions for a given thing over a full understanding of the thing itself (Spinoza's synthetic method). That is, a thing is known better through its conditions (Spinoza would say causes) or through what it expresses, than through an isolated examination of what it is, followed by a less secure investigation of its causes and effects. In the language set out earlier, Deleuze asks, 'What does this actual thing repeat or synthesise, in habit and memory?' and, more importantly, 'What is it driven to repeat or synthesise, in terms of intensities or difference in itself?' These questions are justified on the basis of arguments that show that the three repetitions are necessary conditions for a given thing and that thing is only thought properly, according to a principle of reason, through a complete approach to the three syntheses.

The work on conditions allows for a Deleuzian definition of reasons as the necessary conditions for a thing to appear. This puts great pressure on the work on conditions. If these do not take a form that allows for specific conditions for specific things to emerge, then he will be left with a highly sceptical philosophy that merely has some general and abstract conditions for the appearance of things that limit any further higher knowledge. Higher knowledge would apply to conditions as opposed to a merely speculative and insecure commitment to causality or other laws at the level of the things independent of how they must appear, or things in themselves. For example, if the sole condition for an appearance turns out to be that there is an abstract form of intuition that allows for any appearance and this form is the same for all appearances, then the highest reasons would be the same very thin reason for all appearances. In fact, for Deleuze, in great contrast to Kant's work in the *Critique of Pure Reason*, we will see that conditions are appearance-specific in the sense that the abstract form of conditions turns out to be that there must be specific conditions for each thing, rather than general ones for all of them. It is as if the conditions for seeing things turned out to be specific vision apparatuses for each viewer and thing, as opposed to a single form of apparatus for all viewers and viewed things (*Cézanne's 'eyes', different from Van Gogh's, different from mine, different from yours*).

In practice, Deleuze's method can be seen as guided by the principles of maximising connections defined in terms of reasons and of forgetting those things, including connections, that hinder this maximisation. These principles allow his philosophy to be seen in its widest scope. From a more theoretical point of view, concerning the method specific to the development of his own work and arguments, these principles have to be translated into a more precise conception of Deleuzian dialectics that includes the following methods:

1. Critique
2. The reciprocal search for actual and virtual conditions
3. The search for completeness in terms of reasons determined by conditions
4. The dice throw, or creative and destructive forgetting, that moves beyond what is already discovered or expressed

These methods can be seen as components of a method that allows us to express the intensities of life, of individuals, as best we can. The methods have to be seen as interdependent, that is, each one cannot be fully understood, indeed, gives a mistaken view of Deleuze's dialectics, if is it not only considered with the others but applied alongside them.

The role of critique is to ensure the passivity of the synthesis, that is, through a critique of illusions of identity we allow ourselves to become open to the expression or thought of virtual becomings and to their structural relation to actual individuals. Critique clears the way for the other methods by allowing us to divest ourselves of the strong tendency of thought to return to identity and representation. This explains why so much of *Difference and Repetition* is spent on critical work in the history of philosophy and on the methods from the history of philosophy. Deleuze seeks to undermine the strong relation between common-sense views of the world as based on fixed things (selves, objects and values) and the philosophical reliance on identity (in representation, in the concept, of the subject or object). In particular, chapter 3 and the concluding chapter of the book insist on this critical work within the history of philosophy and with respect to the sciences, allowing only rapid and somewhat mysterious allusions to the other components of Deleuze's method. Chapter 3 criticises the dominance of a particular 'image of thought' in the history of philosophy, an image based on the subjection of our differing senses (imagination, sensibility, memory and so on) to a unified self-consciousness and to its capacity to represent and reflect on representations. The conclusion goes over the many ways in which difference in itself and repetition for itself have been missed or seen as secondary to the illusions of identity that result from this dominance of representation.

The search for conditions has already been outlined above in terms of the search for the intensities that are expressed through the sensations of any actual identity. 'What are the signs of intensity here?' is the important question. This explains why Deleuze spends a lot of time on the relation between intensities or difference in itself and signs or 'dark precursors' in *Difference and Repetition* and *The Logic of Sense*. Put very simply, this is somewhat like the questions asked by someone seeking to quell or tease an unruly individual or mob when they wonder, 'What rising and falling emotions are driving this situation?' This focus on unsure signs of intensity and on precursors also explains why Deleuze puts so much weight on the concept of learning in *Difference and Repetition*. He wants to show how real learning and teaching involves a search for signs that will trigger learning as a radical change in another or in oneself, as opposed to the concepts of learning by rote or acquiring knowledge of facts and procedures associated with correct moves on those facts. This explains the relation between critique and the search for conditions. He criticises learning through the repetition of the same, in order to clear the way for learning as the triggering of intensities. The only way we move towards a complete learning is by expressing the intensities locked up in a situation in a new way (*How can I make the industrial revolution live for them?*). An interesting paradox is worth pointing out at this point. It may be that forcing someone to repeat and learn by rote is the best way of setting down signs for a more intense learning. This explains Deleuze's longstanding interest in humour in the way an overly mechanical repetition undermines the act that it repeats (*Charlie Chaplin on the assembly line in* Modern Times).

Through its repetitions, through the way it creates the new by selecting what to repeat, any individual is not only the expression of virtual intensities and ideas but also an event that alters them. Deleuze does not explain the way in which things occur repeatedly on the basis of actual relations of cause and effect (*Their brains came to associate flowers and pain as the neural pathways became more fixed.*) but on the basis of the connection between individuals and the virtual (*Her resistance to jealousy diminished its intensity and made the idea of trust live more strongly.*). So the search for conditions takes place in both directions of the construction of reality: from the virtual to the actual (what Deleuze calls 'differenciation') and from the actual to the virtual (differentiation). The use of 'from' here indicates the way in which different intensities are related in an idea as they are expressed in actual individuals – the chaos of the virtual becomes determined in this way. It also indicates the way in which a given individual comes into existence and becomes a sign for other individuals: chaotic series become determined in an individual. The search for conditions is then a search for the reciprocal determination of the virtual and the actual. It is justified by Deleuze's transcendental deductions and by his view that the complete view of a thing must be actual and virtual. Hence the third method given above: we must search for complete determination.

But what does complete mean here? We have already seen the kind of problems raised by this question in the paradox and problem that lie between the two principles of connection and forgetting and between the first and second synthesis or repetition and the third. Complete determination cannot mean knowing the thing as something fixed and well determined. A learning that moves towards complete determination cannot mean knowing something in all its parts and in terms of what species and categories it belongs to (*If you know yourself, you know yourself as dying. Know your love and lose it.*). On the contrary, if we are to move to a sense of completeness and learning that capture the virtual side of things, then it is exactly not as actual identities or fixed things. We have to learn about them and ourselves as things that are the expression of difference in itself, of pure intensities. This can only be done by the risk-laden dice throw, that is, by experimenting with ways of repeating and synthesising differently. That is why Deleuze's dialectics tempers the first three methods of critique – the critical and constructive search for conditions and completeness. It adds a creative method that is destructive of the results they arrive at. We have to forget in order to be truly complete, in order to experiment with the ways in which individuals

21

are reciprocal determinations of the actual and the virtual and the ways in which they resist representation and identity.

I have followed Deleuze in naming the conjunction of these methods a Deleuzian dialectics. This is despite the fact that the method is connected with philosophers that he is assumed to be opposed to: Hegel and Aristotle. Dialectics captures the intricate calculations and reciprocal relations that must govern thought as it works with the four sub-methods in order to emerge as an overall method. Unlike Hegel and Aristotle's dialectics, Deleuze's method cannot be seen as progressive either through a logic dependent on a movement from contradiction to synthesis or through a refinement of categories. In the first case, this is because of the demand to destroy any emergent progress or refinement, to forget it, in the risk-laden dice throw. In the second case, it is because categories are illusory from the point of view of the emergence of individuals with respect to difference in itself – no matter how refined and mobile your categories, they will not capture reality. So, though Deleuze draws a strong distinction between Nietzsche's affirmation and Hegel dialectics, in his *Nietzsche and Philosophy*, this dialectics, as contradiction and negation, is not the destructive and creative one of Deleuzian dialectics.

READING DIFFERENCE AND REPETITION

How should we read *Difference and Repetition*? The most important point, in answering this question, is to realise that the book is an application of the methods it explains and justifies. *Difference and Repetition* is a series of varying repetitions. These involve a critical method against representation, a learning of the reciprocal determination of actual individuals and virtual intensities, a search for completeness and a chance-driven experimentation with new concepts and ways of expressing intensities. This experimentation deliberately complicates the outcomes of the first three methods. In each of these, the book also involves justifications for the methods, through transcendental deductions and arguments based on the principle of reason as applied to a synthetic method. So the book is a product of Deleuzian dialectics – an intricate combination of critique, synthesis with a view to completion and destructive creativity.

We are presented with a complicated work, not only in the sense that it does not proceed linearly, building on secure foundations and then proceeding, secure step by secure step, upwards to a conclusion, but in the sense of a work that undermines its partial achievements with a view to more complete ones. This means that a reading that takes any specific section of the book as the last word on a given matter (for example, by concluding that Deleuze is, above all, a critical philosopher) is likely to miss the significant input of other methods and sections of the book on that section. In practice, this kind of reductive reading is rather difficult and unsatisfactory anyway, since each section and chapter of *Difference and Repetition* involves elements from later sections and chapters and from all his methods. To use an expression favoured by Deleuze when he explains how a member of a repeated series harks back to and looks forward to other members, each section of the book is a 'contraction' of the rest of the book. That is, each section develops others to lesser or greater degrees of density. So each section is the complete book, but more or less clear (and obscure) on each aspect. In particular, this contraction into greater clarity or obscurity demands that similar points are made very differently in terms of style and context throughout the book. *The book is, therefore, like the world, each living thing – each individual – is a contraction of the world, a connection with all of the world. But it is individual through the way it connects by forgetting different perspectives on the world, by the way it selects a world.*

The importance of contraction means that the rather standard conclusion to the book is to be treated with considerable suspicion. The concept of finally summing up a given application of Deleuze's method runs counter to its spirit – it cannot be securely summed up in terms of specific conclusions about actual matters of fact. In order to respond to this problem, I have chosen to introduce the book through a study of principles, structures and methods. Specific conclusions about this or that real thing or event or faculty are always open to a different repetition, one that must take account of those conclusions but that must risk them anew in a differing repetition (*How can these conclusions be intensified again?*). The continuity of the book and of Deleuze's philosophy, the way it hangs together, is methodological and structural rather than a matter of knowledge or specific findings about things. This mirrors his views regarding learning set out above. In this context, his comment in the preface that readers need only read the conclusion are a sign of Deleuze's humour and irony – frequently encountered traps in *Difference and Repetition*. Readers need only read any part of the book, since each is a contraction of the others, but, if they read that part as the final word, then they will have fatally missed the point.

However, these views concerning the priority of methods over actual facts are controversial and must be approached critically. *Difference and Repetition* spends a lot of time on topics in the sciences, social sciences and the arts. This time has to be viewed as justified in terms of inspiration, illustration and exemplification rather than as a core aspect of Deleuze's argument or philosophical methods and structure. He does not touch on biology, literature, mathematics, psychology or linguistics in order to validate the philosophy, either in terms of sources of truth, justification through successful applications or as a source of correct methodology. His recourse to other disciplines does not depend on the foundational validity of specific scientific discoveries, mathematical deductions or the relative value of art-works.

On the contrary, his turn to them is in terms of points of interest – the science and art-works give rise to a set of ideas and illustrate them. So, if it appears that Deleuze is critical of a given theory or work in another discipline, it is solely on the grounds that it appears to depart from his philosophically justified principles, methods and structures. The critique is not on the grounds of a deeper scientific or artistic understanding or sense – that is for scientists and artists. There is a temptation to view him as arguing for a philosophy–science–arts hybrid that overcomes the specificity of each. To give into it is a mistake, since it commits us to the theory that the hybrid, general thinker, covering scores of topics, has a better grasp of truth, validity and value than the individual specialist. Deleuze's philosophy embraces the singularity of each individual and individual discipline as places for creative thought but it advocates a structure and series of principles for the extension of that thought to a thought about the lives and values of individuals.

2

Outside Repetition, Generality and Laws

THE SIMULACRUM

In the preface to *Difference and Repetition*, Deleuze sets his work in the context of contemporary philosophical concerns. He gives initial definitions of key terms, as well as setting down the main topics and aims. In some ways this clarity is deceptive since these opening remarks will be greatly complicated later in the book and later in the preface. It is also deceptive since the preface says nothing directly about the philosophical principles, methods and arguments that the book depends upon. It is a mistake, therefore, to take his opening remarks at face value. The preface is significant as much for what it hides as for what it reveals. Despite these reservations, three areas of interest stand out: the sense of the book's position in the history of philosophy; the way in which it responds to modern life; and how it contributes to the movement towards a new style of writing and thought in philosophy.

Deleuze situates his work in the philosophical context of the turn to difference that gathers pace through the twentieth century. He singles out Heidegger as an example of this turn. This is important because it allows us to think of Deleuze alongside other thinkers of difference influenced by the German thinker, most notably Jacques Derrida. If we are to reflect on the links and differences between Deleuzian dialectics and deconstruction, *Difference and Repetition* will be a central work. Deleuze's encounter with Heidegger occurs sporadically through his books but here it is at its most sustained, unlike the more aggressive remarks in *Foucault* or the more ironic and humorous ones in *Essays Critical and*

Clinical. Broadly, the contrast between Deleuze and Derrida lies in the former's preparedness to adopt systematic forms, arguments and concepts from the history of philosophy and then to cast them, still fully functional, in a new and disruptive setting. The latter shies away from this inclusive approach, preferring to undermine historical arguments from the outset and replacing them with a much looser methodological framework. Deleuze offers us principles and methods for a philosophy of difference, whereas Derrida offers us an ethos and style of writing about difference explicitly resistant to the emergence of principles or methods.

These oppositions notwithstanding, the common threads in this new philosophy of difference are a reaction against the dominance of representation and, hence, of identity in the history of philosophy and against the relegation of difference to a negative position with respect to identity. Deleuze speaks of a generalised anti-Hegelianism as a way of characterising this philosophy. This is the first trap of the book. The new turn to difference in itself is opposed to a definition of difference as the way in which self-identical things differ (*Spot five differences between the two pictures...*). It is also opposed to a view of difference as that which can be overcome (*The opposition of man and woman is overcome in the concept of humanity.*). But these characteristics can only be attributed to the most crude reading of Hegel. What we find later in *Difference and Repetition* and, indeed, in Derrida's works, such as *Margins of Philosophy*, is that Hegel must not be viewed as having a position that can be simply dismissed as wrong in this way. In fact, this notion of wrongness, wrong as opposed to right and eliminable in favour of right, does not belong in deconstruction or Deleuze's dialectics.

The clue to the proper role of the remarks on Hegel lies in Deleuze's description of the contemporary shift to difference in terms of signs and as a spirit of the times. Anti-Hegelianism and the turn to difference are only signs that must be thought through. *Difference and Repetition* is a site where that thinking takes place – Heidegger's work on ontological difference is another. Neither should be identified with a crude opposition to representation or to definitions of difference in terms of sameness. Instead, the preface to the book draws us in to the much deeper philosophical position of asking what made this turn possible and what the sense of the turn is. It is not so much 'This is wrong, let's do things differently.' as 'Under what conditions has this occurred?' and 'Given those conditions, where do we go from here?'.

The same point is also true of Deleuze's opening remarks on life in the twentieth century. When he speaks of the way we try to insert small variations in our repetitive lives (*I wear mine long.*) and the way in which modern art works depend on similar variations (*Marilyn1, Marilyn2, Marilyn3*), he is not giving us evidence to support a thesis. Instead, the observations are merely 'hooks' designed to introduce us to a conceptual innovation, the simulacrum, and to a related thesis about the inseparability of Deleuze's novel concepts of difference and repetition. Contrary to appearances, his work has nothing to do with empirical methods of contemporary cultural criticism or empirical sociology or psychology. The concept of the simulacrum resists those methods where they seek to identify trends with a high degree of objectivity. Not only that, the Deleuzian principles that respond to the concept are designed to resist a world based around that illusory objectivity.

The concept of the simulacrum plays an important role through *Difference and Repetition*. Put simply, it means a member of a repeated series that cannot be traced back to an origin of the series (*It differs from the original Boeing 737 200 in this way.*) or back to an origin outside the series (*It differs from the basic Boeing model plan in this way.*). Neither can the simulacrum be situated precisely with respect to the way it differs from other members of the series (*The 737 400 is longer than the 737 200.*). The difficulty of what Deleuze is trying to get us to accept jumps out here. If I identify a difference between a buttoned shirt and an unbuttoned one, or between the shades of pink running through Warhol's Marilyn series, if those differences can be conceptualised in terms of differences in predicates, then they are not simulacra. So how can I ever be in the presence of a simulacrum? What is the sense of a difference that cannot be identified? Are we not on the verge of the worst kind of mysticism when we begin to speak of real but not actual differences?

As I have already indicated in the introduction, answers to these questions depend upon Deleuze's deduction of a virtual side to all actual things and on his claim that there are significant differences in the virtual intensities expressed in our actual sensations. These differences do not correspond to actual recognisable differences. That the shade of pink has changed in an identifiable way is not all-important. It is that the change is a sign of a re-arrangement of an infinity of other actual and virtual relations. The unbuttoned shirt or the repetition of green, red or black ones or the variation of pinks is not the whole difference. This lies in the infinite series of other changes and reactions that the describable actual difference is only sign of or expresses – *something like a shift in emotions and what they drive us to do . . . Another black shirt on the street . . .*

Similarly, the statement on the inseparability of difference and repetition can seem quite a straightforward claim – no difference without repetition, no repetition without difference. However, it is a mistake to understand this slogan as if it depended on the thought that we have to be able to identify actual similarities between two repeated things in order to identify their actual differences (*Though similar, the two pictures differ in this way.*) or the thought that, in order for us to become aware that something has been repeated, some actual thing must have changed (*Same point of the circuit but a little lower on fuel*). These thoughts must be wrong, at least on Deleuze's terms, since they return difference to something that must be thought of in terms of identity, that is, in terms of an actual difference between two well-defined things. In addition, it defines repetition in terms of the repetition of things that are broadly the same and this would make Deleuze's claim that a repetition repeats all other repetitions impossible to sustain.

The correct reading of the inseparability claim is that repetition, understood as the variation of things that cannot be identified in actual things, always accompanies difference, understood as a variation that does not depend on identity. The repetition of pure differences underlies all actual identities – in Deleuze's words, it is disguised in them. But, in return, the repetition of actual identities is disguised in any determinate idea of pure differences. This claim is paradoxical from the point of view of a philosophy that includes the statement that differences must be identifiable. How can we know that something has varied in a repetition if we cannot recognise a difference? *Because they differ, these pictures are different in all aspects. Same but utterly different point on the circuit, because fuel is lower.* But how, then, do you know that they differ? How do you know that fuel is lower?

The concept of the simulacrum and the thesis on inseparability are not ends in themselves, as if Deleuze is only interested in uncovering hidden truths about difference and repetition. Two incongruous phrases of an ethical and political bent, from the preface, betray the overriding concern with principles for life and methods for thought: 'The task of life is to make all these repetitions coexist in a space in which difference is distributed' and 'The simulacrum is not just a copy, but that which overturns all copies by also overturning the models: every thought becomes an aggression.' (DR, pp. xix–xx, 2–3) The Deleuzian principles of completeness and forgetting or creative destruction discussed in my introduction emerge as results of the simulacrum and the inseparability thesis. In a brute and still relatively unclear manner, Deleuze is counselling us to create simulacra or to become individuals that show actual well-defined things to be illusions with respect to pure differences, that is, with respect to differences that cannot simply be identified. At the same time, we ought to seek to express the comprehensive aspect of repetition. That is, we ought to express all of the series of pure differences and actual things implicated in a given event but, in order to do so as intensely as possible, we ought also to forget all of these series by reconfiguring them.

The task of *Difference and Repetition* is then: to argue for the existence of these pure differences; to explain them, as well as other related terms such as simulacra, virtual, individual, disguise and so on, further; to justify the account of reality as a structure of the virtual and actual; and to deduce how to act best given this account of reality. Failing such explanations and arguments, his philosophy must remain wildly speculative. The preface only offers suggestive and peripheral remarks on the way to such answers. I have singled out the three most prominent ones. Each one introduces an important theme from the book but, again, in a shorthand version. These are: the response, in terms of selection and cruelty, to the accusation that a philosophy that seeks completeness is that of the 'beautiful soul'; the redefinition of empiricism as the creation of concepts expressing pure differences; and the consideration of the effect of selection and creation on the style of philosophy.

According to Deleuze's definition, the beautiful soul can be seen as a combination of a determinist fatalism and an indiscriminate romanticism – everything is necessary and to be made beautiful through my reaction to it (*Look at the pretty street urchins!*). His attempt to separate his philosophy from this definition is critical to its success since, in urging completeness in connecting with everything, he appears to flee judgement (*never that again*) and hence to move towards a simple endorsement of perverse loves – from a political modernist point of view. Deleuze's answer is to accept that he flees judgement and seeks out a maximisation of connections but that this does not prohibit selection. On the contrary, his second principle, to forget through creative destruction, is neither fatalistic nor inclusive of all actual states. Deleuze is committed to

29

a revolutionary philosophy, against the accusation that his work is that of a 'beautiful soul'.

The form of his revolution is given by a strange definition of empiricism. Deleuzian empiricism is the creation of concepts in response to individual problems but individual problems are a take on the whole of the actual and of the virtual. To experiment is to introduce thoughts and acts that change an individual perspective on the whole and, thereby, to change it for all individuals, with an eye for the expression of hidden intensities and the destruction of illusions of fixity. This empiricism must not be confused with the empirical methods associated with scientific experiments. Instead, the sense of experiment is more like a provocation with a view to a change and a re-intensification. This explains Deleuze's definition of philosophy, in his preface, as a kind of Duchamp-like troublesome irreverence: a moustache on the Mona Lisa; a clean-shaven Marx; but a bearded Hegel. There is a necessary cruelty to this creative selectivity but it is not the smothering inclusiveness of the beautiful soul. Instead, it is a cruelty with respect to the situation that is destroyed and forgotten when another is affirmed and with respect to other situations that the change will necessarily impinge upon.

Unlike modernists in politics, Deleuze cannot justify these forms of cruelty on the back of a universal utopian view that atones for current violence in the promise of final just state or, at least, a tendency to approach such a state. The relation of actual to virtual is such that there is no shared logic that would allow for valid judgements with respect to progress on both sides of reality. Instead, forward-looking movement depends on creative experiments by individuals. These cannot be compared in terms of actual outcomes since there is no common set of values or norms that applies to each. Rather, individuals must experiment in a way that expresses reality as the virtual and the actual, and according to principles that apply to all individuals, but with no guarantee of success. So any comparison relies on questions of whether one has experimented well in terms of reality and principles, rather than in terms of actual or promised outcomes.

All writing that responds to the need to experiment with concepts, all writing responsive to Deleuze's principles, must then work against the fixing of a world in set concepts or a fixed real world. This is why he speaks of a writing in tune with 'impersonal individuations' and 'pre-individual singularities'. The former are the simulacra that must replace the illusion of the persistence of the same actual self and subject through time. The latter are the pure differences expressed through the movement, the changes of the simulacrum, of a 'dissolved self'.

According to Deleuze, we are not fixed selves or subjects. Un-derlying those identities are mobile individuals, set in motion by unidentifiable intensities. In relation to this view of the self and the subject, philosophy should not seek to fill the world with secure truths and norms. On the contrary, since it must be in experimen-tal touch with the impersonal and the pre-individual, it will always have to work with an obscure edge that it can only experiment with, rather than grasp. How exactly that experimentation should take place is a further key concern for the rest of the book. The answers that Deleuze gives are often counter-intuitive: history of philosophy as collage, the most faithful readings allied to dramatic estrangement through strange juxtapositions. However, even if we can understand the direction of these brute assertions, a lot turns on whether Deleuze can back them up with convincing arguments. His preface gives us few clues as to these arguments, yet they form the core of *Difference and Repetition*.

[margin note: subjectivity]

REPETITION AND GENERALITY

Unlike the preface, the introduction to *Difference and Repetition* re-sponds to three clear philosophical objections and, thereby, offers counter-criticisms of the positions that ground these objections. First, Deleuze considers the criticism put in the following ques-tions: 'Doesn't repetition presuppose a form of generality?' or 'How can we recognise that something has been repeated without referring to a general form that emerges through repetition and allows it to be recognised?' *What has been repeated?* Secondly, he responds to a more subtle form of this first objection that avoids the question of the necessity of generality by viewing repetition as the result of a freely adopted regularity or moral law: 'Doesn't repetition emerge out of our acts based on a freely adopted moral law?' *Shouldn't we adopt a consistent pattern guided by the good?* In the move from the first questions to the second, there is a shift from generality concerning characteristics, the scientific search for laws of nature, to the search for repetition according to laws that are not laws of nature but moral laws (from 'It's the same' to 'It be-haves in the same way because of this moral law'). Thirdly, Deleuze

31

answers questions concerning his use of the concept 'Shouldn't a concept be determined and not this vague experimental thing you speak of?'.

In order to justify a definition of repetition independent of generality, Deleuze seeks to show that the right concept of repetition must not involve equivalence or substitutability. He claims that, when the repetition of members of a series is understood as the continuity of general characteristics, these are seen as either equivalent in each member – if the characteristic is one of quantity (*They are all the same shape but in different sizes.*) – or they are seen as substitutable – if the characteristic is one of quality (*This part is the same here and here.*). This approach is behind the strong critical question against Deleuze's view of repetition as the repetition of something unique – how do we know that this unique thing has been repeated? We are not going to get Deleuze's full answer at this point. But his answer contains its germ. He claims that the question 'How do we recognise repetition?' is of the wrong sort. We should be asking 'Why does repetition matter?', 'Why is it significant?' and 'How do we repeat well?'. This is a very odd reversal in the common-sense order of these questions. Shouldn't we have a clear concept of repetition before having a sense of its significance?

Deleuze's philosophy goes counter to this seemingly obvious point. Put simply, his view is that we have intimations of significance prior to well-defined concepts and to knowledge, not the opposite. What is more, these intimations are irreducible and critical elements of the concept. So he is not only picking up on the rather standard point that something has to be different for there to be repetition, since there must be some way of distinguishing two repeated things. Rather, he is insisting that this difference is what is significant in repetition, that is, there is repetition because there is pre-conceptual difference and that difference is what makes repetition matter.

The reversal depends on seeing value as prior to the question of being – the answer to the question 'Why?' is constitutive of the answer to the question 'What?'. (The power of Deleuze's apparently haphazard chapter construction is evident at this point since, at the end of the chapter, there will be a reprise of this issue in a redefinition of the meaning of essence and the importance of the question of essence in philosophy (see final section below).) The importance of value explains the rather odd selection of examples of repetition in the opening pages of the introduction to the book.

Reflections, doubles, soul sisters and brothers, acts of celebration and commemoration are all cases where the repetition or the experience of repetition is accompanied by intense reactions allied to the persistence of difference (*And still we can never be one. Please let that not be me. Bring it back. The moment lives on in the celebration. It's gone...*). In each case, the emotions are double – something is sensed in the same way but there is also a sensation of a profound difference, for example, in the feeling that a celebration could become a betrayal.

But aren't these examples merely recalcitrant or marginal cases of a more straightforward repetition – one where value does not play a central role? Wouldn't it be best to start with the standard, more simple and uncomplicated case, in order then either to eliminate the deviant cases or to discover that, in fact, they are in accord with the standard despite appearances? These questions flush out a key aspect of Deleuze's argument. For him, all repetitions are of the marginal kind – it is just that the simple cases hide this and thinking about repetition, in terms of equivalence and substitutability, strengthens the illusion. This is because repetition is not an objective fact but an act – a form of behaviour towards that which cannot be repeated. Thus we make things the same, even the most simple things, against the background that they could be very different (*I can't believe the bolt failed...*). So each bolt, each simple same thing, matters because it carries with it the possibility that it could be different. More importantly, for Deleuze, the repetition of the same carries forward the condition for that possible difference – a virtual world of significant differences with intense ramifications (*I wasn't in my usual seat on that fateful day... Our paths crossed...*).

However, that argument does not seem to counter the objection that repetition is not mainly about acts of construction but objective acts of observation – not a question of making it the same but different, but of checking that it is the same and defining what that check is looking for, that is, equivalences and substitutability. The answer to this objection lies in Deleuze's concern to distinguish repetition and resemblance. We can never say that two things are the same because of the difference implied in any repetition. Not only are they not exactly the same but that difference can take on immense significance (*Why don't you just take the same plot of land at a different but similar geographical location?*).

So, when we say that they are the same, we are saying that they are sufficiently alike, that they resemble one another enough for a given purpose: 'For generality only represents and presupposes a hypothetical repetition "given the same circumstances then..."' (DR, pp. 2, 10). This claim is then not objective but a matter of convention (*To all intents and purposes they are the same.*). But this convention is open to a Deleuzian critique through the principles it depends upon and presupposes. Is supposing that things are alike and acting as if they should be alike the best way to proceed? It is partly to put to these questions that Deleuze then moves on from the resistance of repetition to natural law to its resistance to feely adopted regularity.

REPETITION AND LAW

In his consideration of law and repetition in the introduction to *Difference and Repetition,* Deleuze is not primarily concerned with laws of nature but moral laws that are based on acts meant to be independent of laws of nature. His target is not science but a Kantian approach to morality. This is a strength in the sense that it allows him to develop a critique of approaches to reality that argue that we must act as if our actions can be fixed according to a law of our choice, given certain constraints. These approaches also imply that we can decide to bring repetition back under the rule of equivalences and substitutability, despite objective evidence to the contrary.

However, this focus on morality is also a weakness. It means that, at this stage of his book, Deleuze continues to evade legitimate questions concerning the role that science may have to play in the development of his own concepts. Does it make sense to speak of intensity, of individuals and of their acts without putting these terms to scientific scrutiny, in the form of experiments, and to scientific criticisms, in the form of comparison with what is known about these concepts (*Emotions are produced by these chemical reactions. This individual has these properties. The reasons given for these acts are... The chemical genetic and physical explanations for them are...*)? I have already argued that Deleuze views this kind of knowledge as incomplete and illusory with respect to arguments about the conditions for actual things. However, until these arguments are fleshed out in a reading of Deleuze's two key chapters on synthesis, these arguments can only be seen as speculative and as swimming against the orthodox view that, if you want to know about and speak with security about phenomena, then you should turn to science first and foremost.

Deleuze's argument against the role of laws in morality focuses on the rational decision to lead a life according to laws or rules. He is opposed to this decision for two reasons: first, it perpetuates the illusion that life is something that can be thought of as repetitive in the sense of a repetition of resemblances; second, in perpetuating this illusion, it turns us away from the real source of intensity in our lives, that is, the creative experimentation with simulacra or as individuals caught in a process of change. This explains why he picks on Danton's rail against the sapping repetition of morning rituals and on Kant's fondness for exactly such patterns and strictures (*Woke up. Got out of bed. Took a cold shower... as usual.*). We consciously adopt these rituals in order to give moral worth to our lives but end up subjecting ourselves to actions bound to boredom and despair. But what if they do not end in this way? What if this end was the right price to pay for good morals? Or what if the rational selection of good morals cannot be considered in the same way as ends with respect to pleasure and pain?

The crux of Deleuze's argument is not directly a concern with these ends or with the worthiness of moral endeavour. Rather, it is that we never really repeat according to a law that we adopt consciously. The conscious act must be played out in a different way that belies it. We play out the law through acts that must become habitual rather than conscious:

> Conscience, however, suffers from the following ambiguity: it can be conceived only by supposing the moral law to be external, superior and indifferent to the natural law; but the application of the moral law can be conceived only by restoring to conscience itself the image and the model of the law of nature.

> (DR, pp. 4, 11)

Why is this distinction between conscious and unconscious repetition significant? Can Deleuze demonstrate that natural law, that is, the unconscious acquisition of habits, underlies every adoption of a moral law?

For Deleuze, relying on his argument against generality outlined earlier, a habitual repetition is never the repetition of the same. In other words, habit cannot be understood in terms of generality but must be understood in terms of a constantly altering scene where either an action has to change in order to reinforce the intention to acquire a habit (*This time do it as if you mean to caress it.*) or where the action remains the same but in a different context (*It's the same caress on any surface.*). So the argument is that we can never consciously repeat the same act because the act must be part of a responsive refinement to something that cannot be identified. There is no free rational selection of a moral law because that selection must take place against a background that is beyond the grasp of any rational consciousness. In the study of repetition of habit in the chapter on repetition for itself, Deleuze expands on this argument with the claim that pure differences are a necessary condition for repetition and for habit.

Yet his preliminary observations allow him to introduce two essential aspects of his method and of the application of his principles – humour and irony. Ironic and humorous creations respond to the demand to act according to Deleuze's core principles of completeness and forgetting with respect to moral laws. Humour and irony combine connection with creative destruction. He explains this in the context of a reversal of the laws. Deleuze frequently returns to these aspects and develops them through *Difference and Repetition*. Here, they function by either showing the sources of the law that run counter to it or by ridiculing the law by too great an obedience. The former is the ironic form encountered in, for example, Nietzsche's *Genealogy of Morality* where Kant's moral philosophy is also one of the main targets. Though the law is supposed to be selected by free rational choice and to encourage the same, it is shown to come out of much more base impulses resulting from evolution, that is, drives that must be thought of in terms of repetition as the repetition of difference. Irony shows that we really follow the law for base 'reasons', through hidden desires. In Nietzsche's ironic ridicule, but with a serious lesson, Kant's moral law is a product of his strange obsession with efficient garters and with regular walks, rather than the other way round.

Humour, on the other hand, can be found in the comedians of silent cinema, where moral laws are followed to the letter – for example, where Laurel and Hardy are so keen to obey an order that they end up bringing about events that the law is meant to avoid. Their concern to cooperate turns into the most disastrous kind of disobedience. Ordered to deny any knowledge of a thing – 'You have not seen me. Right!' – they pursue that order in situations where an admission of knowledge is now required – 'Have you seen this man before?' 'Never, officer!' 'Arrest that man!'. Or, when given an order that needs to be loosely interpreted – 'Never get your gun dirty.' – they turn unflinching obedience into the worst kind of subversive action – 'No don't fire, you'll tarnish the barrel!'.

More recently, Homer Simpson, echoing Laurel and Hardy, also allows us to see the funny and, thereby, fragile side of moral laws when he follows commands and laws too closely or out of context or when he adopts absurd moral codes, only then to lapse back, vindicated, into his more immediate and haphazard instinctive or pragmatic attitude to events. Like irony, humour functions with the moral law rather than by simply opposing and then replacing it. It satisfies the principle of seeking completeness by following the law, rather than avoiding it, or replacing it with something different – we are left with the law but its status has changed and the context within which it is applied has been added to.

Humour also functions by discarding an important property of the law, that is, by undermining its claims to purity and to universality. So humour also satisfies the principle of forgetting or constructive destruction. Sure, we have to work with laws but they are only part of the story. They are also a restrictive part if they are seen as free-standing or as implying that they can be applied universally. We can begin to see that it is wrong to attribute to Deleuze the poor but common caricature of anarchism, where it is defined as utter opposition to the law. Humour and irony work within the law. They transform the law and our relation to it but they are not simply against it. In order to allow a space for his concepts of repetition, simulacra and individuals, his philosophy advocates an uncovering of the absurdities that the moral law has to conceal so it can stand as pure and universal. Works of irony and humour affirm the transforming emotions they trigger, while undermining the laws they work through.

REPETITION AND CONCEPTS

Deleuze follows up his remarks on the role of irony and humour with a study of the way Nietzsche and Kierkegaard use repetition, allied to theatre and drama, in a similar constructive resistance to moral laws. I will cover these moves in the next section, in order to be able to develop Deleuze's philosophical arguments about concepts first. My separation of Deleuze's arguments is justified on the grounds of ease of explanation. It must not, though, be seen as a defence of the thesis that Deleuze's different arguments are independent. On the contrary, in *Difference and Repetition*, lines of argument complete and illustrate one another to the point where they ought to be viewed as complementary.

In the work on concepts, Deleuze does not participate in the debates about generality, universality and law as pursued by the two dominant ways of contemporary professional philosophy. He does not contribute to a detailed historical study of the issues and texts by responding to the vast array of studies of, for example, Kant. Neither does he return explicitly to a detailed reading of Kant's text. On the other hand, he does not follow the analytic tradition and take sides in the careful and often rarefied debates around the definition, truth and validity of concepts or laws. These arguments come out of a view of philosophy as a profession very close to the natural sciences, where many specialised practitioners participate, often in small and detailed ways, to the overall development of a subject area in learned journals subject to peer review and through specialist conference proceedings. In the first model, philosophy comes close to history as an academic discipline. In the second, it is closer to one of the models for the correct development of physics, biology or medicine. Yet, at least in the first sections of *Difference and Repetition* and, in fact, through the book, the visible arguments must be seen as poor in terms of history of ideas and in terms of the close analysis of concepts and arguments – or, if not poor, at least thin.

Deleuze's philosophy is inimical to the model of philosophy proposed in the history of ideas and to the professional model of the analytical tradition. This can be seen in his determination to forget, to destroy and move beyond established truths because they obscure deeper truths about reality. However, it is not the case that the close historical study of texts or the analytical approach to concepts cannot arrive at the same sceptical conclusions as Deleuze, probably with greater scholarly and formal logical validity or with a more general consensus among experts. Neither is it the case that a strongly historical or analytic approach cannot point towards realms outside established fields of knowledge.

If there is an opposition to these approaches in Deleuze's work, it has nothing to do with findings but how they are arrived at. That is, the methods of history of ideas and analytic philosophy go against Deleuze's principles, methods and structures. This explains, at least at a superficial level, why *Difference and Repetition* does not fit easily alongside the methods dominant in academic philosophy that developed from common roots, in Kant, for example, through the twentieth century. This does not mean that there cannot be fruitful and open relations between these methods, rather, it means that all of them will have to evolve as they encounter different approaches. Indeed, they are evolving as each encounters different, but related and worthwhile, types of argument and ideas.

Deleuze's argument on concepts is designed to show that a concept cannot correspond to an actual object, that is, the claim that a concept can successfully represent an actual object is false. This is important because it shows that representation through concepts cannot give a satisfactory account of Deleuzian repetition – we do not have the right idea of repetition if we define it as the repetition of objects that correspond to the same concept. His line of argument is as follows. First, he argues that, in order for a concept to represent an object, it must correspond to that object alone (its extension must be equal to one). If this were not the case, the concept would represent more than one object and, thereby, fail to successfully represent one of them (*I am going to Paris. Do you mean Paris, Texas or Paris, France?*). Then, he argues that, for this to be the case, its comprehension must be infinite, that is, the concept must have an infinite number of predicates or determinations that correspond to properties of the object. My concept of this chair represents this chair alone because the infinite set of properties belonging to this chair and this chair alone corresponds to the infinite set of predicates in the concept.

At this stage, Deleuze seems simply to assume that objects have an infinite set of properties resistant to systematisation in a finite manner or, at least, he gives no clear argument why this should be the case. A weakness of his approach comes out here insofar as the reader is forced to fill many gaps that would have benefited from, for example, a debate with the Fregean analytic tradition, where a great deal of work has been done on the problem of reference. This link could be made through Deleuze's reliance on Leibniz for arguments about predicates and properties and the connection this draws to Russell, Frege, the early Wittgenstein and to the arguments within analytic philosophy that follow from these foundations. Deleuze gestures towards this connection in *The Logic of Sense* and, poorly, in *What is Philosophy?* but he leaves a careful study of the problem of reference to his reading of Plato in chapter 3 of *Difference and Repetition*. Another connection could be made through Deleuze's remarks on names and naming a little further down in his argument. Here, a reference to Kripke's *Naming and Necessity* and to the debates that followed it would have been very useful.

In fact, Deleuze returns to the question of infinity and to the related question of chaos frequently through *Difference and Repetition*. He does so in relation to differential calculus and Leibniz and to Hegel's discussion of infinities (see Chapters 3 and 6 of this book). There, he argues that infinity must not be thought in terms of scale, the infinitely big or small, or in terms of number, an infinite series of natural numbers. Instead, infinity is the resistance found in pure difference to identification as scale or as number. An actual thing is infinite because of its capacity to change through the expression of virtual ideas, or multiplicities of pure differences. I shall go into these difficult metaphysical claims later. Put simply, Deleuze's view is that no object is fully accounted for through its actual properties since the changes that it has undergone and will undergo, and the differences implied in those changes, must be considered to be part of the object.

Setting aside his assumptions and arguments regarding infinity, the next step in Deleuze's argument is to claim that concepts can be blocked either artificially or naturally. By blocked, he means fail to have an infinite comprehension. So a blocked concept 'chair' would be one that only involved a limited number of predicates – say, 'has four legs' and 'can be sat on'. That blocked concept is useless when I want to get you to get the chair with the blue back among a stack of black ones. If we accept Deleuze's assumption that a particular thing is determined by an infinite set of properties, then a blocked concept never satisfactorily corresponds to a particular object. Though, again, we could ask why a satisfactory correspondence would have to be one free of the possibility of error (*OK, so you brought the wrong one. What extra predicates do we need to get the right one?*). We could also ask whether a satisfactory answer was ever possible, that is, whether Deleuze is operating with an implausible definition of representation (*Look, it is possible for me to get her to fetch the single blue chair in a limited set of black chairs with the right blocked concept, so where's the problem?*). As in the case of infinity, we have to wait for arguments developed much later in the book in order to have these questions answered fully. However, in the introduction, Deleuze gestures towards the depth of the problem in moving to harder cases of blocked concepts.

In fact, the artificial or logical blockages of a concept are of no concern to Deleuze since these cover cases where we choose to limit the set of predicates, for example, in order to make comparisons and establish categories and species based on resemblance (by defining chairs as having four legs and a back, for example). The possibility of this kind of blockage does not necessarily bring conceptual correspondence into question. However, Deleuze goes on to speak of natural blockages, that is, blockages beyond our control that force concepts to fail necessarily in corresponding to one actual object and one alone. He introduces the two most important methods of the book at this stage to describe the processes that lead to an understanding of this blockage – transcendental deductions and Deleuzian dialectics. He makes no effort to define these methods at this stage – they are merely pointers to important arguments later in the book. In his introduction, he only gives three cases of blockages. These cannot constitute valid arguments by themselves since the accounts they give of their key terms are far too short and sketchy and since no evidence is given that these cases exhaust all possibilities.

The first case of a blocked concept is the concept for a particular word (an example Deleuze deems to be more successful than that of Epicurus's atoms since such completely alike atoms may not exist). Words must be defined in a limited manner (X means A, B and C). 'We have here a reason why the comprehension of the concept *cannot* extend to infinity: we define a word by only a finite number of words.' (DR, pp. 21, 22) Words and their definitions are always open to alteration as they are used in language and no word can be said to represent a sole object since the word may represent many. Not only that, the way words come to be associated with things allows them to alter in what they represent. Deleuze calls this kind of blocked concept nominal concepts and they have a finite comprehension or set of predicates. The concept or definition of a word can never correspond uniquely to a given actual word.

The second case of a conceptual blockage he calls concepts of nature and their comprehension is indefinite. What this means is that the concept is limited in its predicates but not in principle, that is, they can be added to infinitely with respect to the object they correspond to (he calls them virtually infinite). Deleuze argues that any concept of nature can always be shown to correspond to two or more identical actual things. Therefore, the concept can never be said to correspond to one thing however much we add to its comprehension. He turns to a Kantian argument from the *Prolegomena to Any Future Metaphysics* to justify his claim. For any given concept of nature there are further non-conceptual spatio-temporal properties that allow it to correspond to a plurality of objects that are identical from the point of view of the concept.

In the *Prolegomena*, Kant explains this point in terms of 'inner differences' between things that can only be revealed through 'outer' spatial relations. His aim is to show that space and time are not real qualities 'attached to things themselves'. (*Prolegomena*, p. 42) We cannot put the left-handed glove on the right hand, yet the gloves are the same in terms of their concepts in the sense that all their internal properties are the same or they are isomorphous:

Here are no inner differences that any understanding could think; and yet the differences are inner as far as the senses tell us, for the left hand cannot be enclosed in the same boundaries as the right (they cannot be congruent) notwithstanding all their mutual equality and similarity.

(*Prolegomena*, p. 42)

Right-handedness and left-handedness are outer relations – in Deleuze's version they are extra-conceptual.

The reference to Kant is designed to move the argument on to non-conceptual differences and the way in which they show that a concept of nature is always incapable of corresponding to one thing and one alone. For Deleuze, differences in themselves or what he has called, by this stage, pure differences or intensities are non-conceptual differences. For any given concept, there are differences in the relation between the things that correspond to the concept and pure differences that cannot be accounted for by the concept. For example, given identical gloves in terms of concepts, it is not only the case that the actual glove could be right- or left-handed but also that its significance could vary due to the intensities or pure differences expressed in actual gloves. The same glove can mean and lead to different events for non-conceptual reasons. Later in the book, he is going to deduce the necessary existence of these differences (see my introduction on the importance of transcendental deductions). If his deduction is successful, then he will have shown that, for any given concept of indefinite comprehension, there is a multiplicity of actual objects, defined according to pure non-conceptual differences.

Finally, Deleuze introduces a third case of blockage and a second argument for the impossibility of a concept corresponding to one and only one object. He remarks that the second case concerns concepts that are present to consciousness as concepts of theoretical objects – that is, they are not concepts of objects that we remember having experienced. This is what makes them indefinite·

Such a situation may be better understood if we consider that concepts with indefinite comprehension are concepts of Nature. As such, they are always in something else: they are not in Nature but in the mind which contemplates it or observes it, and represents it to itself.

(DR, pp. 14, 24)

But then what about concepts that depend on memory? Can these be blocked too?

According to Deleuze, concepts that depend on memory can be blocked because of the gap between the original event and our memory of it. Concepts of remembered things do not correspond to one and only one thing that we remember. On the contrary, because a memory is constructed, the correspondence of original thing and memory is always broken or blocked. This is a necessary property of memory due to the difference between the consciousness of experiencing an event and the consciousness of remembering that consciousness. The immediacy of the former becomes an object open to free manipulation by the latter. He will make much of this difference in his books on cinema. Cinema shows how memory is a form of construction that blocks or destroys the immediacy of memory. But it is also an art that thrives on that blockage, by accepting that remembered events must be constructed.

When we experience a thing or an event, we cannot know how our future memories will manipulate our conscious experience by adding or removing conscious and unconscious elements. What we are conscious of recording is accompanied by other unconscious records set down for the future. In addition to his point on self-consciousness, Deleuze will claim later that this unconscious elimination (or, following Freud, repression) is inevitable. So the concept does not truly repeat or represent the original object and Deleuze's repetition for itself will have to take account of 'the unconscious of representation'. (DR, pp. 14, 24) In a link to his work on irony and humour, he argues that this unconscious explains tragedy and comedy in theatre since the hero acts without either a terrible knowledge, in the case of the former, or a plain and common-sense one, in the case of the latter (*She's your mother. Don't open a porthole in a storm.*). So the arguments against the perfect correspondence of concept to object are not only critical, designed to disarm thought about repetition in terms of concepts,

43

they are also a lead-in to a way in which we ought to respond to this conceptual failure and insufficiency.

TRAGEDY

I am not going to go into the detail of Deleuze's points regarding the similarities that bring Kierkegaard and Nietzsche together in a thought and style that affirms Deleuze's repetition against generality, law and concept. In short, they write and think in ways that respond to the detail of Deleuze's arguments, as I have explained it above. More important and difficult is the way in which the two philosophers give rise to Deleuze's concept of the theatre or of philosophy and metaphysics as theatre. (At this stage, we have to stick guardedly with the word concept, despite only having his critique of a certain misuse of it, rather than his own very different sense – something like a complex relation of thoughts, feelings and contexts.)

The Deleuzian concept of theatre responds to the problem of how to create without representing. Initially, he speaks of the movement of Kierkegaard's and Nietzsche's works, contrasting it with Hegel's logical movement, as a way of explaining their violent reaction to his philosophy. Much of this argument goes back to Deleuze's *Nietzsche and Philosophy* and, indeed, is rather light when compared to it – apart from the extra work on Kierkegaard. Hegel's logic moves from a representation to another that negates it (*This is not that.*) and on to a synthesis (*This as both that and that.*). Whereas Kierkegaard's and Nietzsche's theatre do not allow for a representation to emerge. Instead, the movement is not from one thing to another but in one changing individual:

Rather, it is a question of producing within the work a movement capable of affecting the mind outside of all representation; it is a question of making movement itself a work, without interposition; of substituting direct signs for mediate representations; of inventing vibrations, rotations, whirlings, gravitations, dances or leaps which directly touch the mind.

(DR, pp. 8, 16)

But how is this possible since Deleuze has argued that words and concepts fail to capture the movement of the thing or its difference – that is, its resistance to repetition as repetition of the same?

Many of the pages that follow the statements on movement read like empty posturing and prevarication in the light of this question. However, this rather heavy literary style is designed to dramatise Deleuze's point in line with his views on the necessity of dramatisation, as developed later in his book. Notwithstanding his rather inelegant efforts at making us sense his point, he argues that Kierkegaard and Nietzsche do not theorise theatre – they do theatre in philosophy. He insists that their theatre is real movement and real repetition. This does not get us very far at all, in terms of arguments and evidence. On the other hand, Deleuze makes interesting claims when he describes the detail of their work. Two points stand out. First, their words call for a reading that has to re-enact them. The reader is an actor following Kierkegaard's and Nietzsche's script and stage directions.

This re-enacting becomes a central concept of his philosophy through the concepts of vice-diction and counter-effectuation. To vice-dict or counter-effectuate the script is to say it in a different way by expressing how it works on us. To do so is also to change the script. Second, the script is loose with respect to the specification of characters – they are merely layers of masks that need to be fleshed out. So the texts force the reader to put new voices and feelings and new contexts and thoughts into them. In that sense, the reading is not a literal repetition, in the sense of being able to say: 'I know what Hegel means by the beautiful soul in *The Phenomenology of Spirit*.' The reading must be: 'This is how I play Kierkegaard's aesthetic life or Nietzsche's superman.'

More importantly, when we play Kierkegaard's and Nietzsche's characters, we are set in movement in terms of our voice, feelings, contexts and thoughts. Reading their works is not a purely intellectual exercise. It is a complex process that undermines our sense of self and our capacity to act as a pure subject – that is, one that is fully conscious of its intentions and driven by them alone. The fact that we have concepts when reading them must be seen with the fact that those concepts do not stand alone but emerge with an emotional, physical and environmental background. Deleuze claims that the latter are not themselves represented and cannot be. They are direct:

In the theatre of repetition, we experience pure forces, dynamic lines in space which act without intermediary upon the spirit, and link it directly with nature and history, with a language which speaks before words, with gestures which develop before organised bodies, with masks before faces, with spectres and phantoms before characters – the whole apparatus of repetition as a 'terrible power'.

(DR, pp. 10, 19)

45

Important arguments for the necessity of this directness and its resistance to conceptualisation emerge later in *Difference and Repetition*, in particular, in terms of intensity and difference in itself. A way into the spirit of these arguments is to understand emotions, bodies and contexts as movements that are not fully captured when they are conceptualised because they become something different when they are seen as having a fixed identity (*The hurt and anger are not the same when I tell you about them. The record books say 100mph – but that could never capture the first thrill of achievement in that tiny Triumph.*).

This emphasis on movement and directness allows Deleuze to separate Kierkegaard and Nietzsche. He says that the first jumps, in an allusion to the leap of faith that he calls for, whereas the latter dances, in a first indication of the importance of Nietzsche's eternal return and the importance of his idea of rhythm for *Difference and Repetition*. In the leap of faith, Kierkegaard risks a return to identity in God and the knight of faith, though this remains only a risk since there is no promise of successful leap and since the leap is conveyed through philosophy as theatre. Nietzsche, though, never even makes such a promise in a philosophy that comes after the death of God and 'the dissolution of the self'. Instead, we only ever play the same parts differently. At this stage, Deleuze is not prepared to select one thinker at the expense of the other. From the point of view of his philosophy, it does not even make sense to speak of selecting a whole thinker – we select concepts, styles, intensities when we enact one or the other or both.

FREUD AND MASKS

Deleuze's discussion of Freud adds two important refinements to his work on the blocked concept and on repetition in Kierkegaard and Nietzsche. It also begins his far-reaching thought about death that carries through the whole of *Difference and Repetition*. Deleuze is concerned that, up to this point, he has introduced the main concepts of his philosophy in negative terms: 'But natural blockage itself requires a positive supra-conceptual force capable of explaining it, and of thereby explaining repetition.' (DR, pp. 16, 26) His critique of the concept and of the claims that concepts can correspond accurately to real things lead to a negative definition of his own concepts of repetition and of difference in itself. More seriously, he is aware that the discussion of masks and re-enacting is open to the criticism that we are still acting a well-defined part through masks. In short, his work, up to this point, is vulnerable to the criticism that his picture of reality, though complex, must still be thought from the point of view of identity. What is the positive sense of repetition and of re-enactment that save them from this attack?

In order to sketch a preliminary answer to this question, Deleuze suggests a role for death in the play of masks and disguises. His discussion relies heavily on Freud. The claim is that, after his *Beyond the Pleasure Principle* (BTPP in my references), Freud no longer explains repression as repetition from the point of view of an actual act of repression and actual repressed things (*You are stopping this from being repeated by doing this.*). The context for this claim is the relation of the pleasure principle to the death-drive. Put simply, the pleasure principle is the drive to seek out practices that diminish tension or an unpleasant intensity (*Satisfy your hunger.*). Whereas the death drive is to seek out practices that increase such intensities (*Head out into the cold.*). It can, therefore, be seen as a destructive drive – though Deleuze will dispute this.

According to Deleuze, in *Beyond the Pleasure Principle*, Freud goes beyond the explanation of repetition, as based on specific events and on the pleasure principle, when he shifts his discussion of repetition and the death-drive towards instincts and to a 'daemonic' power: 'It may be presumed too, that when people unfamiliar with analysis feel an obscure fear . . . what they are afraid of at bottom is the emergence of this compulsion [to repeat] with its hint of possession by some daemonic power.' (BTPP, p. 30) Instead of being the flip-side of a pleasure principle, where pleasure is seen to necessitate destruction, the Freudian death-drive becomes a 'positive originating principle for repetition' (*You are doing this because of the instinctual death-drive, that has nothing to do with the relation of actual past events to present ones or to a need for different pleasures.*). It is not the case that, because pleasure involves the elimination of tension and, therefore, its own exhaustion, we are driven to seek out new sources of tension, in order subsequently to eliminate them in new pleasurable acts. According to Deleuze, the death-drive is the condition for actual repetition and not the other way round. But then what does he think the Freudian death-drive is?

The answer relies on the work on Nietzsche and Kierkegaard and theatre but also serves to explain why it resists definition through identity. However, the answer also shows the way in which Deleuze is prepared to depart from orthodox readings, in this case of Freud, to make his own philosophical point. It is also an early statement of Deleuze's critical stance on Freud, developed later with Guattari in *Anti Œdipus*. Deleuze moves against the direction of Freud's enquiry in *Beyond the Pleasure Principle*, where instincts are explained by reference to biology as 'an urge inherent in organic life to restore an earlier state of things which the living entity has been obliged to abandon under the pressure of external disturbing forces'. (BTPP, p. 30) The death-drive must not be thought through the opposite forces of the self, the pleasure principle and earlier states of organic matter. Instead, the death-drive is internal to each mask we put on. It is the drive to move on from it to the next one and so on:

Death has nothing to do with a material model. On the contrary, the death instinct may be understood in relation to masks and costumes. Repetition is truly that which disguises itself in constituting itself, that which constitutes itself only by disguising itself.

(DR, pp. 17, 28)

So we repeat because, as masks, that is, as combinations of actual things, sensations, virtual ideas and the intensities that light them up, we are driven to play different aspects of ourselves in different ways, again and again. This play must not be explained in terms of a drive to return to an origin. Neither must it be explained in terms of the need to renew the pleasure we take in resolving tensions in our characters in a destructive moment. Instead, it is a result of the 'fact' that we are a necessarily unstable combination of actual things and pure differences. The Deleuzian definition of a mask is, then, something that represents nothing but, instead, puts significant components of other masks into play again in new ways (*a sadder smile, faster tears, less furrowed brow – this time round*). But why can't this account of masks be explained in terms of origins? Can there be a clearer definition of masks than this very narrow one (supplemented by elliptical references to Nerval and Proust, thereby linking *Difference and Repetition* to Deleuze's Proust book, *Proust et les signes*)? What arguments are there for the existence of such masks? None of these questions are answered at this point in *Difference and Repetition*. We are led to understand a definition, a set of claims and a structure, but not yet to follow the validity of any underlying arguments.

Despite the absence of these arguments in this section of *Difference and Repetition*'s introduction, Deleuze gives further indications of his critique of Freud. These are interesting since they carry through an interest in a redefinition of heath and cure that can be traced back to *Nietzsche and Philosophy* and that carries through to *Essays Critical and Clinical* if not right to Deleuze's last and very beautiful essay 'L'Immanence: une vie'. He notes how Freud's move to the death drive in *Beyond the Pleasure Principle* takes place when he reflects on the transference that happens during psychoanalysis. Patients repeat their troubles during analysis and transfer them to the analyst. But Deleuze disagrees on the nature of what is repeated and on whether anything is actually transferred. It is not actual events, persons and passions that become identified (*'It's not my mother': therefore, we conclude that it is.*). Instead, analysis 'works' because roles and masks are authenticated. So, controversially, at least from the point of some branches of psychoanalysis, Deleuze claims that analysis does not work because it recovers original trauma. It is a site where a way of creating masks that respond to the significant points of other masks is given a seal of approval.

For Deleuze, due to his work on death and repetition, curing and health are not entirely about actual injuries, whether mental or physical, they are about how to repeat well: 'It is in that sense that repetition constitutes the selective game of our illness and out health'. (DR, pp. 19, 30) This surprising philosophical and perhaps medical view is put across in its most shocking, but also most clear, form in *Logics of Sense*. Great philosophy has often allied itself with revolutions in medicine – for example, in Descartes (an alliance that he returns to later in *Difference and Repetition*). The challenge here, though, is that his philosophy seems so far removed from contemporary medicine, though perhaps it marks the move to a more holistic and less purely trauma based medicine – in the same way that his later works move towards a view of the world in terms of the interdependence of all environments. Thus, in his later works such as *Essays Critical and Clinical*, Deleuze describes the different ways in which a life can be studied as an attempt to live with the events that give it consistency but also tear it apart (*How can this life be intense without disintegrating as any expression of intensity?*).

SIGNS AND THE ESSENCE OF REPETITION

The penultimate section of the introduction to *Difference and Repetition* begins with an important presentation of Deleuze's method and argument. This is a response to the critical question that has grown in importance through my reading of the chapter: Why can't repetition be thought of in terms of the repetition of the same things? A variation on this question is: Why can't the members of a series be identified satisfactorily? His answer turns on the central methodical principle of the book, as I have already outlined it in my introduction. Deleuze's argument combines a principle of sufficient reason, Spinoza's synthetic method and Kant's transcendental conditions. This combination may seem rather baroque and, indeed, Deleuze's methods are profoundly baroque. His reflections on folding and unfolding later in *Difference and Repetition* indicate the importance of rhythmic complexity for his work long before they are returned to in greater detail in Deleuze's book on Leibniz and the baroque, *The Fold: Leibniz and the Baroque*. Certainly, the practical application of the Deleuzian dialectics is often necessarily complicated, as Deleuze combines different responses to the demand for completeness with the demand to forget, in way that brings different clear and obscure perspectives on individuals into harmony.

However, the underlying argument for that practice, his principle of reason, can be put simply. Completeness can only be achieved by taking account of all the conditions for an actual thing and event. In terms of repetition, conditions are not what accounts for a given actual property of the thing, but the signs of its individuality. Conditions make the thing individual not only in how it has come about but also in how it is going to change. So the notion of cause is profoundly transformed by Deleuze. He criticises the traditional concept of cause, in order to replace it with the concept of condition – though at times he retains the word cause in its new sense of condition. This sense has nothing to do with the causes of general characteristics (*What makes humans talk?*). It is about what makes an individual different (*What makes her voice affect me so?*). This explains Deleuze's opening to the passage in question through the question of essence. He intends to overturn the traditional concept of essence and its relation to causes that develop from Descartes into our modern scientific conceptions of causality and scientific explanation. This revolution is designed to free Deleuze's concept of repetition from a model of thought that is inimical to it.

Here, we can return to Deleuze's own use of irony in the preface to his book. When he says that 'unfortunately' he has not been able to speak of science in a 'scientific manner', his apparently laudable self-critical stance is a joke based on the fact that his method has to be, and is unashamedly, anti-scientific and opposed to a dominant model of science with respect to truth and explanation. This is because the hegemony of scientific observations and the idea of causality that allows us to explain them is questioned in *Difference and Repetition*. In his introduction, Deleuze only explains this move with respect to cases of repetition. His point is this: in three important cases of repetition, the reason why repetition matters has nothing to do with the repetition of the same thing but, rather, with the repetition of difference that can only be approached through indirect signs and not actual differences. This does not mean that the scientific approach to causality has no use – as if we could not trust Deleuzian bridge-builders to study the laws of metal fatigue. Rather, it means that any understanding of bridges, from the point of view of general laws and concepts, is incomplete from the point of view of questions of significance or repetition.

In *Spinoza and the Problem of Expression* (pp. 140–7), Deleuze contrasts Spinoza's and Descartes' methods by claiming that the former works under the assumption that the cause of a thing is known better than the thing itself, while the latter claims the exact opposite. Therefore, Spinoza works back to a cause, known only indeterminately in the thing, in order to gain better knowledge of the thing through better knowledge of the cause (*What brought you here, stranger? What do your reasons say of you?*). Whereas Descartes seeks clear knowledge of the thing – only then to work back to a necessarily less clear knowledge of the cause (*Who are you, stranger? What do you allow us to learn of your reasons?*). The contrast in the clarity and distinctness of the starting point explains Deleuze's turn to signals and signs in the thing and his fascination with the problem of expression in Spinoza and Leibniz (*How does the thing express its causes? In what way is it a sign of its conditions?*).

Deleuze's originality lies in the context of repetition that he gives to the longstanding enigma of Spinoza's synthetic method. So long as we think in terms of identity, the method must seem inferior to Cartesian analysis since we cannot know the identity of the absent causes of something better than we know the identity of the thing. To follow Descartes, too many reasons to doubt our reflections on the identity of the cause would persist. But, if we allow the assumption that repetition is about differences running through a repeated series, then what matters for an understanding of a member of the series with respect to repetition is how that member allows us to pick up on the variation.

For Deleuze, the actual members of a series and the variations belong to different orders that are related because each is the condition for the other but in different ways: 'By "signal" we mean a system with orders of disparate size, endowed with elements of dissymmetry; by "sign" we mean what happens within such a system, what flashes across the intervals when a communication takes place between disparates.' (DR, pp. 20, 31) We can perceive the work of pure differences in actual things (signs) but we cannot identify them except through signals or observable differences.

Later in *Difference and Repetition*, he will seek to demonstrate this dissymmetry in terms of relations between the different structures of actual and virtual and in terms of the way in which the virtual is the condition for change and evolution in the actual. In return, the actual is the condition for determinacy in the virtual. I cover and criticise these numerous and detailed transcendental deductions in later chapters. At this stage, it is enough to insist on the insight that things relate to one another in a different way than their conditions. So, underlying the relation of cause and effect between actual things, and undermining it as a sufficient explanation or reason, there is the relation of their conditions and the 'effect' of those conditions on actual things and on their causal relations. Note that this puts immense strain on those later arguments, from a sceptical point of view that regards effects that are non-causal with suspicion (*How does this work exactly? Can you reproduce it under laboratory conditions?*).

Signs never allow the variations to be known completely, they only express them under a form of actual difference that also obscures them. Later in the book, in chapter I, Deleuze attempts to secure this statement and the assumption regarding repetition by giving ontological arguments for the necessary universality of repetition (Everything is repetition of difference but this repetition requires actual identity and, hence, is open to the illusion that identity returns and that pure difference is the illusion.). In the introduction, though, he merely gives cases to support the claim that signs are the key to repetition and the way in to the proper form of causality in a synthetic method.

The first case is repetition in art. More accurately, it is repetitive decorative art on the borderline of nature, understood as regularity, and artistic freedom, understood as that which can break with law. This interest in decorative art is a loose echo of Kant's work on the difference between decoration, nature and the work of genius in his *Third Critique*. It also provides an interesting link to Walter Benjamin's work on repetition in art in 'The work of art in the age of mechanical reproduction'. Deleuze argues that repetition in art is not simply the repetition of a motif, as in wallpaper, for example. Instead, each apparent repetition picks up on an element from the previous member of the series and alters it slightly. This dissymmetry is accompanied by sensations that express the underlying movement of intensities and ideas. All of these things together make up a sign.

For example, small changes in the actual colour red from member to member of a series may be accompanied by a sensation. This sensation is the expression of a change in the way in which different intensities envelop or cover each other. In turn these re-configurations in intensities are accompanied by a change in the way in which an idea is clear and obscure. The sign is the actual change in reds, the virtual changes in intensity and the changes in the clarity and obscurity of ideas. This definition of the sign is an echo of the combination of signifier and signified in the sign as defined in structuralism.

However, Deleuze's signs are not signs for someone, rather, they are signs within an individual (*What is happening to me and hence to the whole world?*). So signs are not a matter of correct interpretation or reading, they are a matter of a necessary experimentation with what the sign triggers in the individual (*What if I try this?*). Signs are, therefore, dynamic due to the ongoing processes of reciprocal determination between the elements of the sign, between its actual side (the change in the colour red) and, its virtual side (the change in the envelopment of intensities and the clarity of ideas). This dynamic relation is present in musical and mathematical rhythm and, indeed, in any other rhythm, including natural cycles and the repetition of words and syllables. A virtual dissymmetry always underlies a merely illusory repetition of the same actual thing. The dissymmetry is an expression of virtual movements in intensity that he calls its cause. It is a cause insofar as it gives sense to the dissymmetry (*Why does this small change in reds matter?*). Later, in *A Thousand Plateaus*, Deleuze expands on these remarks on expression and sense in rhythm art, music and nature at great length, in particular, in the plateau on the ritornello.

In the remainder of the introduction, Deleuze links this point on signs and repetition to his earlier remarks on theatre and death and to later work on difference in itself. However, one new remark stands out on the relation between signs, learning and teaching. He argues that, given the dynamic structure of signs, successful teaching does not depend on imitation, where exactly the same gesture or act is repeated from teacher to pupil. Imitation takes place against a background of movements that have already begun. This means that good learning and teaching should work to come into harmony with those movements and with those of the thing to be learnt. So it cannot be a case of imitating the same gesture as a block. Instead, we learn and teach well when we find ways of triggering signs through dissymmetry in repetitions from teacher to pupil and within the repetitions asked of the pupil. This dissymmetry is what Deleuze calls the remarkable points of the actual things brought into play, for example, the body of the swimmer, the wave, the body of the teacher:

> We learn nothing from those who say: 'Do as I do'. Our only teachers are those who tell us to 'do with me', and are able to emit signs to be developed in heterogeneity rather than propose gestures for us to reproduce.
>
> (DR, pp. 23, 35)

It is important, though, to stress the speculative aspect of all these remarks. This is recognised by Deleuze in the last paragraph of his introduction. He raises two related questions that have not been answered yet. What is a concept of difference that cannot be thought of in terms of identity? What is the essence of repetition as something that does not need to be defined negatively with respect to concepts and as distinct from a repetition of the same thing? That these questions remain at the end of the long introduction shows the preliminary nature of the points raised in it. Deleuze has introduced us, often vaguely, to some of the key concepts and ideas but, in offering only the bare outlines of his arguments, he has merely shown us a rich set of links rather than a valid structure.

3

Difference

DIFFERENCE IN ITSELF

The central problem of the 'Difference in itself' chapter of *Difference and Repetition* is how to determine difference without defining it in terms of identity or representation. Deleuze is searching for a way of thinking about difference that does not view it as a meaningless chaos (*Difference is undetermined – it is everything and nothing.*) or as the negation of identities or of things we can represent (*If difference is to make any sense, it must be as 'the difference between two things' or 'not this thing'.*). More precisely, through his critical readings, Deleuze detaches difference from four key moments in the history of philosophy. First, against Aristotle, difference must not be thought of as that which defines divisions within being: categories, genres and species (*As existents the difference between plants and animals is... As animals the difference between humans and apes is... As humans the difference between men and women is...*). Second, against Hegel, difference must not be thought of as that which subsumes all identities and their antitheses – that is, as the never to be reached end of an expanding process of contradiction and synthesis (*Each synthesis has its contradiction and each contradiction has its synthesis, in an ever wider infinite spiral of difference.*). Third, against Leibniz, difference must not be thought of as infinitely small differences (*Each thing can be subdivided at its limits. No thing is the same as any other at these limits.*). Fourth, against Plato, difference must not be thought of as that which departs from an original (*It differs from perfection in this way.*).

Each of these critical moments is also an opportunity to approach a positive thought of difference. The critique of Aristotle leads to an important Deleuzian ontology that defines being as something that resists categorisation – that is, that resists judgements dividing things into sub-categories according to analogies (*These are alike but different in this way.*). Instead, categories are always illusory from the point of view of being (*'To be' is said of all things in the same way.*). This ontology is part of the thought of completion in Deleuzian dialectics – there is no ontological bar to complete connection (*It is wrong to say that there is something essential to humans that separates them radically from animals.*). The critique of Hegel and Leibniz leads to a clarification of the thesis that difference underlies identity and representation and not the opposite.

But 'to lie under' does not mean 'to be the foundation for'. Difference is not a limit that stands as the origin or the end of a process of identification (*We can represent all but the smallest things.* or *We can represent all but the biggest thing.*). Rather, difference is that which turns all representations into illusions – identity is only a cloak thrown over deeper pure differences. This approach to difference is the result of Deleuze's transcendental method whereby the conditions for actual and virtual things are deduced. Difference is the condition for changes in actual things and actual things are the condition for the expression of difference as something that can be determined.

Finally, and perhaps most importantly for the development of a consistent Deleuzian philosophy of difference, the work on Plato seeks to define virtual ideas with respect to difference rather than identity (*The idea is not a perfect origin with no internal differences or contradictions.*). This leads into the later chapters of *Difference and Repetition* where Deleuze argues that purely differential ideas are the condition for actual things in terms of reciprocal syntheses (chapters four and five of *Difference and Repetition*).

So the six main sections of the chapter are:

1. the presentation of the problem of how to think difference as determinate in a positive manner – hence the search for difference 'in itself'
2. the critique of Aristotle
3. the argument for Deleuze's 'univocal' ontology (being is said of all things in the same way)
4. the critique of Hegel and Leibniz

5. the definition of difference as the condition for identity but not as a foundation or a limit
6. the critique of Plato

Each of these includes moments where Deleuze's original concepts are developed, notably, the concepts of eternal return and of transcendental conditions with respect to the self. I shall deal with each of these sections individually, beginning with the first, here. Each original moment will be emphasised in relation to the critical and constructive arguments that put it into context.

Later in the book, Deleuze will define a problem as something that does not have a single simple solution – that is, there is no way to resolve the problem once and for all. Instead, a problem is something that defines a field of different drives or pressures as problematical for an individual, in the sense of involving an irreducibly complex set of different and conflicting challenges (*I'm pulled towards all of these, yet I cannot have them all, yet if I choose one it must be at the expense of the others.*). Each solution merely transforms the problem and throws up new challenges, rather than finally breaking the spell. A problem is a series of tensions that must be met with a constructive act – something like a way of living with the problem, rather than solving it.

Solutions have to be added to the roll call of illusions that *Difference and Repetition* seeks to reveal. For example, there is no solution to the question of how to live an individual life, as if somehow all its tensions could be dispelled if only we lived properly. To think in terms of the proper is to invite the most damaging of illusions into an individual life (*If only I knew who I was ... What would M do? ... How to be a good mother, father, soldier, servant, boss?*). This helps to explain the enigmatic first section of the chapter on difference in itself. Deleuze cannot present the problem of the determinacy of difference in an overly simple way since this would encourage a view to a straightforward solution. On the contrary, he needs to show that, for the specific task of constructing a philosophy of difference, determinacy must be thought of in a new way and in a way that resists any notion of finally determining difference.

This new approach has two significant aspects. First, determinacy must not be confused with distinctness, where to be distinct means to be well-defined with respect to limits that preserve a thing from other undetermined things. For Deleuze, a thing is determined because it cannot be distinguished finally from a chaotic state – to be determined it must appear with a chaotic state. Second, indeterminacy must not be viewed as an evil that can be escaped, as if the goal of philosophy were to render all things determinate and thereby 'save us' from chaos. Therefore, the first two paragraphs of the chapter generate images and examples of a determinacy that depends on a backdrop of indeterminacy, rather than other determinate things. This explains the strange images of floating organs and the references to Goya's aquatints and Odilon Redon's use of chalk effects. It also explains the concern with cruelty and monstrosity in the latter parts of the second paragraph. Due to its association with a chaotic backdrop that generates emotions resistant to knowledge and reason, difference has been seen as something to be avoided or tamed. Goya's and Redon's works capture this emotional response by playing on the relation between a thing that is differentiated and an ungraspable, undifferentiated backdrop.

This, in turn, explains Deleuze's interest in cruelty, not only here but through the book and his works as a whole (for example, in *Essays Critical and Clinical* and in his work on Sacher Masoch). He associates the belief that things can be determined independently of a chaotic backdrop, and the belief that we should move towards a complete determination of things and away from chaos, with the belief that it is possible to finally do justice to things, to act without cruelty. His counter-view is that difference as chaos is necessary and compels acts of determination to a necessary cruelty. His precise understanding of cruelty is, then, the generation of emotion and change as things are determined in relation to an indifferent background. The hard to bear cruelty of Goya's *Caprichos* or *Desastros* is, therefore, not only in their violent subjects but in Goya's style – in the way in which he animates individual things with pain, fear and lust by setting them against an indistinct ground. In Goya's works, defenceless bodies or figures teeter over pits or hover slightly above an oblivion that we sense as horrific but without understanding the nature of the horror. This state is universal according to Deleuze's approach to difference.

It would be a mistake, though, to move too readily between actual forms of cruelty and Deleuze's definition. He does not mean that we cannot avoid actual specific acts of violence, as if we could only shrug our shoulders at images of torture. His work for a group concerned with prison conditions, the *Groupe Information Prisons*, in the 1970s, alongside Foucault, testifies to the belief that philosophy can be engaged against cruelty. But this engagement does not mean that philosophy can somehow aim to be pure or that it can bring ever greater purity to the world. Even when we determine something as wrong and something as better, we have to throw others back into indistinctness and we carry something of the indistinct forward. So Redon's floating, dream-like, peaceful figures, achieved through abstract chalk lines with no clear boundaries, capture the same cruel effect as Goya's. In content and style, Redon's works force beauty and innocence to appear against and out of a chaotic background, half-way between blissful sleep and an airless submergence.

So difference in itself is vivifying, in the sense that to live is to be determinate, but that living intensity has an indistinct ground as its condition. To live is to live in horror of the ground – difference is cruel. According to Deleuze, in reaction to this 'terrible' state, philosophy has mistakenly attempted to 'tear difference away from this damnation'. In order to tame difference, philosophy has posited an original happy state free of cruelty. This state is found in classical Greek philosophy and it is what difference must be returned to – that is, difference must be defined without recourse to the undifferentiated background and hence to cruelty. In this fictional, odyssey-like account of the history of philosophy, Deleuze is following his own study of theatre and drama outlined in my previous chapter. Thanks to Goya, Redon and a tale of origins and fall, he has dramatised the opposition between difference defined in itself and difference defined in terms of identity and representation. The drama is designed to convey the emotional and philosophical stakes of this opposition. The precise philosophical arguments behind it begin with his study of Aristotle.

ARISTOTLE

Deleuze aims to show that Aristotle's definition of difference misses a deeper understanding of the term. At stake is the question of whether difference ought to be thought of in terms of prior categories or whether categories presuppose and illegitimately ignore a deeper form of difference. Later in the book, Deleuze will highlight the way in which the Aristotelian approach has become imbedded in thinking and common sense – for example, in the way learning involves exercises of attribution in the early stages of development and, indeed, much later, in the form of tests (*Where does this thing belong? In which of these boxes would you put this thing? What is the difference between this set of things and that one? Circle the torque wrench. Is Heidegger a hermeneutician or a phenomenologist? Tick one box.*).

If the philosophical justification that underpins these questions is that the correct distribution of things into sets has to be the first way of approaching them, then Deleuze argues that this is a mistake based on the wrong view of difference. Through *Difference and Repetition* he develops a counter-view of teaching and learning. He constructs it around the definition of difference as that which sets things in movement and as that which can only be approached by resisting thought in terms of the proper and in terms of categories (*Where else could it belong? What if we think of it as something else? In what ways can we make it fall outside its proper category?*). So differences between things, based on which sets they belong to, are not the important or primary differences. Rather, real difference is a matter of how things become different, how they evolve and continue to evolve beyond the boundaries of the sets they have been distributed into (*It is not what you are or what this is, it is what you are becoming and why this becoming is significant for others and other things.*).

The first move in Deleuze's argument is designed to show that Aristotle is, indeed, involved in the definition of the essence of difference. This is shown through the leading question of his work in *Metaphysics X*: 'What is the greatest difference?' According to Aristotle, difference is more than otherness or diversity – it is opposition. In opposition, it reaches its greatest form in contraries. Furthermore, the greatest contraries are those that hold between species of a same genre (for example, in the difference between animals capable of flight or earth-bound). Outside these oppositions, difference becomes less strong, in the sense of less well-determined and, therefore, imperfect. So completely different things – that is, things that cannot be said to belong to the same genre in any way – are merely other. This otherness cannot be captured in a concept (*Is this moon creature better than a truffle-hunting dog? How should I know? It's just different.*). Similarly, different individuals differ only in insignificant ways – that is, ways that cannot be thought of in terms of general concepts giving rise to species (*Yeah, OK, this one's a bit more 'handsome' but they're both excellent truffle-hunters and that's what matters.*).

Deleuze's critique of the definition of difference as the contrariety of species within genres turns on the roles of conceptual identity, representation and judgement. His aim is to show that true difference is not a matter of contrary predicates that allow for the determination of subsets within greater sets defined by more general concepts (*In the set of dogs determined by the general concept, we find the subsets fighting dogs and pets determined by the predicate 'bred to kill'.*). The role of thought with respect to difference, defined according to contrary predicates, is to distribute individuals into sets and subsets – this is judgement as common sense. It is also to divide sets into hierarchies – this is judgement as good sense. Judgement depends on representation since the individual we are faced with, in fact or imagination, is subsumed under a representation for judgement to take place. *As you sneak over the garden fence, a shadow moves and you hear a growl. What predicates are present here? Those of poodle or mastiff (representation and common sense). Which is worse (good sense)?*

But why is this way of thinking about difference mistaken? Specific difference or the search for species and sub-species in terms of contraries seem to be confirmed by practice and conventional wisdom about practical success. Categorisation seems pretty effective and important, whether you are on an illicit assignation, defending your chickens or breeding dogs for sale. Why is Deleuze opposed to the distributive nature of judgement and its capacity to unite us and our senses around agreements regarding common and good sense?

His answer is formal and practical. Formally, Aristotle has not found the greatest difference and the greatest difference is presupposed by specific difference. Practically, specific difference is incomplete and cannot account for the evolution and mutation of species, where contraries are, in reality, related. Neither can it account for the significance of individuals within that mutation. Against the definition of essences, the proper and categories, Deleuze suggests a critical and creative method concerned with evolution and transgression. For example, in his *Foucault*, he combines archaeology and genealogy as the study of the elements that explain past evolution. These elements serve in the creative movement that goes beyond present categories and genres. This study is reflexive – the past is recovered but only where it is also created by future change.

The execution of Deleuze's critique of Aristotle is extremely dense. I have set out my version of its main points in more simple form covering paragraphs three to five of the second section of the 'Difference in itself' chapter. Deleuze's arguments aim to show, in turn, that species, genres and Aristotle's definition of being cannot be the basis for determining greatest difference:

1. Specific difference, the difference between species, is not the greatest difference since it cannot account for differences be tween genres, where differences are not a matter of contrary predicates. *Rocks are different from animals but not in the same way as fighting dogs are different from toy poodles.*

2. Specific differences depend on the definition of general sets or genres that provide the series of predicates within which specific contrariety occurs. *You cannot subdivide the set of dogs without knowing what dogs are.*

3. So specific difference cannot be difference in itself since some differences elude it and since the definition of difference depends on the definition of concepts that itself depends on the definition of genres. Aristotle has not arrived at the essence of difference.

4. It is wrong to think of difference in terms of predicates since the term is used in ways that preclude that definition.

5. According to Aristotle, being is not a genre because differences exist (so things that do not have a predicate *are* in some way).

6. But, by defining existence in terms of analogy, Aristotle, then, misses this opportunity for defining difference in terms of being and free of the condition of prior concepts. That is, for him, things *are* in different ways and not in the same way. An analogy holds between the existence of different things – when we say that rocks and animals exist we mean that to be a rock is to satisfy the predicates of the concept rock in a similar way as animals satisfy the predicates of the concept animal. Rocks and animals exist but only according to an analogy that holds between the ways in which they are.

7. This move to analogy sets philosophy in the context of judgement concerning the correct definition of genres and species (common sense) and the correct definition of the hierarchies of genres and species (good sense).

8. Aristotle's philosophy does not give us the right definition of difference because it renders it secondary to the determination of conceptual identity.

The metaphysical conclusion of this critique of Aristotle's definition of difference is the distinction drawn between an equivocal definition of being (*All things are but how they are differs and that difference depends on what they are.*) and a univocal definition (*All things are in the same way, independently of what they are.*). The more practical result of the critique is the connections drawn between concepts, predicates, analogy and perception when difference becomes a reflexive concept – that is, when it operates after the definition of genres or sets, in order to subdivide them and organise them.

> As a concept of reflection, difference testifies to its full submission to all the requirements of representation, which becomes thereby 'organic representation'. In the concept of reflection, mediated and mediating difference is in effect fully subject to the identity of the concept, the opposition of predicates, the analogy of judgement and the resemblance of perception.
>
> (DR, pp. 35, 52)

Deleuze's counter is that there are non-conceptual differences. They resist the demand for representation in the determination of parts or subsets according to opposition and differences in predicates.

DELEUZE'S ONTOLOGY

In the context of his work on Aristotle, the challenge that Deleuze's ontology has to respond to is the following. All things cannot be in the same way since things are different. It is different to be a rock and an animal – they are in different ways. Therefore, to be is to be what you are and not simply to be. Being is equivocal and the relation between different existents is analogical. This challenge hits at the very engine room of Deleuze's philosophy since it displaces his principle of connection in favour of a principle of determination of identity – it's what you are, not what you connect to. What you are disconnects you from other things, once and for all, and positions you in a hierarchy of distinct sets or categories. In turn, this returns Cartesian analysis to favour, against Spinoza's synthesis – know the thing clearly and distinctly, then move to its causes, rather than know the thing through its causes.

So long as we persist in thinking of existence primarily as the existence of a well-defined thing, Deleuze will not be able make his case and Aristotle will prevail since, however esoteric the definition of what being is as a property of the thing, we will always come up against differences between things with respect to this property or predicate – hence Deleuze's constant objection to thinking in terms of concepts and predicates as the foundation for thought. But, then, how can being be defined if not by reflecting on the existence of things we can identify and define conceptually?

Deleuze's arguments for being as univocal (the third section of the 'Difference in itself' chapter) is a dialectical response to this challenge. He draws us to a difficult and counter-intuitive ontology by tracing the way in which different attempts at an univocal ontology can be dragged back into the demand for an equivocal definition of being. The section constructs a subtle ontology on this gradual refinement following a pattern of arguments through historical debates. Put simply, two related movements allow us to follow the direction of the dialectic. First, to be is not to be a well-defined thing with recognisable limits – on the contrary, it is to be a pure movement or variation in relation to well-defined things. Being is both being and becoming, where becoming is the condition for being. Second, the section and, indeed, *Difference and Repetition* as whole are moving towards a definition of those pure variations as things that are but that cannot be identified. Finally, once Deleuze has defined the ideal synthesis of difference and the asymmetrical synthesis of sensation, to say that something is is to say that it is an individual – a changing re-enactment of the whole of ideas, intensities and actual things through singular sensations.

The first move in the dialectic is to look at propositions in order to put the claim that being is not a genre or category. A proposition, let's say 'This picture is blue.', has a sense or meaning – what we mean when we utter the proposition. It designates something – the picture. It has designators that allow it to refer to the picture – 'this', 'that'. The sense may vary for the same referent. When we say 'This picture is blue.', different senses of blue – this picture is sad or of a blue colour – apply to the same existent. Designators may refer to any number of distinct things. However, whenever we say 'This is X.', 'is' has the same meaning. So, although the senses and referents can vary without limit, what we mean when we say that they are remains the same. Being cannot be a subset of referents or meanings. It is not a category or genre – that is, a way for things to be in a certain sense or as a member of a certain set. So, even though referents and senses are different, they are the same in terms of being: 'We must add that being, this common designated, insofar as it expresses itself, is said in turn *in a single and same sense* of all the numerically distinct designators and expressors.' (DR, pp. 35, 53)

It is important to stress that Deleuze's discussion of propositions can only be seen as an explanation of a position rather than a justification for it. As justification, it would merely beg the questions 'Is *to be* really said in the same way of all things?' and 'Even if it is, is it right to do so?'. From the point of view of the analytic tradition, we would look askance at Deleuze's pronouncements and point him to the works of Meinong, Frege and Quine, among others. The justification comes out more clearly in Deleuze's arguments for the necessity of sensation in relation to sense and understanding in chapter 5 of *Difference and Repetition*. That the remarks on propositions are only a provisional step is made clear by the next point that expresses a counter to the claim that being is said of all things in the same way.

Though he does not voice it, Deleuze goes on to respond to the objection that, even if being is said of all things in the same way, it is said of different things. In other words, there is a division of existents that means that, when we say that all things exist, we mean nothing more than all things can be divided into categories (*Yes, flying pigs exist but only as creatures of fantasy. They do not exist like real pigs except in the sense of existing as X or Y.*). It is worth noting that this objection allows for many of the logical and analytical objections to Deleuze's rather throwaway statements on propositions – for example, that, when we say that something is, we mean different things, depending on what we say exists. His response to these objections is to draw a distinction between two different types of division or distribution, in order to allow for the possibility of distinctions between beings that do not depend on different categories of existence.

A distribution that divides that which is distributed must be distinguished from a distribution where an open space is occupied. Deleuze calls the first a sedentary distribution where judgement operates by allocating things to different pre-established categories (*Where does this belong?*). The second is called a nomadic distribution, where space can be cut up, but only contingently, and after a space has been opened up by a distribution operated from within that which is distributed (*Look, they seem to accumulate here and here*). According to Deleuze, the nomadic distribution is resistant to external or general hierarchies since the things that distribute themselves cannot be compared legitimately to one another – that is, they are not measurable according to the categories they are supposed to fit into. This is because he defines a nomadic distribution as one where we do not have access to the principle guiding the distribution or to the power that generated it. Put simply, we can never know that a nomadic distribution is over in terms of generating new principles and distributions. Instead, things are only answerable to the demand to distribute nomadically – that is, to go beyond and undo an emergent order.

This distinction between nomadic and sedentary distributions reappears and becomes very important in Deleuze's later work, most notably in *A Thousand Plateaus* with the concepts of the nomadic war machine and the relation of smooth and striated space. The nomadic war machine is a nomadic distribution in a smooth space undoing a fixed, well-determined striated space – that is, a space given an external ordering that always returns to be undone again. In *Difference and Repetition*, though, the terms have a strongly ontological function, rather than the more practical and experimental aspect of the later work. Being is univocal and the 'is' is said of all things in the same way because all things distribute themselves and are only answerable to themselves in overcoming their internal limits and the way they become fixed. In other words, any fixed definition of categories of existence cannot account for the way in which things evolve and have evolved outside those categories. Things distribute themselves in a way that must remain opaque for an understanding that attempts to fix categories.

However, the argument for an equivocal view of being returns at this point. Deleuze puts it through a series of questions that insist that, even if being is said of all things in the same way in terms of a nomadic distribution, when we designate individual existents, their relation to the distribution is still one of analogy (*This one is like this one and unlike those ones...*). So, although we cannot legitimately distribute things into pre-set categories, we must establish such categories after the fact and we must do so using analogies that establish different categories of existence.

Deleuze's response is that this view is mistaken because it fails to take account of the initial distribution. It compares that which has been distributed as recognisable individuals, in terms of categories, but it cannot account for what makes them individual in a positive way – that is, for the way in which individuals have evolved and continue to evolve independent of the categories we ascribe them to. 'We must show not only how individuating difference differs in kind from specific difference, but primarily and above all how individuation precedes matter and form, species and parts, and every other element of the constituted individual.' (DR, pp. 38, 56) The problem is, though, how do you show this individuation without making recourse to judgements of likeness based on concepts? The rest of the section on ontology shows how such a demonstration has evolved from Duns Scotus, through Spinoza and on to Nietzsche.

Deleuze wants to show that 'to be' is not simply an empty term that must be supplemented by a series of different 'to be an X'. In other words, all things are in the same way and this way has substantial attributes – it is not an empty category that only acquires sense once it is divided further. According to him, the first philosopher to provide ways of showing this precisely was Duns Scotus in his definition of formal and modal distinctions. First, formal distinction does not imply a numerical distinction – that is, there are some distinctions, for example, different attributes, that do not imply any sort of division within a being that possesses them: 'God can possess these univocal attributes without losing his unity'. (DR, pp. 39, 58) There are differences in God (thought and extension, say) but not different parts of God (he is indivisibly thought and extension). The same is true of being. Things are in different ways but to be remains the same.

Second, modal distinctions distinguish an attribute and the ways in which it can vary. There are many different modes of an attribute – that is, ways in which it is found in actual things (there are many different ways of being extended) – but these do not alter extension as an attribute of being. Things are in different ways and those ways vary in things but to be (God) remains the same. Scotus's distinctions counter the objection that, if two things are different in a specific way, then they do not exist in the same way with respect to that difference.

The problem with Scotus's definitions is that, in Deleuze's words, being remains neutral. That is, it is no longer empty – it has attributes – but these are held at arm's length from their actual expression in varying modes. God is an abstract neutral being at one remove from actual beings. Spinoza develops Scotus's insights by extending being to the modes. His *Deus sive natura* (God or nature) is attributes and their modes. Actual things are, then, only modes of attributes and everything is in the same way but to varying degrees: 'From this follows a determination of modes as degrees of power, and a single 'obligation' for such modes: to deploy all their power or their being within the limit itself.' (DR, pp. 40, 59) To be is said in the same way of all things but to varying degrees. However, this idea of varying degrees still maintains some kind of distinction between attributes and modes – between being (every attribute), attributes and modes (variations of attributes). These distinctions are still an opportunity for the return to an equivocal definition of being and to analogy (being varies differently in actual things; these differences allow us to define sets or genres; things are alike in their variations; genres are alike in the way their things vary).

Only Nietzsche overcomes the equivocal definition of being and its relation to judgement by insisting that being is only the modes. To be is to become and things only acquire identity because they become, because they express pure variations. Deleuze's interpretation of the doctrine of eternal return, that only becoming returns and not identity, is the culmination of his dialectic opposing univocal and equivocal definitions of being. When he says that to be is said of all things in the same way, he means that all things are as the return of pure differences and only as pure differences. There are no attributes and there is no substance independent of them. You are because you express pure variations in a different way, in different combinations and to different degrees. Your identity, as a different individual, depends on the way you express pure variations (*her mother's anger but softer*):

That is why eternal return is said only of the theatrical world of the metamorphoses and masks of the Will to power, of the pure intensities of that Will which are like mobile individuating factors unwilling to allow themselves to be contained within the factitious limits of this or that individual, this or that Self.

(DR, pp. 41, 60)

So there is no need for analogy. It is the same pure becoming that returns but one that has no identity other than in its repetitions. There is also no need for judgement. Since they have no identity, pure differences cannot be categorised and, hence, neither can the identities that express them. Instead, new creations repeat these differences by passively selecting some at greater degrees than others. But do pure differences exist? Is eternal return true? More importantly, why aren't the things that express pure differences open to a legitimate treatment in terms of categories? That is, is it not possible to think of Nietzsche's doctrine of eternal return in terms of an equivocal definition of being? Perhaps the answer to this last question is that these things are secondary and illusory from the point of view of their condition in pure becoming but Deleuze does not flesh out the argument at this point. The full argument only occurs with his comprehensive definition of individuals in the fifth chapter of *Difference and Repetition* where he claims that reality must be thought of in terms of individuals resistant to categorisation.

Once again, he has taken us through a dialectical argument that fits into a much wider dialectic – this time, on the possibility of a univocal ontology in the context of the definition of difference in itself. This argument draws in a series of important historical references and makes plausible points, such as the critique of Aristotle from the point of view of questions concerning the genesis of categories and the possibility of evolution. But we must wait for later arguments to be able judge the validity of the enterprise as a whole due to the conjectural nature of the statements on eternal return and on pure differences.

HEGEL AND LEIBNIZ

In his critique of Aristotelian ontology and in his alternative account, Deleuze has distanced himself from definitions of difference that treat it as secondary to definitions of identity based on concepts and representations. But what occurs when a more Deleuzian definition of difference, such as that which undoes representation and identity, is combined with concepts and representations? He considers this possibility in the 'Difference in itself' chapter through encounters with Hegel and Leibniz. Put simply, his claim is that their philosophies attempt to put pure difference at the foundation of identity by defining the limits of identity in terms of the infinite. In other words, at its limits, any supposed identity is, in fact, ill-defined because it cannot be represented due to the infinite, ungraspable nature of the limit.

According to Deleuze, Hegel and Leibniz differ in the nature of the infinite limit. In Hegel's case it is that anything is always subsumed, in a greater and contradictory thing, to infinity. So, each time we think we have arrived at the final identity of all things, it is open to a contradiction: 'Even though it is said of oppositions or of finite determination, this Hegelian infinite remains the infinitely large of theology, of the *Ens quo nihil Majus*.' (DR, pp. 45, 65) In opposition to this Hegelian infinitely great limit, Leibniz posits infinitely small differences at the limit of anything, so that, whenever we arrive at a final identity, it is undone by tiny but significant variations. For Hegel, as read by Deleuze, whenever we arrive at a well-ordered understanding of the world, ordered, finally, by the greatest entity that holds it all together, then a contradictory but also subsuming entity shows the first order to have been temporary and subject to retrospective re-assessment. For

Leibniz, on the other hand, whenever we arrive at a well-defined representation of a thing, we find in it the smallest traces of what the definition is supposed to exclude and these traces also show the first representation to have been insufficient.

Given the way in which the infinite undoes identity and representation in Hegel's and Leibniz's philosophies, it seems odd that Deleuze should want to criticize them. However, as befits his dialectical method, he is concerned to show that, whilst there is much to learn from them, neither philosopher goes far enough in putting pure difference at the foundation of identity. His claim is that, in both cases, representation returns to tame the infinite: 'In both cases, as well, it seems that infinite representation does not suffice to render the thought of difference independent of the simple analogy of essences, or of the simple similarity of properties.' (DR, pp. 49, 70) More importantly, this return is inevitable due to the different ways in which they set up the structure of limits, identity and infinite. This allows Deleuze to develop his own arguments and concepts, in particular with respect to Leibniz, whilst criticising the two earlier philosophers. The concepts that stand out in this dual argument are power, contradiction and 'vice-diction'.

Deleuze uses the concept of power to explain how an infinite limit is related to and undoes established identities. Difference, defined as an endless process of 'disappearance and birth', is no longer something beyond the boundaries of well-defined entities – it is at play in their genesis and destruction. This is the great contrast with Aristotle's fixed categories since things must not only be approached through what they are but also in terms of how they have become and how they are undone. It also responds to Deleuze's strongest criticism of Aristotle since evolution can be explained as an intrinsic aspect of all categories and as something that all things participate in.

Difference is, then, something powerful in itself. The question of how to participate in and understand the way in which things evolve in relation to infinite processes replaces judgement in relation to categories, hierarchies and fixed concepts. Deleuze calls the first 'orgiastic' representation, picking up on the indifferent promiscuity and bacchanalian senses of the term. Such representation comes out of a chaotic ground or foundation, as opposed to the second, organic representation, or representation in terms of proper parts and sub-parts. Through the section on Hegel and Leibniz, he will reproach them for allowing thought in terms of the proper and essences to return in orgiastic representation: 'In short, orgiastic representation has the ground as its principle and the infinite as its element, by contrast with organic representation which retains form as its principle and the finite as its element.' (DR, pp. 43, 63)

The first step of Deleuze's critique is to note how the introduction of the concepts of infinitely small and infinitely big differences re-introduces measure, judgement and representation in difference as chaotic ground. In Hegel's case, this takes place through the role of the concept of contradiction. According to Deleuze, Hegel rejoins Aristotle in defining the maximum of difference as contradiction. However, unlike Aristotle, Hegel pushes contradiction to infinity and, thereby, goes beyond contradiction defined as an opposition within a wider category that brings the contradictories together (*Whether capable of flight or earth-bound, they are both mammals*). The overarching category, in Aristotle's case of an equivocal being, is never present. So contradictories are never brought together as the same in ever greater but stable categories. Each time contradictory categories are subsumed under a further one, it is as different categories – each differs from itself in the subsumed contradiction (*A flying squirrel is a mammal in a different way than an earth-bound one and flying or earth-bound differ in the category of mammals in a different way than in other categories.*). This process of differing in contradiction is endless, so no definition of categories or of contradictions is final.

However, Hegel ascribes a value to this differing in the contradiction. That is, the essence of a thing lies in its real contradiction and in the contradiction of that contradiction – the synthesis. So the task and direction of philosophy is to lift contradiction in ever wider cycles of real contradictions and syntheses: 'Difference finds its own concept in the posited contradiction: it is here that it becomes pure, intrinsic, essential, qualitative, synthetic and productive; here that it no longer allows indifference to subsist.' (DR, pp. 45, 65) Identity then returns in the definition of the essence of a thing as its real contradictions and syntheses, in terms of what it subsumes and what it is subsumed in. This is not a closed, finite identity but it is closed in the logic that governs the endless spiral of contradictions and syntheses. In this way, difference loses the indifference that Deleuze values, despite its definition in terms of the infinite.

If Hegel's infinite has to be understood as the infinitely great, Leibniz's must be understood as the infinitely small. From

Deleuze's point of view, Leibniz's advantage over Hegel lies in the way difference is thought of without having to make recourse to contradiction. Two things are not different because what is essential for one is negated in the other (*capable of flight, not capable of flight*) but because what is inessential for one is related to what is inessential for the other. So the inessential, an infinitely small difference, turns out to be critical in determining difference universally. There are at least two ways in to this work on Leibniz and difference. The first is mathematical. The second draws on Leibniz's famous idea of possible worlds and his examples of Caesar (as having crossed the Rubicon or not) and Adam (as sinner or not) from the *Discourse on Metaphysics*.

Infinitely small differences, from the point of view of a life, can lead to utterly divergent worlds. *At the moment of greatest decision between two loves, your sensations drive you to a momentous decision. But just as the decision begins to crystallize an acquaintance happens to stumble into the process, snapping you back into the normal flow of your life. You opt for safety and decency, deciding against expanding a brief encounter into a whole life.* Two possible lives start from that moment – the one that you live and the one that you have sacrificed. You were the same up to the jogged moment of decision but the smallest most insignificant detail brought out two vastly different worlds (*Why did she have to walk in then?*).

For Deleuze, significance does not lie in the chance encounter with the blundering acquaintance but, rather, with the two possible futures lying dormant in an apparently settled life and the way in which *apparently* insignificant events switch between those possibilities. The two worlds do not contradict one another. In Deleuze's words, following Leibniz, they vice-dict each other or play the life in different ways. From the point of view of each life, the occurrence or non-occurrence of the disruption seems infinitely small. Chance interventions occur all the time – some serendipitous others disastrous – and there will be many other more significant events occurring alongside each one. But, from the point of view of the difference between the two possible worlds, the event is all important.

Deleuze explains this point by referring to Leibniz's work on differential equations. Leibniz and Newton discovered that, for the variables x and y of an equation, an infinitely small difference of x, called dx, is insignificant with respect to x and, hence, to the value of the equation for given values of x and y – similarly dy to y. However, the relation dy/dx reveals significant points of the relation y/x and significant points of the initial equation – for example the points at which a curve changes inflexion. Here, Deleuze returns to two terms that are of great importance for his work later in *Difference and Repetition*. The equation reveals the reciprocal determination of x and y. However, the knowledge afforded by that equation is incomplete with respect to the relation of x and y until we include the information garnered from successive differentiations (work on the relation of dx to dy and ddx to ddy and so on).

In a life, variables are in a relation of reciprocal determination, which we must work with, but, in order to get a view of the complete life, we must also work with information that is insignificant with respect to the variables but critical for an understanding of their relation: 'The inessential here refers not to that which lacks importance but, on the contrary, to the most profound, to the universal matter or continuum from which the essences are finally made.' (DR, pp. 47, 67) The lesson that Deleuze wants to draw in his contrast of Hegel and Leibniz is that the greatest difference, that is, the most significant difference, is in fact insignificant from the point of view of contradiction and essence.

The differences we can draw by negation (*To contradict this is to negate its essence*) and the representations that are necessary in order to be able to draw them (*What is its concept? To what category does it belong? Who am I?*) fail to grasp the power of insignificant differences in determining and undermining identity and evolution. A possible world or an individual emerges where a significant point ensures the continuity of the series of events that come together to make that world or individual. On the other hand, a significant point may also mark the divergence of a series of events.

According to Deleuze, this divergence is what is meant by the concept of incompossibility.

That is to say, for each world a series which converges around a distinctive point is capable of being continued in all directions in other series converging around other points, while the incompossibility of worlds, by contrast, is defined by the juxtaposition of points which would make the resultant series diverge.

(DR, pp. 48, 68)

These are the Leibnizian roots of Deleuze's later development of the concept of haecceity (notably, in *A Thousand Plateaus*). The haecceity is the inessential event that defines an individual or world (*For me, she'll always be the still dry heat of a Mediterranean midday.*).

These Leibnizian roots are also an important element of Deleuze's dependence on passivity and the concept of the dice throw with respect to the creative destruction element of his method. The significant point or haecceity cannot be discovered through a conscious representation of the self, only through experimentation, because that significance may lie in infinitely small differences. Indeed, even if it lies in apparently obvious and gross aspects of an identity, these will be transformed and will participate in evolution in ways that cannot be predicted. This openness to unpredictable and apparently small-scale events is explained best in terms of Deleuze's concepts of the event (developed later in *Difference and Repetition*) and of the events and the cracks that run through and disrupt lives and things in his *Logics of Sense.*

Yet Deleuze remains critical of Leibniz. This is because his treatment of infinitely small differences is still approached from the point of view of identity. Thus, in the way Deleuze has explained Leibniz, difference is still defined as infinitesimal and significant from the point of view of an identity that it presupposes.

> Between Leibniz and Hegel it matters little whether the supposed negative of difference is understood as a vice-dicting limitation or a contradicting limitation, any more than it matters whether infinite identity be considered analytic or synthetic. In either case difference remains subordinated to identity, reduced to the negative, incarcerated within similitude or analogy.
>
> (DR, pp. 50, 70)

For Deleuze, this relation of the infinitely small to an identity is a mistaken account of the event. The event is not only merely an actual event for an identifiable person (*the bumbling acquaintance, the unsettled decision*). The event must be thought of primarily as an occurrence at the level of the virtual – as something that resists identification and not the actual. The event is a relation between actualities and a sensation (*I cannot do it.*) that expresses an intensity that envelops others (*The intensities in duty, embarrassment and fear grew and overshadowed passion, devilment and bravery.*). This reconfiguration of intensities lights up ideas in different relations of clarity and obscurity (*The idea of order – to serve, to repress – became clear. The idea of freedom – to move, to taste – receded.*).

But is this not fanciful invention and unnecessary complication? Isn't identity a necessary and primary condition for speaking of difference and of the significance of events? How is it possible to speak of difference without making such a move? How can we judge that something is infinitely small, if not by reference to larger identities?

DIFFERENCE AS EXPERIMENT AND EXPERIENCE

Following his discussion of Leibniz, Deleuze is able to give his first lengthy definition of difference as he sees it. The definition is unusual since it is extensional rather than intensional – that is, he gives practical applications of the term, rather than a list of its properties or characteristics. Following the critique of Aristotle, we should not be surprised by this since Deleuze has voiced a strong opposition to the reduction of a thing to a fixed concept or set of predicates. The practical exposition of difference returns to Deleuze's concern with principles and method. We find him refining the ideas of completeness and forgetting with respect to difference, as well as developing a more precise sense of how we should act positively with respect to them. This contrasts with the negative effects that he finds in Aristotle's, Hegel's and Leibniz's approaches, where the privilege assigned to identity has negative practical consequences because real difference is ignored. The practical definition of difference in itself covers the following areas:

1. There is a right way of experiencing difference.
2. Opposition and contradiction work against real difference.
3. Difference must be affirmed.
4. If affirmation follows negation, real difference is missed.
5. Given eternal return, the affirmation of difference must be prior to identity and negation.
6. Representation works against affirmation.
7. There is an aesthetics of difference that escapes representation.
8. The idea of the identity of the self works against real difference.

The first of these points is perhaps the most accessible but it is still counter-intuitive. If there is a manifesto on difference in *Difference and Repetition*. It is the paragraph that begins 'There is a crucial experience of difference ...'. (DR, pp. 50, 71) But, as the paragraph unfolds, it becomes clear that Deleuze means that there is a right way and a wrong way of experiencing. This is very odd both from a view of experience as the experience of brute facts, beyond the actions of the subject – something like the experience of sense-data in Russell or primary qualities in Locke – and from the point of view of Deleuze's passivity, where we could assume that we have to let experience happen. The correct understanding is, in fact, between these two positions. We have to work in a certain way in order for a fundamental experience of the multiplicity of pure differences, or the absence of facts, to be expressed in us.

The form of this action is questioning with respect to conditions: 'There is a crucial experience of difference and a corresponding experiment: every time we find ourselves confronted or bound by a limitation or an opposition we should ask what such a situation presupposes.' (DR, pp. 50, 71) I have kept the additional qualification 'and a corresponding experiment' from the Patton translation. It makes sense to translate *expérience* by experience and experiment and to add to Deleuze's words, in order to render the two French senses of the term. However, Deleuze only writes *expérience*. So it remains a crucial matter of interpretation since it could have been better to have insisted that for Deleuze all experience is an experiment or that some experiences call for experimentation. Indeed, by putting this degree of interpretation into his excellent translation, Paul Patton could be accused of having let down his otherwise very high standards of literal accuracy allied to clarity. Here, though, the introduction of experience/experiment split has very strong philosophical grounds.

When we experience difference by experimenting, Deleuze claims that experience becomes a radically multiple thing – that is, it is no longer the experience by a self of a set of objects. It is the temporary coming together of an infinite series of pure differences into areas of more and less clarity and obscurity, according to the experiment. His difficult definition is necessary in order to go beyond the sense of experience as an opposition (experiencer/experienced) and a related opposition of identities (identity of the experiencer and of the experienced). Instead, away from this deeply embedded presupposition, we have to think of experience as, for example, a particular pattern of waves forming on a sea in turmoil but without someone experiencing it. The experience is the connecting pattern that occurs when different perpetually shifting wave heights, lengths, colours and shapes combine for a moment into something more fixed before disappearing into new combinations. In Deleuze's later work, with Félix Guattari, this idea of a temporary combination of differences becomes the important idea of the rhizome or network of differential relations that cannot be viewed in terms of fixed boundaries, measures and origins. Real difference and rhizomes connect but do not connect identities. Real experience of difference connects with as much as possible but it does not connect objects in consciousness or memory.

If this definition of the experience of real difference is correct, then we can see why Deleuze goes on to claim that thought, in terms of oppositions, presupposes it and does it damage. The damage occurs because, each time we fall back on to a thought in terms of oppositions and contradictions, we cannot experience real difference. The movements captured in the wave are not contradictory but merely other. An experience does not lie in the opposition of subject and object, or experiencer and experienced, but in a coming together that requires neither subjective nor objective identity. Oppositions and contradictions arise because we fix the movements of real difference. Without these movements there would be nothing to fix and without them we could not explain why 'fixed things' change. But, according to Deleuze, any treatment of difference that begins with a negation (for example, with movement defined as the negation of fixity) cannot approach difference as pure movements. Thus, when Leibniz and Hegel attempt to explain change through infinite limits, identity returns either in the concept of the greatest – that in which all contradictions are subsumed – or it returns as the identity of the thing that allowed for infinity at its limits.

To counter the treatment of difference as the negation of identity, Deleuze states that difference must be affirmed in itself. He contrasts a false or quasi-affirmation that comes out of negation (*We are not-this!*) with real affirmation (*This becoming!*). The first carries with it a remainder of what it negates, like Zarathustra's ass in Nietzsche's *Thus Spake Zarathustra*. This is to burden affirmation with the identity of that which has been negated and opposed. It is to carry an ever growing weight of things, as each successive affirmation negates earlier ones and their negations (*This time I am going to get my life right!*).

So the affirmation of real difference must be a shedding of ballast that neither affirms a well-defined thing or identity nor negates one. This again explains the importance of Deleuze's turn to Nietzsche's eternal return, where affirming is an action that allows pure difference to return and where only pure difference actually returns. The doctrine of eternal return is at the heart of Deleuze's principle of forgetting, where to forget is to leave things behind through the affirmation of something that is itself not carried on (*When she sings, her thoughts are erased in the harmony of body and tones.*). Forgetting as affirmation can, therefore, be seen in negative terms since something is left behind. But there is no immediate consciousness of that thing – no conscious rejection of it. We can become conscious of the erasure of identity in eternal return but only after the fact (*I do not sing to forget. I forget when I sing.*): 'The genius of eternal return lies not in memory but in waste, in active forgetting.' (DR, pp. 55, 77)

Representation is, therefore, counter to the affirmation of real difference and counter to eternal return. Affirmation, in Deleuze's sense, cannot involve the conscious representation of the thing to be affirmed or of the subject of the act of affirmation. In his claim that representation 'mediates' everything, he means that the affirmation becomes secondary to the consciousness in which there is a representation and to the demand that the represented thing coincide with a concept. This is true even when representations are multiplied to infinity, in the sense where there has to be a representation of that multiplication: 'Infinite representation includes precisely an infinity of representations – either by ensuring the convergence of all points of view on the same object or the same world, or by making all moments properties of the same Self.' (DR, pp. 56, 79) But what kind of act or event can avoid representation? In the remainder of the section on the definition of difference, Deleuze suggests that the multiplication of destabilising perspectives found in works of art can affirm difference without having to depend on representation. He also returns to the example of theatre and drama, outlined in Chapter 2, above.

However, once again, the form of his presentation remains one of a somewhat turgid description of art as transcendental empiricism or experimentation with respect to the expression of the conditions of the given. For precise accounts of how this experimentation works and why it is justified, we must again wait for later chapters. In this case, the delay is worthy of criticism. At times, Deleuze seems to go against his own method in describing concepts and processes without the precision, with respect to conditions, critique and completeness, that would allow the descriptions to stand out as determined against an indistinct ground.

The answer to this critique is that Deleuze's method requires creative moments, where key concepts and ideas must be dramatised, in order for other individuals to sense them and work with them, rather than understand them in a pure intellectual manner. This leads to a great contrast in *Difference and Repetition* between the 'strong' critical sections and creative arguments, and the 'overblown' moments of more arty descriptions or clumsy sloganeering. That is not to say that the style of the book is ever attractive in either a poetic or literary sense, or in the sense of an economical form of argument. Rather, it is that some sections of the book repay close analysis in terms of argument and structure. Whereas others, though difficult, remain superficial, in the sense of adding very little in terms of understanding the ideas and sections they connect to, either in terms of Deleuze's work or in terms of other texts. This is because they are meant to transform that understanding into a sensation, adding creativity with respect to the senses to a critical intellectual grasp. It is up to each individual reader, to each individual, to detect whether these dramatisations work. According to Deleuze's doctrine of chance-driven selection, there will be successes but also failures, in his attempt to dramatise concepts, as well as to define and justify them.

PLATO

At the end of his work on difference in itself, Deleuze returns to his carefully argued definition of difference through the critique of key figures in the history of philosophy. There are two fatal misunderstandings lying in wait in the work on Plato. Both are possible from the very first line of the section: 'The task of modern philosophy has been defined: to overturn Platonism.' (DR, pp. 59, 82) In the sentence, the French word '*renversement*' has at least two possible senses. The first sense is that of a reversal or inversion. The second is that of an overturning. If the line is read in terms of overthrowing or wiping out Platonism or if it is understood as positioning Deleuze as straightforwardly opposed to, or even as distant from Plato, then the consistency of the arguments of *Difference and Repetition* and the detail of Deleuze's definition of difference will have been missed. The sentence must be understood as advocating an inversion of Platonism that remains faithful to its key structure, as defined by Deleuze. Perhaps the best translation of his slogan would then be: 'The task of modern philosophy has been defined: to reverse Platonism.' This would maintain both the sense of an inversion but also of a reversal of the results of Platonism. The aim is to tweak the Platonic structure in order to avoid an error with severe consequences regard to difference, in an otherwise important and more powerful structure than those put forward by Aristotle, Hegel and Leibniz.

So, in the chapter on difference, Deleuze's work on Plato has a dual function of responding to questions that come out of his earlier critiques of Aristotle, Hegel and Leibniz, and of refining the definition of difference. One aspect of that refinement lies in criticising one, albeit crucial, aspect of the content of Plato's structure. The problem that Deleuze is responding to is: How can pure difference interact with actual well-defined things when the former are radically different from the latter? How do things with nothing in common belong to the same system? This is one of the core problems of Deleuze's philosophy. The structure that Deleuze is interested in is the following: 'The four figures of the Platonic dialectic are therefore: the selection of difference, the installation of a mythic circle, the establishment of a foundation, and the position of a question-problem complex.' (DR, pp. 66, 91) He will criticise the third of these and the way it fatally damages the positive roles of the others. Put simply, the structure is right, as is the dialectical method, but they depend on the wrong kind of foundation, one based on identity, when it should be based on pure difference.

Each of the figures of the Platonic structure corresponds to an aspect of Deleuze's own work and responds to the critical questions put to him. Thus, the emphasis on the selection of difference is a response to an Aristotelian question: Is difference not a matter of dividing things into smaller and smaller oppositions and contradictions? The Platonic answer, as interpreted by Deleuze, is that difference is not about oppositions and distinctions but about selection. This means that the division does not operate according to the question 'In what way do these things differ?' but according to the question 'Which is the best?'. Each of these options must be understood as operating prior to the other. We search for opposition prior to searching for value or we search for value prior to having an understanding of oppositions and contradictions. Platonic and Deleuzian selection is about making differences out of valuations. They depart from an indistinct ground and look for higher values. But how do you select without making recourse to prior identifiable oppositions and contradictions?

In answering this question, Deleuze parts from Plato. According to him, the basis for selection in Plato is a myth. The myth allows us to choose between the good or the true and the bad or the false (*the mythical racehorse, the mythical leader, artist, lover*). The difference between this mythical basis and the prior division into genera and species is that the mythical one is not present in that which has to be selected – they are only pretenders to the perfection found in the myth. The connection between the myth and the pretenders is through what Deleuze calls the circle of myth – that is, the myth tells of how things were originally divided and it allows that division to return later (*Shergar's stride allowed him to glide over the turf in a way that will never be matched, though many horses may remind us of it. You must search for your Romeo or Juliet.*). In tune with this circle that divides and returns, dialectics is a matter of selecting the best by returning to a foundation where the idea of the best was cast first (*What is the ideal horse? What is the ideal lover?*).

This foundation is the idea, a concept that Deleuze takes from Plato to fulfil a different role in a similar structure. Though actual things cannot be equal to the idea, they participate in it to greater or lesser degrees. In Deleuze's work, in particular when it is inspired by Spinoza, the term participation is replaced by expression (when it is inspired by Nietzsche it becomes affirmation). Actual things allow the idea to return and do so well or poorly. That is how the idea allows for a double selection: the selection of the ideas that return and the selection of the actual things that allow those ideas to return well. Deleuze describes this second selection as a test that takes the form of a question and a problem, again drawing a strong parallel with his own reliance on the concept of the problem:

Neither the problem nor the question is a subjective determination marking a moment of insufficiency in knowledge. Problematic structure is part of objects themselves, allowing them to be grasped as signs, just as the questioning or problematising instance is a part of knowledge allowing its positivity and its specificity to be grasped in the act of learning.

(DR, pp. 63–4, 89)

A problem shows a tension at the level of ideas that cannot be resolved, only participated with, affirmed or expressed well.

This Platonic tension corresponds to the irresolvable tensions between pure differences, intensities or becomings in Deleuze's philosophy. The tension does not show a lack or contradictions in ideas defined as Being, but an essential problematic structure that is the ground of all things: 'This (non)-being is the differential element in which affirmation, as multiple affirmation, finds the principle of its genesis.' (DR, pp. 64, 89) In other words, affirmation must not be reducible to affirmed identities or negations because the condition for affirmation as creative destruction is that it avoids resolving original tensions between pure differences. In an interesting note, Deleuze goes on to link this concept of (non)-being to Heidegger's work on Being and to the misunderstandings of his work that continued to think of being in terms of negation or contradiction. However, Deleuze still criticises Heidegger for retaining a negative element in describing being in terms of the Nothing, thereby erasing the problematic structure of positive differences. In so doing, Heidegger continues to represent being through this negative slant – for example, in his reading of Nietzsche's eternal return as nihilistic.

Thus, in parallel to Plato's structure of selection, mythical circle, ideal foundation and problems, we find Deleuze's structure of selection through affirmation or expression, of eternal return and dramatisation, of ideas as multiplicities of pure differences and problems. That this is only a parallel and not an exact correspondence can be explained through Deleuze's main criticism of Plato. For Deleuze, ideas do not have an identity – they are multiplicities of pure differences. Therefore, dramatisation is not the myth of a well-defined origin but the demand to dramatise the fact that there is no origin that can be identified. Selection is, then, not between true and false pretenders but between simulacra and only simulacra. There is no genuine article and simulacra are selected with respect to the relation of a given actual situation to the expression of pure differences, with a view to maximising their number and intensity (connect) and in line with the need not to perpetuate the illusion of fixed identities or values (forget).

Deleuze and Plato cannot be reconciled on this issue since it carries through the structure as a whole and distinguishes the principles of their dialectics:

Plato gave the establishment of difference as the supreme goal of dialectic. However, difference does not lie between things and simulacra, models and copies. Things are simulacra themselves, simulacra are the superior forms, and the difficulty facing everything is to become its own simulacrum, to attain the status of a sign in the coherence of eternal return.'

(DR, pp. 67, 93)

But where the Platonic form allows him to account for selection through the comparison of the identity of the thing and the identity of the form, thereby allowing the true form of all things to emerge through dialectics, Deleuze seems to plunge us into a destructive relativism. Are all situations and simulacra equal? In a void of judgement and identity, how do we make decisions at all? Does the true and the truth of things survive the replacement of Plato's secure foundation with an absence of measure and direction: 'Everything has become simulacrum, for by simulacrum we should not understand a simple imitation but rather the act by which the very idea of a model or privileged position is challenged and overturned.' (DR, pp. 69, 95) Deleuze's answers to these questions regarding the specificity of differences and situations with respect to acts in his chapter on repetition. There, he provides arguments that explain how it is possible to move correctly in one direction or another. Through repetition, things become located in space and time despite their constant lack of ground with respect to difference in itself and despite the illusory nature of the active subject.

4

Repetition

REPETITION FOR ITSELF

If the concept of difference in itself allows Deleuze to move away from fixed definitions and values, the concept of repetition allows him to develop the mechanistic and materialist aspects of his philosophy. These aspects have already been encountered here in the guise of Deleuze's principles regarding passivity. Pure difference happens to us – it is not the result of direct actions. This explains the central role taken by the forgetting of identity in *Difference and Repetition*. Repetition is a process that underlies all identities. Free will is, therefore, an illusion. Things are not simply made to happen – they also always emerge through an unconscious repetition. It is tempting to see this opposition to free will and materialism as informed solely by Deleuze's reading of Spinoza but, through the chapter on repetition, we find all of Deleuze's earlier philosophical influences combining in his concept of repetition.

The concept also allows Deleuze to answer pressing questions put to his philosophy after the creation of the concept of difference in itself. How do things acquire any determinacy at all, given the founding role of pure difference? Why is there this world or set of things and not another, given the apparently chaotic and random nature of differences in themselves? It appears that all things are equal or equally far removed from pure differences. Given this, is any guidance on how to act and how to act well possible? The concept of repetition allows Deleuze to begin to explain how things become determined and what the exact role of difference is in that process. It also allows him to select which acts are true to this role and which acts hide it damagingly. Put simply, Deleuze

84

believes that we have to find the right ways of acting in terms of underlying processes of repetition that we cannot fully control or understand. He calls these acts the vice-diction, doubling or counter-actualisation of virtual events. There is a way of repeating well with respect to the pure differences that give life its intensity.

The chapter on repetition also has a strong and necessary critical edge. It is present in the title of the chapter since, in insisting on the 'for itself' of repetition, Deleuze develops two related critical lines of thought. Firstly, he answers the critical question 'Is it not necessary for there to be an identity, for example, a consciousness of repetition, for there to be repetition at all?' In other words, doesn't repetition have to be for someone? He will show that it is possible to think of repetition as straightforwardly 'for itself'. Secondly, by showing that repetition underlies the illusion of fixed identities, including consciousness, Deleuze can criticise the founding role given to the well-defined subject and self in the history of philosophy. He can also criticise strongly empirical and objective approaches in disciplines such as psychology. In both cases, he will argue that, despite the importance of understanding actual processes, identities and evidence, we must also look deeper than this understanding, to the underlying processes of repetition that cannot be thought of in terms of identities or objective facts.

The core argument behind this work on repetition for itself is a series of deductions concerning passive syntheses of time. These syntheses are the condition for a series of actual processes analysed from the point of view of repetition. For example, Deleuze can be interpreted as asking what the condition is for a consciousness of repetition or what the condition is for repeating a genetic character or a historical event. His answers come to view these conditions in terms of syntheses of time. This complex but deeply rewarding and important philosophy of time will, no doubt, come to be viewed as one of the most important developments of that philosophy. It stands against contemporary philosophies of time that situate time in the sphere of narrative or intentionality. Yet it also reacts against philosophies of time that defend an objective linear historical time, within which events have to take place according to a well-measured sequence and subject to an irreversible direction of past to future.

The four strands of Deleuze's method, as presented in my introduction, work together to construct a consistent Deleuzian philosophy of repetition and time. There is a response to problems in the concept of difference through the creation of a concept of repetition and other associated concepts. There is a critique of the role of the subject and self in the history of philosophy and in other disciplines. There is the deduction of the conditions for experiences and cases of repetition. There is the extension of Deleuze's philosophy into a more complete structure through the argument that three passive syntheses of time are at work in all events understood through the concepts of difference and repetition.

FIRST SYNTHESIS OF TIME

The most pressing critical question concerning repetition for itself turns on the part of Deleuze's method that searches for transcendental conditions. In particular, it asks whether there is an actual 'given' that can be taken without difficulty as the starting point for a search for conditions or a transcendental deduction. Is this given merely hypothetical, thereby reducing Deleuze's work to conjecture, easily falsifiable through scientific approaches to that given? Or is there never such a given, merely an endless and ungraspable trail of differences, perhaps something like the concept of *différance* developed in Jacques Derrida's early work? More classically, is Deleuze caught in a vicious circle since it appears that he must assume a determined given in order to deduce determination through repetition? Later, in Chapters 6 and 7, I will argue that Deleuze must embrace a contingent ground for his philosophy and that this is consistent with some of the most important concepts of his philosophy, notably, sensation and individualisation. This, then, puts his philosophy on a hypothetical footing. However, in order to grasp the significance and range of such conclusions, it is important first to follow the trail of his arguments through *Difference and Repetition.*

The starting point or given selected by Deleuze is the 'living present' (*présent vivant*). This is not given an abstract and general definition. Rather, it is narrowed down to particular cases of life. He is interested in cases where living things show or experience what I will call an expectancy. In the case of an experience, this may be discovered negatively in experiences of shock or disquiet or stumbling where an expected thing is not there or has been replaced by something else (*He crashed his head against the lowered beam and resolved then and there to sue that builder.*). Or it may be shown through questioning (*What do I or you expect to come next?*). Deleuze looks at two famous examples of expectancy from two philosophers already studied in his earlier books: Hume's example of the repetition of couples of events AB AB AB AB A . . . , where we come to expect B to follow A; and Bergson's example of a clock striking a particular hour, for example, 4 o'clock A A A A, where we expect the fourth strike to follow the third.

The significance of these examples lies in their relation to repetition. There is a relation between expectancy and repetition. What is it? What is the condition for expectancy as a particular product of repetition? Repetition is not a property of the repeated things since there is no causal relationship between different members of the series (a particular tick-tock does not necessarily cause the next, except in very specific circumstances). According to Deleuze, repetition is, therefore, not an objective property – it is something in the experiencer. But what? He explains it in terms of a contraction of the previous instances in later ones, thereby creating an expectancy. This contraction is passive in the sense that we do not have to think consciously about it for it to take place. Previous instances of AB are contracted passively, as on a photosensitive plate, in order for there to be an expectancy. It would, therefore, be a mistake to associate expectancy solely with the experiences of human subjects. Rather, it is the property of passively acquiring an unconscious relation to the future (*the disorientation of a horse on frozen ground for the first time*).

Deleuze goes on to conclude that the condition for the lived present is the passive synthesis of time where the past is synthesised, or contracted, in the present as a behaviour towards the future. He calls this synthesis habit – it is what gives the present a direction from past to future: 'Passive synthesis or contraction is essentially symmetrical: it goes from the past to the future in the present, thus, from the particular to the general, thereby imparting direction to the arrow of time.' (DR, pp. 71, 97) When we repeat an act in the past (*ascending a flight of steps*), the series of repetitions becomes synthesised in the present (*Even drunk and in the dark, we are a record of the prior repetitions.*) as a forward looking movement (*That record allows us to stand in a relation of expectancy to the future – until a child's toy undoes all the good work of repetition.*).

According to Deleuze, the passive synthesis of time is not the cause of expectation in the sense of particular event X being the cause of particular event Y. It is, rather, that any case of expectation is only possible because there is a passive synthesis of time – the past is projected into the future through the present. So, given that there is expectation, there must be such a synthesis. Any process that rests on expectation must itself rest on that passive synthesis,

where 'to rest on' means that we do not have a complete understanding of the later process without understanding its relation
to the prior one. This set of arguments rapidly leads to the following sweeping conclusion: 'In other words, the active syntheses
of memory and understanding are superimposed upon and supported by the passive syntheses of imagination.' (DR, pp. 71, 97)
This is because we only have a sense of the direction of past to future as expectancy because of the passive synthesis of time, defined
as habit.

But many sceptical questions must be raised at this point: Is it
really the case that repetition is only the product of passive syntheses? Is it not an objective property – given the right conditions
we know the same thing will happen, independent of any particular past record leading to expectancy? Is an 'experience' of expectancy necessary for an understanding of the direction of time?
Could that not be acquired in abstraction, from a knowledge of
the laws of physics (this cause must preceded by this effect) or biology (this plant reacts in this way to this environmental change),
for example?

Deleuze's initial remarks and conclusions are wholly unsatisfactory from the point of view of these questions and their long
history in, for example, Hume scholarship on the questions of
induction and causality. However, answers do unfold through the
chapter on repetition for itself. The apparently haphazard flow of
the chapter on repetition can be viewed more clearly as a series
of arguments that support the validity of the opening paragraphs.
The first of the arguments is based on an important extension of
the concept of contraction. Deleuze expands its scope from the
contraction through repetition of independent experiences AB
AB AB into a habit, to the contraction of A and B into AB, to the
contraction of many different sensations into A and into B. His
point is that expectation is not only a matter of expecting a particular thing to follow another because they have done so in the
past. It is also a matter of expecting a particular conjunction of
independent things to make one. Furthermore, it is to expect a
great number of perhaps unidentified unconscious things to come
together to form a unit.

So Bergson's example of A A A A demands the same treatment
as Hume's AB AB AB. . . . In fact, any A hides in itself a contraction of other events ABCD . . . ABCD. . . . Deleuze's claim is that
any interaction with an actual thing is accompanied by the expectation that the thing will maintain some degree of consistency.

That expectation depends on a contraction that must be based on repetition – a thing is not sensed unless it is sensed as repeated. In response to the claim that his example of expectation is subjective and limited, he argues that expectancy and repetition are not only cases of the living present but are presupposed in any relation to an actual thing, where the consistency of the thing into the future is a condition for the relation. He has deduced the general form of the living present from the necessary conditions for that case. Furthermore, since any experience is dependent on repetition, any experience depends on contraction and the passive synthesis of time as habit.

Deleuze goes on to distinguish different types of passive syntheses and to distinguish these from active syntheses, such as representation. Syntheses can be ordered in terms of priority, in the sense of which are presupposed by others. First, there is the passive synthesis of time as condition. Any passive contraction through repetition presupposes that a series in time can be contracted into the present. Second, there is the passive synthesis of repetitions of sensations into a sense. A sense is an umbrella thrown over many different sensations. These are synthesised as they are repeated to form the sense. Third, there is the passive synthesis of different sensations into the sensation of a thing. The different sensations associated with a thing are brought together so that we may sense the thing as a whole. Finally, there is the active synthesis that we operate consciously.

We move from presupposing the passive synthesis of time to the search for the actual syntheses at work in any event. For example, take the sensation of a chair, where I turn my attention to the chair and judge it according to the predicates of the concept 'chair'. The active consideration presupposes the passive synthesis of time insofar as the activity is directed from past to future and involves an expectancy (*Is this sixties polystyrene purple blob really a chair?*). The past is synthesised in the movement to the future in the present. The active consideration also involves the synthesis of different sensations, say, sight, touch, smell, hearing (*This thing looks great, squeaks horribly, is uncomfortable unless you're very relaxed, smells like cheap plastic.*) into an overall sensation of the chair. Each of these individual sensations is itself the synthesis, in individuals, but also through generations, of prior quasi-sensations into a fully developed sense (*The sense of smell only appeared ten thousand years later... Do you know she can tell if it's an original just by its smell?*). Without passive syntheses there would be no chair to consider.

89

This relation of passive syntheses allows Deleuze to counter questions concerning the regularity of repetition – that is, whether it should be viewed in terms of natural or moral laws. Repetition makes things by altering them. Natural laws only come later and then can only be applied to things at a certain time. Through time, things do not have a fixed identity but must be thought of as the synthesis of varying sensations. Similarly, freely adopted moral laws must be explained in terms of the passive syntheses that they presuppose. However, it is important to note the basis for Deleuze's arguments in the search for transcendental conditions, beginning with the statement that there is a sense of expectancy in the living present and concluding with relations of passive syntheses. His account does not explain how these syntheses work. It pays no heed to empirical work on the senses or on perception or on habit. There is only the thinnest phenomenology of expectancy and certainly no argument for its necessity. I will return to these serious objections later in Chapters 6 and 7, preferring, at this stage, to follow the construction of Deleuze's structure of transcendental conditions.

In terms of this structure, he argues that there can be no overarching set of laws or rules that covers relations between the different levels of syntheses. Instead, each level only contains 'signs' of others – where a sign is only an indication, something like a presentiment. Together, signs and this account of levels amount to Deleuze's idea of life. It is worth quoting at length:

We must therefore distinguish not only the forms of repetition in relation to passive synthesis, but also the levels of passive synthesis and the combinations of these levels with one another and with active syntheses. All of this forms a rich domain of signs which always envelop heterogeneous elements and animate behaviour ... The manner in which sensation and perception – along with need and heredity, learning and instinct, intelligence and memory – participate in repetition is measured in each case by the combination of forms of repetition, by the levels on which these combinations take place, by the relationships operating between these levels and by the interference of active syntheses with passive syntheses.

(DR, pp. 72, 100)

Deleuze's argument, on the lack of laws and on the necessity of signs for the structure of different levels of repetition, depends on a series of far-reaching points. I want to draw them out of the above passage, along with a series of critical remarks:

1. The different levels of syntheses are only conditions for one another and not causes because each level has a radically different content to others (time, expectation or desire, sensations, senses and acts). They involve 'heterogeneous elements' and, therefore, cannot be explained in terms of causal relations.
2. However, there is a relation from one level to another in the sense that what is more or less intense at a given place and time on one level depends on relations between other things on other levels. Signs are an opening on to this relation of differing intensities. This is not a matter of possibility or likelihood but of attraction and opportunity. There is an 'interference' between levels that signs pick up on.
3. Signs are not objects that can be represented and fully conceptualised because they involve combinations of heterogeneous elements that defy representation and concepts (passive syntheses). There has to be a different active approach to signs. The sign disappears when we try to know it as opposed to letting it work through us. Deleuze goes on to conclude that habits cannot emerge out of activity but only out of contemplation, where contemplation means creative, experimental acts indirectly triggering events on different levels. Contemplation belongs to the imagination and not to the understanding.
4. From the point of view of the levels, well-defined subjects and selves only appear on one level and cannot be viewed as well defined in terms of their relation to other levels. The conscious acts of a subject and the identity of a self fail to capture signs and how to live with them.

The most troubling of these claims lies in the conjunction of a claim about heterogeneity and a claim about passages between levels thanks to signs. How can signs pass between heterogeneous things? If they can, why are they resistant to systematisation through representation (*When that happens, you must do this. Then the following will occur*)? Deleuze's answer relies on his definition of difference in itself and on arguments on intensity developed late in the book. Each repetition on each level is not a repetition of the same thing but a variation that must be understood in terms of pure difference. All an act can do is introduce further variations and see what comes of it. It is like playing a game with changeable rules against an infinitely adaptive opponent. Just as fixed rules and a strategic pattern emerge, they lose efficacy, forcing us to begin experimenting anew (*The irony is I thought I knew what made him tick. Then he vanished.*).

So repetitions on a given level are really chance-driven alterations, with only a degree of certainty due to their relation to an individual and to its actual identity, sensations, intensities and Ideas (*I am drawn to this; this intensity is dominating the others; so this set of Ideas – pure becomings – determine me*). Not only that, the relation between levels is also a variation in repetition due to pure differences. Acts or events on one level change other levels in equally unpredictable and open-ended ways. Signs determine and set an individual in motion but they do not determine the outcome of that motion – that is, they only give a sense of the relations that hold on a level and between levels and, hence, give a sense of what is at play in any action.

The most important definition of repetition in the chapter on repetition for itself is that the 'for itself' of repetition is difference – there is no repetition of the same thing for any other thing, only an open variation that occurs with an individual. Acts must experiment in the light of an individual and the signs that work through its sensations. They must be led by the imagination:

Difference inhabits repetition. On the one hand – lengthwise, as it were – difference allows us to pass from one order of repetition to another: from the instantaneous repetition which unravels itself to the actively represented repetition through the intermediary of passive synthesis. On the other hand – in depth, as it were – difference allows us to pass from one order of repetition to another and from one generality to another within the passive syntheses themselves.

(DR, pp. 76, 103)

Deleuze's argument is as follows. Since identities are illusions that cover pure differences, repetition is really the alteration of relations between different pure differences (*The relation of becoming fear and becoming anger is altered through the introduction of a weakening of becoming hungry.*). It is, therefore, about the determination of those relations through their alteration. No representation of those relations of differences can capture them so our proper relation to repetition must be to repeat against the illusions of identity (repeat to forget) and to move towards a complete relation to our locality (repeat to connect).

Deleuze's work on the first synthesis of time and on the relation of different active and passive syntheses allows him to define the living present as a multiplicity of 'contemplations' – that is, as the relation of a series of contractions of pure differences through repetition. For him, underlying the illusion of ourselves as subjects of conscious actions based on representations and the illusion of self-identity, there is passive self or, more precisely, a system of passive selves: 'There is a self wherever a furtive contemplation has been established, whenever a contracting machine capable of drawing a difference from repetition functions somewhere.' (DR, pp. 78, 107) This doctrine of the passive self and associated arguments responds to critical arguments that define repetition in terms of repeated identities and in terms of an identity for whom there is a repetition. However, they do not answer the questions of why this or that passive self emerges rather than another or the questions concerning the value and possibility of selecting selves: 'Selves are larval subjects; the world of passive syntheses constitutes the system of the self, under conditions yet to be determined, but it is the system of a dissolved self.' (DR, pp. 78, 107)

SECOND SYNTHESIS OF TIME

The next step towards determining the living present lies in taking it as a present that passes. In the deduction of the first synthesis of time, Deleuze took expectancy – the projection from past to future through the present – as given. However, there is a different property of the living present that is not fully accounted for by the passive synthesis of past and future in the present. This given is the way in which any present passes. This is no longer the forward-looking expectancy, but the backward-looking sense of something falling away, yet still remaining. Let's call it the sense of archiving to capture the sense of passing into stock but as something different (*It's gone...*).

That which passes into stock is, to some degree, lifeless, with respect to the living present it falls away from, but it is still open to return as something from the past – as archive. This turn to the sense of archiving is very dangerous for Deleuze because it returns him to two explanations that contradict his philosophy of repetition as passive and as a matter of pure differences: Is not archiving dependent on the active memory of subjects? Is it not dependent on objective archiving through identifiable documents and physical traces? An affirmative answer to these questions brings repetition back to identities and repetition of the same (even when this involves a combination of both critical questions: archiving as the subjective take on identifiable traces).

Deleuze fends off both these possibilities through a further deduction of a passive synthesis. It is deeply counter-intuitive since it runs against the grain of common experiences of memory and remembrance, where we remember an archived present through active work on traces, including our own memories as representations (*I went through the old photo albums today... An exciting find has been made in the store of the British library... We deduce this from its fossilised skeleton.*). The enduring intuition is: no trace – no past; no remembering – no memory.

Yet Deleuze wants to claim that there is a pure past, where all events, including those that have sunk without trace, are stored and remembered as their passing away, independent of human activity and the limitations of physical records: 'It is with respect to the pure element of the past, understood as the past in general, as an *a priori* past, that a given former present is reproducible and the present present is able to reflect itself.' (DR, pp. 81, 110) The meaning of pure here should be related to the sense of a difference in itself and to Deleuze's concept of the virtual as opposed to the actual. His aim is to show that the passing away of the present presupposes all the ways in which pure differences are expressed in the present in such a way as to make us sense that the present is passing or to make anything pass away. Again, the argument is a transcendental deduction of an a priori:

In this sense, the active synthesis of memory may well be founded upon the (empirical) passive synthesis of habit, but on the other hand it can be grounded only by another (transcendental) passive synthesis which is peculiar to memory itself.

(DR, pp. 81, 110)

The argument draws heavily on Bergson's work in *Matter and Memory* and can be traced back to Deleuze's book on Bergson, *Bergsonism*. It turns on the sense of passing into archive and three successive explanations. First, if the present can pass away, it is because, in some sense, it is already past or has a past element to it. In other words, every present must have a past aspect in order for it to pass away (*What we are doing now must also be history, if it is to become history.*). That aspect accompanies every present but is not fully that present since, then, there would be no forward-looking present, only a sense of passing away. It is, therefore, not merely the sense of the passing away, which is itself fully in the present, but that which explains that sense. Without such a past side to the

94

present, in all the ways it can be past, there would be a miraculous jump from a present to its past. So, for there to be a sense of the many sides of the present passing away, each must have a past aspect and that aspect is inseparable from the present (*'IT is going', where IT cannot be the present moment from whence that is said nor the IT that becomes archived as a past event.*).

Second, when a present, accompanied by a past, has past away, it becomes a past event for any future present. *All* those past events accompany any new present because they constitute what that present passes away into. When the present passes away, it passes into time as all past events. That time is part of the passing away of the present. Put differently, any present passes away in relation to any present that went before it because the past that accompanied those former presents also accompanies later ones (*He picked up the relic and suddenly felt old . . .*). This means that '*all* of the past coexists with the new present in relation to which it is now past.' (DR, pp. 82, 111) We do not pass away with other present moments but with the passing away of all of them because the presents can never accompany us – only their passing away can (*I'll never be there when her hand passed over the grain of this wood but every hand that has passed over every grain of wood is part of my present.*).

Since the present could not become past if there was not something past in the present and since every present is related to every other as something that passes away, the passing into archive of the present presupposes the synthesis of all the past as the time of past elements of each present, past or future. So, third, the passive synthesis of all the past, as past elements of all presents, is an a priori condition for the present passing away. It does not depend on the experience of the past but is a condition for there being any such experience: the pure past, as opposed to the past of memories and records, 'pre-exists' the present (*The past of her future, of any future, accompanies my present.*).

A fuller sense of the significance of this philosophy of time comes out with its consequences for our views on our relation to time, past, present and future. When we represent a past present, we do not capture the past as a priori condition since we cannot represent the synthesis of all the past. That synthesis must be passive since it does not depend on any form of activity to occur – it accompanies any present, independent of conscious activity. But what is the significance of this condition? What is this presupposed pure past? How does it impinge on the way we think about the present and about activity in the present? Deleuze makes a series of important remarks on the pure past in order to answer these questions.

The first remark is that the first synthesis of time differs greatly from the second, the synthesis of the pure past, since the former is a contraction of a series of distinct elements, whilst the latter is the contraction of the whole past. The relation of the lived present to the two is, therefore, also very different. As projection into the future, the lived present only presupposes a local contraction but, as a passing away, it presupposes a synthesis of the past that itself brings together all past contractions. The pure past, therefore, consists of all the varying degrees of contraction that ground any present: 'The present can be the most contracted degree of the past which coexists with it only if the past first coexists with itself in an infinity of diverse degrees of relaxation and contraction at an infinity of levels...' (DR, pp. 83, 112)

The justification for this claim lies in the view that the pure past must be all the past but must also be amenable to change through the occurrence of any new present. This view follows from the observation that, in order to accompany the passing away of any present, the past includes the way any present contracts with other passed presents. In other words, because each present passes away in relation to all other presents in different ways, this aspect of passing away must be reflected in the pure past (*The passing of empire was but a detail to them – to us it was the beginning of a new world.*). So, although the pure past is independent of the present, it still has a particular relation to each present.

This property allows Deleuze to consider the relation of a particular life to the pure past. He begins with the premise that any life involves many different aspects that may be in opposition to one another and that may be resistant to a reduction to a coherent whole (*She has been a daughter, boss, mother, poor, rich, peripatetic, settled, revolutionary, conservative, optimistic, despairing, healthy, sick.*). Yet we still call that life 'a life' (*she has been*). What gives coherence to a life? For Deleuze, the relation of successive and apparently unrelated presents through the pure past allows us to relate them. A life acquires consistency through the relations between its apparently heterogeneous elements in a relatively consistent arrangement of the pure past (*Her despair and optimism combine to allow us to understand the world she lived through.*).

Deleuze defines destiny as this coherence of the pure past through different presents. Destiny 'implies between successive presents non-localisable connections, actions at a distance, systems of replay, resonances and echoes, objective chances, signs, signals and roles which transcend spatial locations and temporal successions'. (DR, pp. 83, 113) The differences of level in the pure past allow us to explain how aspects may drop out of a life, only to regain importance later, as a new contraction brings it back into focus in a different role. Deleuze uses this work on the passive synthesis of time to great effect in his *Cinéma-1* and *Cinéma-2* books since cinema is able to enact the work of the syntheses in ways that make them more vivid (*Rosebud...*). The work also returns to underpin his claims on the relation of different individuals through the virtual thought of as pure past (see Chapter 7, below).

Two further consequences follow from these remarks on the pure past and destiny. The first is that the relation between the present and the pure past resolves the paradoxes encountered by a materialism that still retains a sense of action. Shouldn't any materialism be deterministic? No, since our passivity with respect to the syntheses of time still allows for actions to alter the localities we are passive to. We can alter where we may acquire habits and to what degree. We can alter where our lives may be contracted and to what degree. Underlying your conscious activity there is a series of passive processes on a physical plane and on a spiritual plane (your destiny as a contraction of the pure past). But your conscious activity has an effect on those syntheses – not in the sense that you can finally determine their outcome but in the sense of opening up and closing down different paths.

In other words, the sign of the present is already a passage to the limit, a maximal contraction which comes to sanction the choice of a particular level as such, which is in itself contracted or relaxed among an infinity of possible levels.

(DR, pp. 83, 113)

The second consequence of the relation of the pure past to the present supports Deleuze's concern with the connections that hold between all things. Each present, each life, is connected to all others but to greater and lesser degrees of contraction. The way in which any life presupposes all the past brings very different lives together, against the Aristotelian desire to categorise lives: 'Since each is a passing present, one life may replay another at a different level, as if the philosopher and the pig, the criminal and the saint, played out the same past at different levels of a gigantic cone.' (DR, pp. 83, 113) This does not mean that the actual lives of pigs and philosophers must have causal effects on one another – though, of course, they may. It means that, despite the absence of such actual connections, there will necessarily be connections at the level of the pure past. The life of the pig and the philosopher change the pure past and, through that change, they may be related to the point where we may say that one can replay another or touch the pure past in similar ways.

At the end of the section on the second synthesis of time, Deleuze returns to critical questions raised by his account of the pure past. How do we have any useful access to the pure past in order to make decisions? Even if we do have some access, how can we choose a level since it cannot be accurately represented in the present? He puts these questions in a rather dramatic way: 'How can we save [the entire past] *for ourselves?*' (DR, pp. 85, 115) This question may appear to be a matter of specific practice, in the sense where his treatment of the pure past has given us some conditions, that hold for any given present, but no way of acting upon those conditions. In fact, though, the questions are much more devastating since they pick up on the possibility that, in principle, there can be no way of acting on this account and that, therefore, the deduction of the pure past is an empty exercise, a mere metaphysical diversion. Deleuze only gives preliminary indications as to how to answer these questions. There is something in the relation between forgetting and reminiscence that relates us to the pure past as something that must be re-created (as in Proust's *In Search of Lost Time*). He goes on to dramatise this re-creation in relation to the past through a deeply obscure tale of the relation between memory and Eros. Creation from memory requires a sensual trigger, a sign from the past (*Dunk that cake again... Kiss her lips...*). But he admits that there is no way of explaining why that should be so on his account of time and the two syntheses. A third synthesis must be discussed to arrive at this explanation.

THIRD SYNTHESIS OF TIME

The problems of specificity and activity raised above are resolved through the third passive synthesis and its relation to the future. Deleuze introduces this synthesis by returning to a study of transcendental deductions and to the search for the conditions for a given thing. This work has an historical context through Kant's critique of the Cartesian subject. Deleuze's study of these well-trodden paths is significant because it allows us to reach a better understanding of his take on transcendental arguments and conditions. According to him, Kant corrects Descartes' deduction of 'I exist as a thinking thing' from 'I think' by pointing out that all we can deduce from the given determination 'I think' is that 'I exist' but only where the 'I exist' is undetermined.

How I exist remains wholly open, to the point where the expression 'I exist' must be seen a shorthand for 'There must be something'. Kant's question then becomes 'How can we determine this something at all?'. According to Deleuze, his answer is that we cannot directly know how the something is determined but we can know how it is determinable. That is, if it is to be determined at all, it must be in this form, where the form is time. We must think of the 'I exist' as given in time.

Deleuze draws a series of far-reaching consequences from this conclusion. He does this by returning to the given 'I think' and by applying the conclusions concerning time to it. The transcendental condition allows him to determine the conditioned thing, the given. This method is a constant in Deleuze's work. We have already seen it at work in the first synthesis of time and in his work on habit. As a thing that exists the given 'I that thinks' must be placed in time as passive. We could have thought that the given and apparently well-determined activity of thinking was to be the foundation for thought and philosophy but it is shown to be secondary and illusory from the point of view of a condition that it is passive to.

The synthesis of time is the condition for activity and out of the reach of activity: 'Time signifies a fault or a rift in the I and a passivity in the self; and the correlation between the passive self and the fractured I constitutes the discovery of the transcendental or the element of the Copernican revolution.' (DR, pp. 86, 117) I have modified this translation to underline Deleuze's interest in the relation between structures, as mirrored by the relation between different geological strata ('rift' instead of 'fracture' as the translation of *fêlure*). This move from the condition back to the given, in order to undermine and alter it, distinguishes Deleuze's work on the transcendental from Kant's. The latter does not leave a rift in the I, by securing it in his practical and speculative philosophy (we have to act as if the I has a secure identity) and by securing the given by drawing a distinction between synthetic activity and passive receptivity (the rift is only implied in receptivity and is curtailed off from the activity of the I).

99

The way in which Deleuze's method depends upon, but also goes beyond Kant's transcendental philosophy, can be set down more clearly at this point. The Deleuzian dialectic takes a given with the wider existence implied by it. This is followed by a search for the condition of that wider existence – that is, by a search for what makes the undetermined ground of a well-determined given determinable. In other words, given a particular sensation 'I think' or 'I expect', we cannot draw further conclusions regarding existence (What thinks or expects and how?) except by searching for the necessary conditions for the particular sensation (What forms do thinking or expectation presuppose?). This is the transcendental element of the method. However, it is taken further in the dialectic through the application of the conditions to the original given – what was taken as well determined is reviewed and extended in the light of the conditions (thinking and expectation are not secure grounds and their status as well-determined must be reviewed in the light of the conditions). The dialectic moves to a more complete determination of the given but at the price of undermining its status as given (*connect and forget*).

But isn't Kant right to resist, or find ways of escaping, this application of the condition to the given, to the intuition, since it implies a vicious circle? If the well-determined given is later put into question, then so must the conditions deduced from it. This explains why Kant takes a pure a priori given, independent of concepts and sensations:

In the transcendental aesthetic we shall, therefore, first *isolate* sensibility, by taking away from it everything which the understanding thinks through its concepts, so that nothing may be left save empirical intuition. Secondly, we shall also separate off from it everything which belongs to sensation, so that nothing may remain save pure intuition and the mere form of appearances, which is all that sensibility can supply *a priori*.

(Kant, 1999, p. 67)

Here we can see the great difference between Kant and Deleuze. The former secures the given with great care to guard against any doubts that may assail it, either at the outset (a Cartesian legacy) or in the light of later discoveries or deductions (a Humean one). Thereby, his deductions build on a secure and inviolable foundation. Deleuze, on the other hand, takes a foundation shot through with sensations and concepts, an individual's particular sensation. In so doing, he risks falling prey to a straightforward reductio ad absurdum – the given is well determined and it is not.

It is worth noting, at this point, that this difference between Deleuze and Kant on the given and his critique of Kant with respect to receptivity and to the gulf between faculties is prepared for in Deleuze's *Kant's Critical Philosophy*. Although that book is not explicitly critical of Kant, it concentrates on Kant's work on the given and raises the problem of the relation between passive and active faculties: 'In Kant, the problem of the relation of subject and object tends to be internalised; it becomes the problem of a relation between subjective faculties which differ in nature (receptive sensibility and active understanding).' (p. 14) In this projection back to his early work, right to his first book on Hume, we can see Deleuze's investment in his own doctrine regarding passivity. The early books were preparing for the masterwork but not in a conscious manner. There are signs of the later method in the earlier identified problems but no necessity to its appearance or exact form.

Can Deleuze escape criticism regarding vicious circularity? A solution raised earlier seems to fail at this point. It does not matter whether the given is taken as hypothetical or fact, since the *reductio* will still show that the assumption leads to a contradiction. So, even if the given is taken as fictional, Deleuze's method fails. The correct answer is rather different and controversial. It is that there is no *reductio* at all. The well-determined given taken at the outset ('I expect') is not negated by the conclusion ('the I is fractured'). Instead, the former is *completed* by the latter. But this implies that well-determined does not mean 'completely known' or even 'known with certainty with respect to certain aspects' or even 'sensed immediately and securely' since all of these are untenable in terms of the deduced forms. When Deleuze says completed, he cannot mean added to, but unchanged. So what does 'given as well-determined' mean? Can it stand at the beginning of a valid transcendental deduction?

In order to answer these questions, it is worth returning to the well-determined starting points in the living present in Deleuze's deductions of the passive syntheses of time: expectancy, as in the passive assumption that something will occur, and archiving, as in the passive sense of the present passing away into the past as a stock of passing presents. Added to these, in the work on the third passive synthesis, there is the sense of the openness of the future with respect to expectancy and archiving. When we create a new work, we drive into a future that must be, in some way, independent of what has already occurred. We free ourselves of the past and of the particular ways it has been synthesised in the present creator (*We can make it different!... This discovery will change everything... After Cézanne, painting would never be the same.*).

For Deleuze, in the drive forward to the future and in the struggle to make it different from the past and the present, there is an implied sense of the possibility of that difference. Let's call it chancing, to reflect the sense of openness but also of risk. Later in *Difference and Repetition*, this chancing will be extended to all individual variations from a norm, in plants, animals or rocks (*Individual plants vary in response to climactic change – they chance different adaptations.*). We are passive with respect to this sense of chancing – it does not have to be a conscious component of out creative acts. But it must be there, where we move toward the new as opposed to further occurrences of the known or of the same. Its absence would be betrayed by a pointlessness (*It's all been done before... Here we go again!*) or an inability to adapt. So, although Deleuze does not discuss nihilism at length in *Difference and Repetition*, it lurks in the background every time he develops the concepts of the third synthesis of time and eternal return. The drive into the future must presuppose an open different future or fall into nihilism or inevitable annihilation. (For Deleuze's more extended treatment of nihilism, we must refer back to his comprehensive study of the concept in *Nietzsche and Philosophy*.)

The third passive synthesis of time is the condition for actions that drive towards the new. It has to be presupposed since its absence would reduce the drive to the new to a repetition of the past. The synthesis has three key characteristics. Deleuze puts them in an abstract form but it is useful to view them first in a more intuitive and everyday manner. First, the drive towards the new presupposes a cut in time that orders it in a non-circular way – that is, from the point of view of a sensation of moving towards the new, the present cuts us off from the past and projects us into a completely different future. The pure past of identifiable events is cut off from an open future that does not resemble it. Time is cut into a before and after, 'a pure order of time' (DR, pp. 88, 120) in Deleuze's more abstract formulation.

Second, this cut in time also assembles it since *all* the events of the pure past are cut off from *all* of the events of the future. The feeling that nothing will be the same again (*after the revolution*) presupposes that the past, as a whole, will not return at any part of the future and, thereby, conjures up the whole of time – time is a 'whole'. (I am slightly wary of the translation 'totality' here since Deleuze does not mean to imply that everything is put on the same basis. On the contrary, the whole or group – *ensemble* – is divided into two incommensurable subgroups.) The action that performs this cut in time, therefore, becomes a symbol for time as a whole (*All of Russia's past and all her future is at those gates . . . All of America's past and future is in that Declaration.*).

So, third, time is put into two series with respect to this cut – there are forms that cannot return and that are consigned to remain past for ever and there are forms that return with the cut that are relived with it. There are moments, whether past or future, that are not ready for the cut and those that are up to it, independent of where they stand in terms of historical time (*The revolution can be betrayed later and prepared for earlier irrespective of whether those acts are conscious of the revolution.*). The third synthesis of time is, therefore, much more complicated than a simple collecting of time or sublation of the past in the future. Deleuze insists on this complication many times through the latter stages of his chapter. The synthesis cuts, assembles and orders. This three-fold structure appears to be paradoxical since the cut is contradicted by the assembly and the ordering and vice versa.

How can time be cut in the present and yet also be a whole in terms of the relation of past to future? How can time be ordered but not in terms of the present cut? The answer lies in Deleuze's reliance on the eternal return of difference and the impossibility of the return of the same: identities fall into the past but that part of them that is pure difference returns (a cut between the same and difference that forms a whole); the parts of acts and identities that are differential or in movement return eternally whether they are in the past or the future (*Beckett's plays are always fresh, because, each time they are captured and interpreted in a way that consigns them to history, they metamorphose into something new – they are never what we think they are.*).

This deduction of the pure form of the third synthesis of time as order, whole and series takes few pages but it is a crucial step in the deduction of eternal return in a properly Deleuzian manner, rather than as a Nietzschean provocation or doctrine. The third synthesis of time must be understood as the eternal return of difference. Identities, or the same, from the past and the present, pass away forever, transformed by the return of that which makes them differ – Deleuze's pure difference or difference in itself. As condition for the sensation of a drive into the new, eternal return cuts the past off from the future (gives time an order). It brings all of time into play because it consigns all identified events to the past and makes all of the future different from all of the past (it conjures up the whole of time). But it only does so when pure differences return, when identity is consigned to the past forever and where there is the sensation of the new free of sameness. 'Eternal return affects only the new, what is produced under the condition of absence and by the intermediary of metamorphosis.' (DR, pp. 90, 122 translation slightly modified). Finally, eternal return operates through a selection of two series – the linear time into which sameness falls and the circular time of the return of pure difference. 'In this manner, the ground has been superseded by groundlessness, a universal ungrounding which turns upon itself and causes only the yet to come to return.' (DR, pp. 91, 122)

The insistence on three syntheses of time – habit, the synthesis of the whole of the past and the cut in time that orders, assembles and divides it into two series – account for the importance of a philosophy of time for Deleuze's philosophy and for its wider originality and significance. The philosophy allows him to explain how things acquire consistency free of conscious activity and natural law (first synthesis), to explain how all things are connected but in a non-causal manner (second synthesis) and to explain how the virtual and actual are necessarily related but without being reducible to one another (third synthesis).

Here, we have a philosophy of time that does not have to deny linear time. Instead, it completes it with a circular time of the return of difference that avoids the paradoxes of the relation of past to future through the present in simple linear philosophies of time. (How can the past remain past and yet be connected to the future? How does the present pass away? How is the future unconditioned by the past?) Actual things occur in linear time but they are only viewed as complete in relation to a non-linear time. We have to account for how actual events alter the pure virtual past and select pure differences that return eternally. The scope of an actual event goes much wider than its causal linear effects and causes. It alters the significance of the past and its power to return in the future (*The revolution changed how we thought and felt. It made a world impossible and opened us to new forces and risks.*).

However, although all three syntheses of time are conditions for actions in the present, they all deny that action is prior to passivity. I have already explained this in relation to the first two: any action presupposes physical passive syntheses or habits; any action presupposes the synthesis of the whole of the past, not only that

104

of which we are conscious. In the case of the third synthesis, the present creative activity is part of that which is left behind (*We too will become children of our revolution.*). 'The synthesis of time here constitutes a future which affirms at once both the unconditioned character of the product in relation to the conditions of its production, and the independence of the work in relation to its author or actor.' (DR, pp. 94, 125)

This does not mean that actions must disappear in favour of some kind of passive inactivity. Deleuze's acceptance that activity must play a role is reflected in a long note on Marx, revolution, repetition and the open future in the middle of Deleuze's work on the third repetition. Rather, the priority given to passivity over activity means that any action must take account of the passive syntheses that it presupposes. This is what Deleuze's principles of connecting and forgetting are designed to do. It is a question of where and how to allow passivity into structures of activity. This is a problem in relation to which a thoroughgoing passivity may, in fact, be a terrible error (*You knew it would bring down all that you love and disconnect you from your source of strength.*).

But, still, all these deductions and arguments ask us to give a lot to Deleuze, in accepting that all our living presents involve senses of expectancy, archiving and chancing. Are these universal phenomena? Does it even make sense to speak of universal phenomena? Who is this 'we' that I speak of? Indeed, even if I am speaking of my senses, how do I know that they will endure? It does not take a great leap of the imagination to conceive of beings whose relation to time is very different to our own, yet whose lives resemble ours very closely. A computer does not have senses of expectancy, archiving and chancing, yet it can create the new, its present acts pass into the archive, it performs actions in the present that contract past repetitions (it has been perfected). None of these properties require Deleuze's syntheses of time for their explanation other physical, chemical and mathematical models will suffice. Could we not treat ourselves as automatic beings? Why, in principle, can there not be chemical or mechanistic explanations for our relation to time? When such explanations gain acceptance, senses that appear essential to us may fall away, dismissed as the product of foolish superstition.

The solution to these questions is to accept that the things that Deleuze takes as given are not universal. His claim then becomes conditional – that is, if such phenomena are present, they presuppose three passive syntheses of time. But this still does not resolve the question of whether they are well determined. Quite the contrary since the lack of universality draws our attention to variations and inconsistencies between different cases. These may show Deleuze's phenomena to be an ill-defined ground in any case. Can we distinguish expectancy from a mistaken certainty that simply presupposes a lack of knowledge or from a conditioning that presupposes control by a knowable external process having nothing to do with passive synthesis of a Deleuzian kind?

FREUD AND PASSIVE SYNTHESES

Deleuze follows his short but crucial deductions of the three passive syntheses of time with a long application of his work on time to Freud's work on the unconscious. This section is many faceted and the full detail of Deleuze's engagement with Freud deserves a deeper study that can be given here. Instead, as in the earlier discussion of Freud and Deleuze, their relation will be approached through critical questions, in particular, those raised in the context of the three syntheses of time. Does Deleuze's extension of his work on time to Freud's work on the unconscious allow the following question to be answered more fully? Does Deleuze's philosophy of time offer a convincing account of the need to refer to an unconscious when searching for the preconditions for actual sensations?

Deleuze begins by following Freud's move beyond the pleasure principle. Deleuze claims that this principle presupposes the first synthesis of time as habit. Even if actions can be explained in terms of the search for pleasure, that search presupposes the passive syntheses that have come to make up the searcher and these cannot be explained in terms of pleasure. These comments are re-enforced by remarks on the formation of organs, such as the eye. According to Deleuze, the eye is the result of a series of passive syntheses, of repetitions, that are not the result of the search for pleasure since they lead to greater excitation. Similarly, the refinement of a sensation through repetition is not pleasurable, though it may lead to pleasure (*I know it hurts but keep practising until you get a feel for that sweet spot.*). This excitation is opposed to pleasure, defined as the feeling that accompanies the diminution of excitation. Pleasure is an after-effect of a process that goes beyond it: 'The repetition of an excitation has as its true object the elevation of the passive synthesis to a power that implies the pleasure principle along with its future and past applications.' (DR, pp. 98, 130)

106

This point leads to a development of Deleuze's critical remarks on Kant about receptivity – an indication that Deleuze means to answer the problem of the possible circularity of his work on the given, to the extent that he turns down Kant's solution to the problem of circularity. The restriction of the passive self to receptivity, defined in terms of the pure forms of space and time, cuts receptivity off from activity, in the sense where the latter is a matter of subjective phenomena of pain and pleasure, whereas the former is a matter of objective categories. For Kant, we must, in principle, share the same receptivity but we must be divided in terms of our sensations of pleasure and pain and, hence, in terms of the actions that are grounded in them.

For Deleuze, this does not make sense since we still have to explain how receptivity and activity are present in the same self (*I can see that it is objectively the case but I still don't like it.*). We also have to explain how the same self has two completely different forms of sensibility: receptivity and feelings. In other words, what is the proper relation of objectivity and subjectivity? Deleuze claims that this gulf between receptivity and activity can be overcome if passivity is extended to activity and if receptivity is not viewed as objective but as subjective: 'The aim of the preceding analyses, on the contrary, has been to show that receptivity has been defined in terms of the formation of local selves or egos, in terms of the passive syntheses of contemplation or contraction . . . ' (DR, pp. 98, 130)

The answer is that passivity and activity are always related – they have an effect on one another. But that effect is not of the form where one completely dominates the other, as in the claims that all activity is illusory or that all passivity is in fact activity. Neither is it of the form where a single logic allows us to understand both (*Activity and passivity interact solely according to these common laws.*). Deleuze uses Freud to explain this special form of interaction. He concentrates on Freud's work on activity towards a real object and its relation to a virtual object. This choice makes sense since the given things that Deleuze took as the starting points for his deductions were not Kantian pure intuitions but activities in the living present that presupposed three passive syntheses. The overall structure of the section on Freud is taken from the demonstration that actions towards real objects presuppose the three syntheses in the unconscious in terms of virtual objects.

Whenever we act towards an object taken to be real and, thereby, strengthen our sense of self with respect to that object, two different processes take place at the level of the passive syntheses presupposed by that action. Here, Deleuze is applying his conclusions regarding the different interactions between levels of structures, described earlier in terms of the three syntheses, to Freud's work:

However, the real objects, the objects proposed as reality or as support for the connection, are not the only objects of the ego, any more than they exhaust the totality of so-called objectal relations. We can distinguish two simultaneous dimensions in such a way that there is no movement beyond the passive synthesis towards an active synthesis without the former also being extended in another direction, one in which it utilises the bound excitation in order to attain something else – albeit in a manner different from the reality principle – even while it remains a passive and contemplative synthesis.

(DR, pp. 99, 131)

For any given object and action, there is a virtual object, a particular synthesis of the pure past and a selection of pure differences according to eternal return. Any action on the given object implies consequences at the level of the virtual object, though this relation is not a causal one. The re-arrangement of the syntheses at the level of the virtual object are of a different order from the causal relations at the level of actual objects. The consequences at the virtual level are then played out again at the level of the actual.

As actual things, the real object and the self are well determined but they are not complete. To have a complete view of the object, we have to operate a dialectical synthesis that goes from the actual to the different structures of the virtual. The structures are the transcendental conditions for the actual object as something intense, significant and in movement. The dialectical synthesis must itself be a creative experimental process involving actual acts and objects because any act can only be the expression of a passive synthesis and never its accurate representation or understanding due to the asymmetry between the levels in terms of the relation they imply within each other. In Freud's case, the dialectic purports to approach a determinable virtual object. But Deleuze points out that this is an illegitimate restriction that ignores its unknowable effects on the virtual.

In other words, there is always a hidden side to any well-determined act and object. This is because of the three syntheses that they presuppose and that are 'disguised' in them: 'Repetition is constituted only with and through the *disguises* which affect the terms and relations of the real series, but it is so because it depends upon the virtual object as an immanent instance which operates above all by displacement.' (DR, pp. 105, 139) The actual can be grasped but it is incomplete – that is, we can be certain of it but only in terms of its actual side. The virtual cannot be grasped, only operated on, and the effects of this operation can only be grasped in the actual. Translated into Deleuze's interpretation of the Freudian unconscious, this becomes a claim about the unconscious. It must be viewed as different in kind from consciousness: 'It concerns problems and questions which can never be reduced to the great oppositions or the overall effects that are felt in consciousness.' (DR, pp. 108, 143)

So Deleuze's argument is that there is no vicious circle in his folding back of the condition on to the given it was the condition for because the application of the results of the deductions to the starting point in the given does not undermine its evidence. Rather it completes it in terms of different views. We have a given sensation, such as expectancy, that is then completed in terms of its relation to the virtual. So, when Deleuze asks us to experiment with an actual thing, it is not to destroy it as an actual thing that we can understand and be certain of. Rather, it is to extend that knowledge through a feeling for the connections, selections and changes implied in that given. The Deleuzian dialectic does not take place in one plane but across many – from given to virtual, to given, endlessly.

The three passive syntheses of time give form to that process by making the relation between planes more precise. For example, from the point of view of this dialectic, painting could be viewed as an experimentation with colour where each painter gives an actual truth about the use of colour (that it benefits from careful delimitation, say) but this truth is only local and must be extended into all other virtual connections (that it benefits from seamless blending or from the dominance of one colour or from careful harmonies). Colour actually benefits from careful drawn limits in Gauguin but it also benefits from their absence in Rothko.

However, this still leaves us with the problem that any given actual thing is contingent, a particular event, rather than a universal. Even if the problem of circularity can be avoided by Deleuze, it is far from evident that his method and his deductions can survive the accusation that they are based on contingency. Can he show that his deductions of the three syntheses of time are universally valid, once he bases them on particulars? This question can only be answered through a study of his concepts of synthesis with respect to ideas and the sensible in chapters 4 and 5 of *Difference and Repetition*. But the importance of the question can be seen in Deleuze's resistance to phenomenology and to phenomenological reductions in particular. Deleuze does not seek universal phenomena though a process of reduction – he seeks universal conditions on the ground of the sensations of individuals.

5

Against Common Sense

THE IMAGE OF THOUGHT

Chapter 3 of *Difference and Repetition* shows the critical side to Deleuze's dialectic. It criticises thought defined in terms of identity in recognition and representation, by showing what that definition has falsely excluded or ignored. He claims that such definitions must presuppose what they seek to exclude. Deleuze explains how thinking has been damagingly restricted due to the effect of an 'image of thought' – that is, a particular set of presuppositions about the form thought should take. Without a critique of this image and without an effort to replace it by a form of thought open to difference and repetition, this damaging effect will continue and strengthen.

The image can be understood through eight postulates or eight claims about how thought should work in principle. He describes and criticises each in turn through the chapter. The postulates explain why there is an attraction to thinking in terms of identity and in terms of a priority of identity over difference in its relation to repetition. So the chapter follows up the chapters on difference and repetition by explaining how we come to miss the essence of difference and repetition described in those chapters.

The postulates are traced back to the history of philosophy, to ways of constructing philosophical systems and to mistaken definitions of truth. However, it would be an error to take the work on the idea of thought as simply critical of philosophy or particular philosophers. This interpretation is superficial and fails to take account of the more complicated background to the critique. Put

111

simply, Deleuze's point is that the construction of philosophy takes place against a background defined by the postulates. This background is presupposed by the philosophy and supported by it but it is not the philosophy proper. The image is in the everyday common sense and good sense that philosophies can seem to support and give rise to but these fall far short of the experimental and ground-breaking quality of all great philosophies.

Philosophy always runs the risk of re-enforcing common sense and good sense. At worst, philosophy may adopt this role as its true task. In order to explain how philosophy can counter this danger, Deleuze defines the concept of Idea from the chapter on difference with greater precision, through the contrasts drawn between the postulates and the Idea which they hide. The true role of philosophy should be to forget the image of thought and connect to what he calls Ideas, the transcendental condition for thought and that which vivifies actual lives through intensities, through difference in itself. The capital I is used to distinguish his Idea from our common conception of ideas as any identifiable thought about something. Deleuze's Ideas are not contained in the mind – they are relations between things in the virtual that are the condition for the evolution of actual things. These virtual Ideas are, therefore, the condition for changes in our actual ideas and must not be confused with them.

However, at this stage of *Difference and Repetition* the definition of the Idea is still rather vague; it requires work from chapter 4 of the book to reach its most positive and clear version. The concept of the Idea is of something in movement that does not have a fixed identity. The Idea cannot be known, only sensed *and* known partially as it is expressed. The Idea is resistant to identification as an object of knowledge because its elements are pure differences that cannot identified only deduced on the basis of sensations. In the two preceding chapters of the book, Deleuze deduced Ideas from sensations, for example, the sensation of expectation. Here, he is concerned with the way in which we come to miss Ideas by assuming that no such deduction is necessary. In short, he is answering the question 'Why is the illusion of identity so strong?'.

The question that he is not answering fully, which, in some way, weakens the chapter and makes it the most treacherous of the book, is 'What is reality if it is not illusion?'. Chapter 3 of *Difference and Repetition* can give the impression that Deleuze's philosophy is about the critique of mistaken forms of thought. This gives it an unduly negative function, as if its main role is critique. This is also the case if the question of reality is taken as secondary to the question of illusions – for example, when we ask 'Why is there an illusion of identity?'. For Deleuze, the problem of how to create, given the reality of virtual Ideas, is as important as the problem of illusions.

It is crucial not to confuse his four-fold dialectic with any of its elements and, in particular, with a negative critique. There is no Deleuzian dialectics where there is no destructive creation or no search for conditions or no search for completeness or no critique. Furthermore, if any of these elements is taken independently of the others, then they cannot be taken as elements of the dialectics. Deleuzian critique works with a destructive creation, with a search for completeness and a search for conditions. This means that it is also a mistake to think that his philosophy can ever escape critique, in the sense where there would be a new philosophy that somehow escaped all the problems of old ones, once critique has accomplished its task. Rather, the critical work shows how creative moments necessarily fall back into illusion, thereby necessitating constant critique and new creation.

This point can be understood as the difference between the important question for any philosophy 'Given your definition of truth, how do we fall into error?' and the primary question 'What is truth?'. For Deleuze, truth is always prone to illusion and falsehood is not something that can be eliminated once and for all. Though it appears that Deleuze may be answering the latter question in chapter 3, this is not the case. He is dealing with the effects and subsidiary clauses of the central arguments and concepts of his book developed in the four main chapters (1, 2, 4, 5).

In many ways, the critical focus makes chapter 3 easier than others and, hence, perhaps, a reasonable place to start. But it is a bad place to finish because, when taken alone, it may relegate Deleuze to simplistic and ultimately indefensible oppositions drawn between the true path and the illusory one. When, in fact, his point is that they are inextricably linked. The way to give priority to difference and repetition involves following difficult and paradoxical principles where identity must have a role to play. What is more, this conclusion is supported by arguments and concepts that owe much to the philosophers we may think he simply opposes.

In terms of links to his later work, the chapter on the image of thought is strongly related but, in many ways, inferior to the book, written with Félix Guattari, *What is Philosophy?* The later book is more careful at intertwining that which a philosophy presupposes, with all its attendant dangers, and the concepts of the philosophy. It allows for selections to made among philosophers, to the extent where Spinoza is described as the 'prince of philosophers', due to the purity of the background that his concepts presuppose, where purity can be understood as freedom from common and good sense. The earlier chapter, on the other hand, works against this careful intertwining and, hence, against the more complex idea of philosophy due to its binary structure (Idea-image; principles-postulates). In order to take account of this problem, I will not simply work through the main postulates but, instead, I will work through the lines of argument and analysis that give rise to them, starting with Deleuze's introduction to the function of the image of thought in Descartes.

GOOD WILL

The first step in Deleuze's study of the presuppositions of philosophy is to draw a distinction between objective and subjective ones. He also calls subjective presuppositions implicit. Thus, an objective presupposition is an explicit assumption of a concept (*For A to be the case, B, C and D must also be the case*). The Cartesian method of doubt is designed to ensure that no dubitable objective presuppositions are left in the philosophy. This explains the necessity for the cogito ('I think, I am' in the version given in the *Meditations*) to be immediate in its truth and not to require a further investigation of assumptions about the 'I', the 'think' and the 'am'. Deleuze claims that this further investigation is avoided by defining man as a thinking thing. It is a moot point whether this avoids the necessity to investigate the objective assumptions of this definition but this is not Deleuze's main focus. His argument does not rest on the problems of objective presuppositions but on subjective ones, though he is not entirely clear about this until late in his opening section.

Deleuze's point is that, independent of objective presuppositions, there will always be subjective presuppositions for any concept – that is, ones that must depend on an appeal to feelings and sensations rather than to further concepts or propositions. The key ideas here are those of necessary independence from objective presuppositions and the definition of feelings as independent of propositions. His point is that, irrespective of any errors regarding objective presuppositions on Descartes' part, there are also subjective ones (*For A to be the case, this feeling must be assumed to be universal.*). Deleuze rather ruins his distinction at this point by defining subjective presuppositions in terms of the form 'everybody knows' and by making a rather weak aside that objective and subjective presuppositions may, in fact, be the same thing. The assumption 'everybody knows that' is still objective and open to conceptual analysis. Deleuze is going to pursue something rather different – moral feelings. The assumption that there is something that 'everybody knows' rests on two moral feelings about thought as betrayed in following the proposition that 'everybody knows': First, *in principle, thinkers seek out what everybody knows* and, second, *in principle, what is known ought to be accessible to everyone.*

Philosophers are aware that thinkers lie and that some have greater cognitive powers than others but, when philosophers write or talk about truth and seek to avoid dubitable objective presuppositions, they assume that, in principle, others seek universal truths and can follow valid arguments: 'This element consists only of the supposition that thought is the natural exercise of a faculty, of the presupposition that there is a natural capacity for thought endowed with a talent for truth or an affinity with the true, under the double aspect of a *good will on the part of the thinker* and *an upright nature on the part of thought.*' (DR, pp. 131, 171) These suppositions are postulates insofar as they depend on the abstraction of the 'in principle'. They are moral insofar as they assume that, in principle, it is how thinkers and thought ought to be, independent of how they are. Deleuze does not hark back to his work on Hume and habit and the difference between 'is' and 'ought' at this point. However, the direction of Deleuze's criticism is that the postulates perpetuate the common-sense illusion that there are moral laws, where there are only moral habits.

Each time a philosopher addresses others with statements that assume that universal assent is possible, they encourage the view that thought is about shareable truths that we want to share. Deleuze's extremism comes out at this point since his view is that these assumptions must be undone by philosophy for thought to take place. Indeed, later in the book, he will argue that thought emerges with individuals. What defence is there for this view since a response to the critique regarding presuppositions could very well be that philosophy ought to adopt these presuppositions explicitly and out of necessity or fall into a quietist despair (*You don't want to hear me and you wouldn't understand anyway.*)? He is well aware of this counter and embraces the 'dangerous' and 'immoral' path of destroying all subjective presuppositions

As a result [a philosophy] would discover its authentic repetition in a thought without Image, even at the cost of the greatest destructions and the greatest demoralisations, and a philosophical obstinacy with no ally but paradox, one which would have to renounce both the form of representation and the element of common sense.

(DR, pp. 132, 173)

Two criticisms emerge against Deleuze at this point we have encountered them before in the work on difference. First, from a social and political point of view, it seems that he has gone too far in developing a line of argument without taking account of moral and political values. The destruction of presuppositions may or may not be desirable from a formal philosophical point of view. But, from a prior moral standpoint, that destruction can seem unequivocally bad. If the goals of philosophy are to be the good, tolerance and understanding, then any philosophy ought to avoid the kind of violence and immorality embraced above (or, at least, only embrace it in the name of a higher good). So Deleuze can be accused of a dangerous immorality at the heart of his philosophy.

Second, from a philosophical point of view, Deleuze's error may be in assuming that subjective presuppositions can ever be done away with. Could it be the case that the proper goal of philosophy is to select the right subjective presuppositions, as opposed to seeking to do away with all of them? In criticising all subjective presuppositions, he may be setting himself an impossible target. In so doing, he may have turned away from the right approach to such presuppositions – finding ways of selecting the best. For example, if subjective presuppositions are inevitable, Deleuze has merely missed that he has 'implicitly' adopted pessimistic ones.

Finally, perhaps what Deleuze takes to be subjective presuppositions are, in fact, objective ones. If they are objective, in the sense of shared objectively by all thinkers or agents, then philosophers are correct in claiming that, in principle, good sense and common sense are essential to true thought. The proper attitude, then, would be to reflect on how those objective presuppositions should be translated into ethics and politics, as opposed to criticising them or seeking to undermine them. On this account, Descartes' assumptions would not be mistaken – they might not even be implicit, in the sense of unseen. They would be the proper objective moral premises to adopt and to keep at a distance from the kind of Deleuzian scepticism aimed at subjective assumptions.

KANT, DESCARTES AND RECOGNITION

Deleuze's response to the critical points made above turns on the familiar argument that even the most obvious and apparently universal moral values have turned out be erroneous, restricted and divisive. As opposed to supporting any given value, the proper role of the philosopher is to criticise all emergent 'obvious' values or *doxa*. He accepts that Descartes is aware of this and that this is why the presupposition of the good and shareable nature of thought is only *by right*, rather than *in fact*. By right implies that the good and shareable nature is only formal and does not concern specific empirical content. In other words, Descartes and Kant share the insight that, in principle, thought is about the good and is shareable but what is good and shared cannot finally be known. This does not lead to an impasse where we know what thought should be but where we cannot apply it in practice because both thinkers develop further postulates on the basis of the first that allow us to know how to think, but not what to think (*These are my values. I have arrived at them through a sound thinking but they are provisional because the facts on which they are constructed are necessarily limited – true by right but not in fact*).

However, according to Deleuze, what this line of thought misses is the way in which thinking by right and in principle still establishes 'obvious' values and a doxa with an empirical content. This content not only betrays the purity of thought but it also allows a set of more practical empirical facts concerning morality and politics to return. He is particularly concerned with the strength of the sleight of hand at work here. The false step into the transcendent, supposedly empty, form gives the impression of avoiding contingent empirical content whilst still carrying it through (*Of course human rights apply to any possible human since their basis is purely formal.*): 'To the extent that it holds in principle, this image presupposes a certain distribution of the empirical and the transcendental, and it is this distribution or transcendental model implied by the image that must be judged.' (DR, pp. 133, 174)

Deleuze argues that, for thought to be in principle shareable and good, it must be able to unify, both within each individual thinker and between thinkers. In the first case, this means that different faculties, such as the understanding and sensibility, must, in principle, be treatable in the same way (*The relation between your understanding of this fact and your feelings about it is the following . . .*). In the second case, it means that different selves can judge when

117

thought is correct (*Yes, any reasonable person must agree to that argument.*). This leads to the second postulate of common sense: thought is a common sense that crosses between the different faculties of the same self. Furthermore, there is a good sense allied to this common sense that allows for different thinkers to share the same common sense.

So, how are different faculties united by the faculty of thought? How are we able to judge thoughts? The answer, for Kant, as read by Deleuze, lies in the transcendent faculty of recognition. This faculty transcends all others in operating in all of them, whilst remaining distinct from them. We can actively think about the objects of each different faculty and, hence, reflect on the faculty because we are be able to recognise those objects (*We sense* this *because we recognise it. We understand* that *because we recognise it*). This identification of the proper objects of each faculty depends on the transcendent faculty of recognition. We can judge a thought because we can recognise it; we can judge a sensation because we recognise it. The third postulate to come under Deleuze's critical scrutiny is, hence, that thought depends on an active subject's faculty of recognition. This faculty has access to all others and must be shared, in principle.

But why does Deleuze have a problem with recognition, since it too is formal and empty of content? We make no suppositions as to the content of recognition when we say that, in order to use different faculties, we must be able to recognise their objects. Neither do we make any such suppositions when we say that thought's capacity for recognition allows us to think across faculties and make judgements. Deleuze's point is that we do make presuppositions but in a general rather than a specific way. We can claim that, in principle, nothing is excluded from recognition since recognition is a condition for anything to register as existing. But, in making this claim, we still exclude a general category of things due to the form of recognition – it operates by comparing the new to that which is already known (*Do I recognise this?*).

So the model of recognition is necessarily conservative since it depends on identifying something anew by comparing it with what is already known or what has already been experienced. This conservatism is philosophical in the sense where philosophy refers the form of the new back on to the form of the already known. Deleuze, though, wants to show the politically conservative resonance of the philosophical commitment to recognition: 'how derisory are the voluntary struggles for recognition. Struggles occur

118

only on the basis of a common sense and established values, for the attainment of current values (honours wealth and power).' (DR, pp. 136, 178) Recognition discounts the new as pure difference, whereas Deleuze wants to affirm it through his creative third synthesis and his appeal to the eternal return of difference. This is because recognition must operate by breaking down difference into that which has already been recognised (*There's something there but I do not recognise it. What should I do to make it recognisable?*).

This explains Deleuze's bitterness at what he sees as Kant's missed opportunity in not pushing through his replacement of error by illusion. In Descartes, error is explained as a lack of recognition or the misuse of faculties through a lack of thought on their limits (what they accurately allow us to recognise). Error is, then, not internal to thought, to reason as the faculty of recognition, it stems from its absence (*You let your heart rule your mind . . . Let's keep feelings out of this.*). But the Kantian concept of illusion attributes flaws in thought to thought itself. Thought is prone to illusions and the faculty of recognition can be led astray on its own (*This rational idea can be recognised but it is excessive.*). However, Kant strives to remedy this flaw by defining the limits within which each faculty can proceed free of illusion.

This definition of limits leaves recognition intact and still at the core of thinking. It confirms Kant in his conservatism:

We see to what degree the Kantian critique is ultimately respectful: knowledge, morality, are supposed to correspond to natural interests of reason, and are never themselves called into question. We only question the use of faculties, that are declared legitimate according to one or other of these interests.

(DR, pp. 137, 179)

[translation modified to be faithful to the original sense of calling the faculties into question].

Recognition survives intact from the danger of illusion thanks to the tribunal of reason that determines the limits of faculties in line with the traditional distribution of power within the state.

But why is this dependence on recognition flawed? It is not enough to accuse an argument of conservatism. It may be a good argument *for* conservatism. Indeed, in Kant's case, what Deleuze sees as conservative others may more readily see as progressive in its resistance to the mistaken use of faculties (*Let's leave religion out of science and science out of religion . . . Let's put freedom at the foundation of reason but subject the understanding to causal laws.*). In other words, what's wrong with recognition in itself? What's wrong with the claim that, for anything to be, it must be capable of being recognised?

REPRESENTATION

Deleuze's answer to these questions turns on a further postulate: recognition depends on representation. In order to recognise the object of a faculty, we must depend on representation defined in terms of an identity that we can conceive of, an analogy that we can judge, an opposition that we can imagine and a similarity that we can perceive. Each of these aspects corresponds to an application of representation to different faculties. In terms of the understanding, it depends on the identity of the concept (*What are its correct predicates?*). For judgement, it depends on analogy (*Is the structure the same here and here?*). In terms of the imagination, it depends on oppositions (*What if this is negated or removed?*). Whereas, for perception, it depends on similarities (*Are these the same to you?*).

Recognition is an overarching and legitimating faculty, thanks to representation. Representation operates on different faculties in different ways but unites all of them through judgements based on identity and the exclusion of that which cannot be identified. There are different forms of identity (of the concept, of the structure, of the imagined thing). They allow us to determine the correct scope for each faculty and the laws that apply to them because they can determine their proper use in terms of how representation operates in them. This determination, though, can be ascribed to a transcendent faculty of recognition charged with keeping faculties within their proper limits on the basis of judgements that must depend on identity.

Deleuze's argument against recognition is, hence, the same as the one developed against representation in the first two chapters of *Difference and Representation*. Conservative recognition is to be avoided because it perpetuates a damaging illusion that hides reality in terms of difference in itself and repetition for itself. These conditions for actual identities cannot be identified but they underlie all identities and allow us to explain their changes and evolutions. True difference and repetition are excluded by representation.

The political and moral horizon of this argument is that representation cuts us off from the intensity afforded by acts open to creative repetitions. This is because representation privileges identity, analogy, opposition and similarity over pure differences and repetition. The demand to represent blocks the creative repetitions that intensify a life tending to stasis. So conservatism in recognition is based on an illusion that leads to decadence or to damaging repressions. Deleuze does not rehearse these arguments in the chapter on the image of thought. Instead, through an ambivalent reading of Plato, he shows how an anti-Kantian approach to the faculties allows philosophy to be attuned to difference and repetition. This leads to a definition of thought away from the model of recognition and away from representation.

Put simply, thought escapes the model of recognition when sensation forces thought to take place. This is not the activity of recognition but the passivity of a 'fundamental encounter' (*I have missed something about the rain on these dull grey streets.*). This thought does not involve the division and correct attribution of recognition (*The grey of London or the blue of Marseilles?*). It is a sign that forces us to think with a problem (*I have missed something of those dull grey streets and these blue skies. What new life can be created to express the grey and the blue?*). The force of the problem, as independent of the questions and solutions of recognition, is that it goes beyond any past solutions stored in memory. It is a problem because it does not yet have a solution and because it does not even allow for solutions that cancel it out.

For Deleuze, a problem is something inevitable (hence its expression through signs and sensation) that can only lead to a series of creative reactions rather than to a lasting solution. The sign and sensation put faculties into discord (*I cannot know the answer to this. My imagination must go beyond memory. What I feel is much more than a mere sensation.*):

Discord of the faculties, chain of force and fuse along which each confronts its limit, receiving from (or communicating to) the other only a violence which brings it face to face with its own element, as though with its disappearance or perfection.

(DR, pp. 141, 184)

This discord compels us to think in new ways.

But how can a faculty 'confront' its limits? What sense is there in speaking of forms of thought that depend on faculties going beyond their limits? Either we know or we do not. Either we sense or we do not. When we mistakenly think we know something that by right we cannot, we do not know and there is only the illusion of knowledge. When we mistakenly think we have sensed something that we cannot sense, we have not sensed that thing but merely suffered an illusion or made a mistake. How can Deleuze respond to these core tenets of Kantianism and the way in which they have become central to modern ideas about the limits of disciplines and the proper spheres of different human faculties?

His response depends upon an important distinction drawn between the use of a faculty within the limits that a common sense has set for it and a transcendent use. This latter indicates that the faculty is being used according to what Deleuze somewhat teasingly calls a 'superior empiricism' or 'transcendental empiricism'. But a lot turns on what is meant by transcendent use or use beyond its limits since this seems to be draw out the main contradiction in Deleuze's argument – that is, of a use beyond the limits of proper use (*What do you mean 'That equation is immoral'?*). This challenge is all the stronger given Deleuze's criticism of the Kantian transcendent faculty of recognition. The two uses of the term transcendent must be distinguished to avoid turning Deleuze's argument back on himself.

Deleuze's argument turns on two notions: that there are certain uses of a faculty that can only be accessed by it and that these uses concern the genesis of the faculty. In other words, Deleuze is arguing that, independent of the limits of a faculty that can be grasped by thought defined as the overarching faculty of recognition, there is an internal sense of how the faculty comes about at all and how it evolves. This sense must be beyond recognition since there is nothing to recognise and identify – only a sense of the movement of the faculty (*Look, medicine and healing are not what non-medical people recognise them to be anymore. We are starting to do things differently. Maybe they never were what people thought. Maybe what they are and were has always been changing through what they become.*).

Deleuze uses the term 'transcendent' to describe an overarching faculty or the use of a faculty beyond its limits. These must be distinguished very carefully. A transcendent faculty of recognition operating over other faculties is criticised due to its dependence on recognition and on illusory identities. According to Deleuze, the true use of a transcendent faculty beyond its limits is with respect to its own evolution through connections with other faculties. It is, therefore, not a matter of the fixing of faculties and determining their proper fields but of transforming those faculties and fields by transgressing established boundaries and laws. That use depends on a transcendental work on the conditions for change in any given faculty in relation to others. This transcendental work is experimental both in the sense that only experiments on the evolution of the faculty can reveal the significance of its evolution in the past and in the sense that the future of the faculty must be a matter of experimentation rather than a question of already established knowledge.

The Deleuzian appeal to the transcendental is, thus, very different from the Kantian. It turns on the questions of where they begin, what they take as given and how they evolve through transforming interactions with others. In the chapter on repetition for itself, we saw that the three syntheses of time were deduced from sensations of change, such as expectation. This was no chance starting point since it responded to Deleuze's philosophical instinct to ask about the evolution of things in order to sense how they have become what they are and how they may become something other – as opposed to the Kantian instinct to ask about the most pure state of things in order to understand what they are and where we can determine their limits. Deleuze's point is that Kant's approach actually presupposes more than it needs to about the priority of identity and recognition and that this leads to a mistaken definition of the faculties. The Kantian response could be that Deleuze does not presuppose enough since we cannot grasp change prior to grasping identity. In other words, how does Deleuze know that he is dealing with a faculty, at all, or with more than one or part of one?

Deleuze's answer reverses Kant's approach, giving priority to a sensibility that sets things in movement above the secure foundation of an unchanging given. Later in the book, in chapter 5, he will argue that no such given can exist without implying sensations. At this stage, though, his 'argument' is little more than a credo:

For it is not figures already mediated and related to representation that are capable of carrying faculties to their respective limits but, on the contrary, free or untamed states of difference in itself; not qualitative opposition within the sensible, but an element which is in itself difference, and creates at once both the quality in the sensible and the transcendent exercise within sensibility.

(DR, pp. 144, 187)

No matter how convinced we are about the reality of Deleuze's difference in itself, difficult questions remain. Can faculties be carried to their limits? If they can, how exactly is this achieved by the intensity of the transcendent exercise of sensibility? Deleuze uses examples from literature (an exchange of letters between Artaud and Rivière) to support his case. But, for every example of great literature coming out of particular sensibilities rather than a well-established thought, there will be counter-examples and counter-explanations of the creative process that stress classical order over loose creativity. A contingent view on the question of the value of different processes in art cannot ground Deleuze's far-reaching claims on the nature of faculties.

ERROR AND ILLUSION

The chapter on the image of thought does not provide satisfactory answers to these problems as a whole but it does develop in particular directions in terms of further postulates explaining the resistance to sensibility and the dependence on recognition. The next postulate concerns the definition and source of error. When the model of recognition holds sway over the faculties, error is defined as a case of false recognition. This falsification is, itself, explained in terms of an interference from outside a faculty, including the overarching faculty of recognition. Errors occur because we do not think within the limits of a faculty, as in Descartes' explanation of error through the interference of an infinite will on a finite but secure understanding (*You wished it to be true when you should have sought to know whether it was true.*). The pervasiveness of this explanation of error supports the definition of faculties within their limits as defined by recognition. According to this view of error, Deleuze's talk of the transcendent use of a faculty makes no sense. So what is wrong with this traditional explanation of error?

Once again, Deleuze points out that the explanation of thought departing from the good and the true through error depends on a distinction between wrong turns taken *by right* and those taken *in fact*. In fact, thought departs from the good and the true for many different reasons that owe very little to abstract definitions of error. Folly, stupidity and malevolence lead to terrible wrong turns but these are not simple mistakes. However, by right, we know what sound thinking is and how it can go wrong. It is a thinking within limits that goes wrong, or errs, when we fail to respect those limits. So, however much folly, stupidity and malevolence fail to resemble error in fact, by right they must be reduced to explanations similar to those of error. This allows them to be considered as things external to correct thinking, in the sense where they depend, like error, on moves beyond its proper limits.

Deleuze's argument is not that the definition of error fails to account for matters of fact but, rather, that error is a fact mistakenly taken as something by right. In other words, it is not that explanations in terms of the limits of faculties are shown to be unsatisfactory when we encounter actual follies, stupidities and malevolence. It is that, when we reflect on what thought must be by right, we realise that it cannot simply be accounted for in terms of error and limits:

> Everything must therefore be inverted: error is a fact which is then arbitrarily projected into the transcendental. As for the true transcendental structures of thought and the 'negative' in which these are enveloped, perhaps these must be sought elsewhere, and in figures other than those of error?

(DR, pp. 150, 195)

In seeking to explain the wrong turns of thought, philosophers are misled by the earlier postulates regarding recognition and representation and the further postulate that thought goes wrong due to errors and that these are external to the correct direction of thought.

They are misled to the extent that they fail to ask a further crucial question in terms of the transcendental or in terms of what thought is by right: What is the condition for follies, stupidity and malevolence? In response to this question, Deleuze draws out a general characteristic of the three, then moves on to its source. His first point starts with a remark on the physical and biological background to folly, stupidity and malevolence but, instead of viewing these as external to thought, he insists that they are a necessary and constitutive background to thought itself. This move chimes with his remarks on repetition and habit from the previous chapter. Thought is made in actual physical and biological repetitions together with the relations they imply in the virtual – it does not transcend them by right. The condition for folly, stupidity and malevolence is the background and the way in which it can rise back to the surface in thought processes that seemed to have escaped them: 'Cowardice, cruelty, baseness and stupidity are not simply corporeal capacities or traits of character or society; they are structures of thought as such.' (DR, pp. 151, 196)

So Deleuze refines arguments from earlier chapters on repetition and later chapters on individuation to convince us of this sometimes disastrous link between the background and thought. Thinking is not a shared universal faculty – it has particular characteristics in each of us. Our thoughts reflect the physical and biological but also the virtual repetitions that have made us

125

individual thinkers as opposed to identical subjects and selves defined by right:

> Stupidity is neither the ground nor the individual, but rather this relation in which individuation brings the ground to the surface without being able to give it form (this ground rises by means of the I, penetrating deeply into the possibility of thought and constituting the unrecognised in every recognition).

(DR, pp. 152)

Error can be stupid or not. It can be cruel or not, depending on the way in which it is related to this inability to give form to the ground. Error cannot, therefore, serve as an explanation for stupidity and cruelty – quite the contrary.

The difference between Deleuze's position and the postulates he wishes to oppose comes out in this demand to give form to the ground. This difference is an instance of his wider criticism regarding the refusal to accept the reality of the ground as difference and repetition. We must express and work with the repetitions that become concentrated in us and come to make us since to repress them or to treat them as something external is to redouble their force. Here, we begin to see the ferocity of the chapter on the image of thought. In the postulates that define the image, philosophy, common sense and good sense become allied to cruelty, stupidity and malevolence in the name of opposing them. The stakes of this engagement are, hence, very high for both sides, where neither side must be associated with a particular philosopher or philosophy, including Deleuze's own. Instead, we are presented with a recurring problem that mirrors the necessary return of the image of thought: How do we give form to difference and repetition without reducing them according to the postulates of the image of thought? How do we give form to that ground, rather than allowing it to work violently within our very attempts to escape it?

PROPOSITIONS AND SENSE

The opposition drawn between recognition and sensibility with respect to signs is developed further in a critique of the postulates that can be discerned in the Fregean analytic tradition. This critique also furthers the points on error with respect to that tradition, in the context of the opposition drawn between questions that allow for solutions and paradoxical problems. Put simply,

Deleuze attacks analytic philosophy of language for privileging designation over sense with respect to truth. He claims that this occurs due to the relegation of truth in sense to either 'psychological flair' – perhaps alluding to the later Wittgenstein – or to 'logical formalism' – perhaps alluding to Quine. This leads to the division of problems defined by propositions into soluble ones – where something is or is not the case in terms of what is designated – and insoluble ones – where nothing is designated – and the latter are relegated into non-sense.

I have already discussed Deleuze's definitions of propositions and his critique of some analytical positions with respect to difference, repetition and concepts in Chapter 2. The chapter on the image of thought adds an important elucidation of the Deleuzian concept of sense to the earlier discussion, though I will argue that the critical work associated with this explanation is sketchy at best. In short, Deleuze's definition of the sense or expressed of a proposition is that it is a problem, but what Deleuze means by problem is highly technical and complex. He uses a rather staged and superficial encounter with some aspects of the treatment of propositions in analytic philosophy to explain this definition.

First, he argues that, as problem, sense has nothing to do with an actual lived meaning that can be explained by analysis of simpler and better understood component parts. This is because the problematic meaning of the first proposition returns in the sense of the second explanatory one. Thus, if the proposition 'War is wrong' is taken to be problematic, then so will the sense of the propositions 'What we mean by "War"' and 'What we mean by "wrong"'. Deleuze does not expand on this remark much further but his point seems to be that, if the sense of the first proposition is resistant to simple definition, then that resistance will be transferred to any proposition that designates components of the first.

At this stage, Deleuze's argument seems to amount to the undefended statement that problematic senses are resistant to analysis or to the breaking down of difficult senses into better understood component parts. Given that there are senses that can be treated by analysis, we might ask Deleuze why all senses cannot be treated in this way. From his arguments on concepts from earlier in the book, we can surmise that Deleuze thinks that sense as problem is non-conceptual and cannot be broken down into predicates or other component parts.

However, Deleuze holds off his positive definition, preferring, instead, to see whether there are other ways of pinning down problematic senses. He suggests that, in order to avoid the regression of senses outlines above, we must avoid treating a problematic proposition in terms of a sense that can be broken up and designated by further propositions. Instead, we must look to what he calls the sense as complex theme. For example, the sense of 'War is wrong' becomes the complex theme 'The wrongness of war'. This theme is not verified by reference to actual wars or to what we mean by wrong and by war but to the idea 'The wrongness of war'. This raises new problems since, if we approach this theme as if it is a proposition or set of propositions susceptible to a logical treatment, then we encounter further paradoxes. For example, 'War is wrong' and its negation not-'War is wrong' have the same complex theme. Furthermore, nonsensical propositions have complex themes: 'The square is round' gives us the idea 'The roundness of the square'. These problems lead Deleuze to the conclusion that the complex theme is a ghost that cannot be captured by logic or according to what the theme designates:

Sense so defined is only a vapour which plays at the limit of things and words. Sense appears here as the outcome of the most powerful logical effort, but as the Ineffectual, a sterile incorporeal deprived of its generative powers.

(DR, pp. 156, 203)

These rather gross steps against analytic philosophy have some merit in raising some general criticisms levelled against the Fregean tradition. But the path is well-trodden and the criticisms have been made much better from within the tradition itself. Indeed, the fact that Deleuze is prepared to include such vague and to some extent ill-informed criticisms regarding the abstraction of analytic philosophy of language is troublesome. Maybe this move to rapid judgements is characteristic of Deleuze's philosophy insofar as his dialectic and synthetic method may encourage rapid moves to wider conditions where straightforward answers are actually available.

On this view, 'transcendental empiricism' would be an excuse to side-step the findings of empirical science. This bungling would destroy the method itself insofar as the given and its conditions would not exist – they would be the product of our over-eager imaginations. Deleuze would have led us to affirm a series of imaginary conditions, such as his syntheses of time, in order to undermine a more widely shared moral image of thought. This raises the possibility that 'Deleuzians' may turn out merely to be followers of a contrarian image, attracted by views that run counter to an orthodoxy and prone to adopting the latest scientific ideas that support these views with little regard to their validity or to whether they are well founded.

The answer to this accusation is that the association of the remarks on propositions and theories with particular scientific theories and philosophies is merely provocative – an aid to the study of the core concepts of his philosophy. These do not bear directly on particular philosophies and scientific theories. This is convincing in the context of his discussion of sense where, as will be shown below, the central concept has little to do with specific analytic philosophies but with an image of thought that serves as their background and that they serve to re-enforce. The work on propositions appertains to the postulates that make up an image of thought which must not to be confused with philosophy, including analytic philosophy of language.

However, a danger remains in the somewhat cavalier example set by Deleuze. His work cannot be implicated in works that take his incidental remarks on philosophy and science as gospel since other more mature responses are readily available in his philosophy and since it is not a valid accusation that a method is not easy to follow, if difficulty is necessary. But the question remains as to whether it is plausible to speak of an image of thought that is neither presented directly in a given philosophy or scientific theory, nor the object of empirical research. This is a serious weakness of his work on the postulates that define an image of thought since it is neither backed up by empirical work (in psychology, for example) designed to prove that such an image does operate, nor is it backed up by the close study of philosophical texts with evidence of a dependency on an image of thought.

QUESTIONS

The criticisms made above imply that Deleuze's work on the image of thought cannot be taken as a basis for a sustained critical engagement with analytic philosophy of language. However, his work in this area is worth pursuing for what it reveals about his own understanding of sense. Deleuze follows the preliminary remarks on propositions with a further possibility for the definition of sense. Perhaps sense should be expressed as a question ('Is war wrong?', for example).

There is little to be gained from this move, if the question is asked with a final answer in mind, since the answer would return us to a set of possible answers. These would have to be treated as affirmative propositions, thereby raising the question of their sense ('War is not wrong' or 'War is wrong') and contradicting Deleuze's claim that problematic sense is resistant to analysis. Yet, from his point of view, the form of the question does have advantages. Each possible answer is only a case of an answer – that is, it carries with it other possible answers and the question itself. Each answer bears testimony to the division of the question into possible answers. The answer's sense does not quite have the final sense that leads into the reductions of sense as problem to more simple senses.

This property of questions leads Deleuze into his definition of sense with respect to problems. Sense is a set of questions and problems and their set of responses and solutions:

Sense is located in the problem itself. Sense is constituted in the complex theme, but the complex theme is that set of problems and questions in relation to which the propositions serve as elements of response and cases of solution.

(DR, pp. 157, 204)

However, this definition is misleading unless we realise that the definition of a problem is, itself, altered by Deleuze. Problems are not cognitive or logical – that is, they cannot be solved or classified according to a logical treatment or according to what we know to be the case. That explains why he relates them to the complex theme, defined as a ghostly idea resistant to treatment as a thing that can be designated or as a set of propositions susceptible to logical analysis. Problems as complex themes resist a seventh postulate of the image of thought whereby truth and falsity are said to apply to solutions of problems rather than to problems themselves.

In other words, it is a mistake to think that solutions are simply true or false solutions to a problem. Instead, a solution makes some aspects of a problem more clear and others more obscure. For example, when we answer yes or no to the question 'Can there be a just war?', we are not giving final correct answers to the question. Rather, our reasons for deciding on a positive or negative answer shed a different light on the problem of war. Deleuze has different ways of arguing for and against different answers and does not fall into a straightforward relativism. He does not allow for final answers to the problem.

Against this postulate, Deleuze holds that, as opposed to solutions, problems must be thought of as true or false. Put simply, a false problem is either overdetermined – that is, it allows its solutions to be judged in terms of truth and falsity (*Is the cat on the mat?*) – or it is underdetermined – that is, it does not lead to a complex set of responses or solutions at all (*Do mice on Mars eat green cheese?*). In defence of his superficial and rather cavalier response to analytic philosophy criticised above, Deleuze's disdain for that tradition comes out of what he sees, with some justification, as its dependence on false problems for the development of its theories. It is not so much that we should care little about cats, mats and green cheese but, rather, that questions about them are a poor ground on which to build a philosophy that will have to deal with true problems (*In what way are animals part of life?*).

Problems cannot be answered satisfactorily or solved by propositions (*Let's not talk about war but about conflict . . . War is wrong when its goals are unjust.*). Instead, a problem is an attribute of the genesis of the act of thought and the use of faculties. In other words, when thinking emerges and changes, it is necessarily accompanied by problems. When faculties, such as sensation and understanding emerge and create themselves, they do so with problems that they cannot rid themselves of but only live with well or poorly. But what does it mean to live with a problem well if it cannot be solved? After all, faculties and disciplines are formed to resolve problems or, at least, to determine our limitations with respect to them. How could we live with a problem without either believing in the possibility of its solution or seeking to define it as redundant. It is not enough to define problems as ghostly complex themes, sets of Ideas, if we are not given a much clearer definition of Ideas. What is an Idea, if not a proposition or a representation?

DIALECTICS, PROBLEMS AND IDEAS

Deleuze's answers to the above question turn on his method defined as a dialectics and on the definition of problems in terms of Ideas. In the chapter on the image of thought, these terms are not defined in full. Yet it is possible to advance a critical understanding of his position and of how it resists the postulates that make up the image of thought. A true problem brings together the four opposed strands of Deleuze's dialectics and, thereby, it follows the principles of connecting and forgetting. A problem connects things to their conditions, both actual and virtual. It does so with as great an extension as possible. It generates critical positions with respect to positions that restrict that extension or hide those conditions. It creates new concepts that allow for the conditions to be expressed with as great an intensity as possible. *What does war presuppose? What is wrong with past definitions of war? Is the problem of war a limited or a highly connected concept? How can we allow new concepts to emerge beyond the boundaries of current limitations? How can we express what is presupposed by war better, avoiding illusions in the current concept? Maybe we should think with two concepts: nomadic war machine and machine of state? Maybe these too need to be allowed to fade, for others to take their place?*

But this means that a problem is in danger of being defined as an overly complex thing. How can one problem stand for so many disparate methods and things (actual and virtual, images and representations, concepts and signs)? The answer is that the problem does not name those things or the structure that brings them together. There is no identity that it could name since the dialectical method is internal to a changing set of contradictions and movements. Rather, the problem, set out as a question, expresses those contradictions and that movement. A true problem is those contradictions and movements and the way they allow for as great a possible extension to the dialectic:

What is missed [by the definition of problems in terms of a field of possible solutions] is the internal character of the problem as such, the imperative internal element which decides in the first place its truth or falsity and measures its intrinsic power: that is, the very object of the dialectic or combinatory, the 'differential'. Problems are tests and selections. What is essential is that there occurs at the heart of problems a genesis of truth, a production of the true in thought.

(DR, pp. 162, 210)

This crucial definition of problems has many important ramifications and perhaps weaknesses. I want to draw attention to the following ones:

1. How does this definition show that it is a mistake to think of problems in terms of a field of possible solutions?
2. The definition leads to a revolutionary Deleuzian definition of truth (necessary, given his resistance to thinking about truth in terms of designation or internal logical coherence). Can this definition of truth operate outside Deleuze's idiosyncratic language and structures? Or is his use of the word 'true' at best contingent or at worst disingenuous (*Your use of the word true plays dishonestly on its earlier force.*)?

132

3. With the use of the term 'intrinsic power', Deleuze brings value into problems. I have deliberately rendered this sense of value in terms of extension due to the twin demands for a connection with and forgetting of everything. But how are we to determine the locality where this value operates, given Deleuze's resistance to the concept of possibility? Can the boundaries of a problem or dialectic be determined without referring to the possible? If they cannot, does it make sense to speak of them at all since how do we ever sense the power of a problem?
4. What is the practical difference between thinking in terms of an image of thought that privileges questions and fields of possible and answers, and a Deleuzian dialectic that must remain intrinsically problematic? Are there good practical reasons for avoiding problems that do not allow for solutions?

A proposition or set of propositions cannot solve a problem as defined by Deleuze because problems allow for many different responses, each of which solves the problem on its own terms but only in a limited way with respect to the problem as a whole (*How to paint? Cubism. Abstract expressionism. Return to classicism. Don't paint – dream ...*). The important point here is that the problem resists any final classification of its responses whereby a direction of correct response or a hierarchy of responses could be determined with respect to a final correct answer or direction of response. This explains why Deleuze stresses the continuity and universality of the problem against the particularity and discontinuity of the responses. Each solution is correct on its own particular terms but not on those of others. With respect to problems, with respect to truth as defined by Deleuze, any given set of propositions is only particular. Universality can only be attained in the fluidity of the problem – it is universal because it allows for a multiplicity of responses.

But this answer merely shifts the difficulty to the question of whether it makes sense to speak of problems according to Deleuze's definition. This comes out very strongly in his association of truth and problems. There are true and false problems in line with their power or extension. These properties are two-sided – a problem is extended through the number of propositions that can stand as particular answers or responses and through the number of other problems it is related to. This is important since it also allows for a sense of the relation of particular responses to the problem as a whole as truth:

It is never enough to solve a problem with the aid of a series of simple cases playing the role of analytic elements: the conditions under which the problem acquires a maximum of comprehension and extension must be determined, conditions capable of communicating to a given case of solution the ideal continuity appropriate to it.

(DR, pp. 162, 211)

But, if it is possible to relate the particular to the universal in the problem, why is there no way of judging between particular responses, thereby giving a direction to the solution of the problem as a whole? If some solutions betray the problem and others are faithful to it, then there is a transfer from the problem as truth to solutions as truthful. This would return Deleuze to the kind of Platonism he criticised in the chapter on difference for itself. There would be true and false pretenders to the claim to have participated well in a given problem. The division into true and false pretenders would depend on an ideal or model for the perfect answer.

Deleuze's answer to this point is that the problem is changed by each particular solution (*Cubism is not better than Impressionism. They are transforming responses to different versions of the problem of how to paint.*). So the structure that Deleuze is proposing is, once again, one of different but related fields that have different internal and external relations. Ideas or problems are related to each other and change according to the actual solutions that are put forward for them but the way solutions relate to one another is different to the way solutions relate to problems and to the way problems relate to problems:

The problem is at once transcendent and immanent in relation to its solutions. Transcendent, because it consists in a system of ideal liaisons or differential relations between generic elements. Immanent, because these liaisons or relations are incarnated in the actual relations which do not resemble them and are defined by the field of solutions.

(DR, pp. 163, 212)

The arguments for this special structure of relations have been developed through *Difference and Repetition*, in particular in terms of the deduction of pure differences as the condition for the genesis of actual things in repetition. More generally, the structure and the way it calls for Deleuzian dialectics are defended by the arguments for the three syntheses of time in their relation to the four different aspects of the dialectics, as discussed in my Chapter 4.

However, there is still no answer to the third question put above. Although Deleuze has given arguments for the general structure, he has not given satisfactory definitions of Ideas and of actual things in relation to Ideas. We know the form of an abstract structure and we know the names of the things it contains. But we do not know what those things are in relation to everyday actual things and to our ideas of possible pure differences. If this situation is not answered, then it is catastrophic for Deleuze's philosophy since its practical dimension, both as method and in terms of guiding principles, depends on a sense of where it has to operate, the 'given' whose conditions we search for and work with and on a sense of what is possible on the grounds of that given (to what extent and how we can connect and forget on the basis of that given). For that matter, deep into a book that makes much of signs and of a sensibility to them, we still do not know what signs and sensibility are for Deleuze. A great weight of expectation and perhaps impatience builds up through *Difference and Repetition* when it is read with an eye both for validity and for practice.

LEARNING

The last section of the image of thought chapter gives some indications of the practical dimensions of Deleuze's privileging of problems over fields of possible solutions. He applies his conclusions to education and draws a distinction between a form of education faithful to the insoluble nature of problems and a final, eighth, postulate of the image of thought. Put simply, his view is that learning does not have knowledge or even fixed capabilities as its final goals. Instead, learning is an essential aspect of problems – that is, problems can only be learnt and only learning allows us to follow on from problems. This following – on is the creation of concepts that respond to the problem in ways that do not fall back into the illusion of having solved it. *Learn to learn – do not learn to know.*

Deleuze is careful to distinguish knowledge as the learning of something, of a skill or facts, say, and learning as a process of apprenticeship with no fixed objective content. This absence of content is conveyed in the sense of the term 'apprenticeship to signs' or to problems and Ideas. To learn is to learn how to be sensitive to and respond creatively to signs and problems, as things that necessarily go beyond what is known or what can be done in a given situation. This sensitivity and creativity are linked – no sensitivity without creation (*You can only sense signs by doing and by doing something different*). Thus, Deleuze insists that learning is necessarily experimental. This necessity is not in the sense of a necessary experimental aspect to the process of learning facts or skill (*You've got to find new ways of keeping them interested or they'll never take the time to learn*). It is in the sense that learning is above all experimentation free of goals in knowledge or skills.

This view of education puts it right at the heart of philosophy and truth. There is no truth without an experimental learning. This does not mean that learning becomes something rare and esoteric. On the contrary, Deleuze has a fondness for the example of learning to swim as an example of the apprenticeship to signs. But do we not learn facts and skills when we learn to swim (*the increased power of relaxed ankles; how to do the butterfly*)? Yes we do. Once again, there has to be an actual identifiable side to our relation to problems, Ideas and pure differences. However, this side does not take priority over the way learning to swim (to sew, to talk, to resolve equations) involves learning how to do something new for us. According to Deleuze, that something new cannot simply be facts or skills since they are the result of going from one state to another, rather than the explanation of how we go from state to new state. Instead, learning as something independent of these results is to be in touch with what allows for the new: Ideas as multiplicities of pure differences; problems as the locus of the creation of truth.

So to learn is to go beyond the faculties that we have by taking them beyond their limits. Learning is, therefore, the form of the transcendent exercise of a faculty, as discussed earlier in this chapter. More importantly, learning cannot be associated with any single faculty or the overarching faculty of recognition because recognition cannot explain the way in which learning involves a move to something new and a going beyond the limits of any given faculty: 'We never know in advance how someone will learn: by means of what loves someone becomes good at Latin, what encounters make them a philosopher, or in what dictionaries they learn to think.' (DR, pp. 165, 215) Two important remarks, consistent with earlier remarks on Kant and faculties, follow from this claim. First, Deleuze cannot hold that faculties are in principle shared and shared within fixed boundaries. Faculties vary with actual individuals and cannot be judged with respect to transcendental faculties of, say, understanding and imagination. Second, how actual individuals and individual situations overcome the limits of faculties is not uniform. With respect to learning we are all different and all learn differently.

Deleuze takes these points and expands them with respect to method and learning:

> There is no more a method for learning than there is a method for finding treasures, but a violent training, a culture or *paideïa* which affects the entire individual... Method is the means of that knowledge which regulates the collaboration of all the faculties. It is therefore the manifestation of a common sense or the realisation of a Cogitatio natura, and presupposes a good will as though this were a 'premeditated decision' of the thinker.
>
> (DR, pp. 165, 215)

His point is that this view limits learning and misunderstands how it takes place. We do not learn consciously since learning must go beyond our conscious faculties (*If I knew how to swim, I'd do it!*). Instead, we have to experiment in ways that connect to the unconscious processes that relate us to water or any other thing we must enter into a new relation to. Every time we think of learning in terms of the final goal of knowledge, we think according to an eighth postulate of the image of thought – thinking knowledge as its end.

6

What is an Idea?

Chapter 4 of *Difference and Repetition* answers the key question left hanging from the chapter on the image of thought: 'What is an Idea?' The answer to this question is all-important because, should Deleuze fail to give a satisfactory definition of the Idea and should that definition fail to be accompanied by a satisfactory deduction of the necessary role of Ideas in actual things, then his account of the importance of difference in itself and repetition for itself will turn out to have been pointless invention. Two questions hang over the first three chapters of his book: What virtual things are specific actual things related to in terms of repetition and difference in itself? How should we act, given this relation?

From the point of view of these questions, up to the end of chapter 3 of his book, Deleuze's work on difference and on repetition has taken a general and abstract form. Without doubt he has developed specific contexts, examples and arguments in that work. He has described how difference and repetition underlie actual things in many different ways. He has also described how they explain genesis and indicate value as intensity. This description allows him to draw a distinction between two forms of thought: the image of thought and thinking as the expression of pure difference. But, through these descriptions and deductions of the necessary role of difference and repetition, he has not given a satisfactory account of how difference and repetition can be treated as well determined and determined with respect to a given situation. It is as if we know that pure differences are real but, also, that they are indistinguishable from an indeterminate chaos of pure differences. It is as if, whenever we have to deal with a given, we must do so with the chaos of all pure differences and all of the ways they have become repeated or expressed in the situation (*Can there be a right way of creating out of a chaos in a way that does not foster the illusion that there is no chaos?*).

So the demand for precise answers comes out of the apparent incoherence of a philosophy that sets the determinacy of a given actual situation against a limitless and indeterminate ground that the situation presupposes in terms of genesis and future direction. Deleuze appears to have given us a useless method and set of principles. His dialectics merely allow for ever more precise arguments for the indeterminate ground (*Look, it is presupposed here and here – like this and like that.*). His dual principles of connecting with everything and forgetting everything fix us in a three-fold paradox. What could it mean to connect to everything (*If I am everything, how am I myself?*)? What could it mean to forget everything (*If I forget everything, how can I be something?*)? How could one do both at the same time (*How can I be both everything and nothing?*)?

In response to these difficulties, the chapter on the ideal synthesis of difference gives an account of how difference is determinable and how it must be thought of as determined, as well as indeterminate. In so doing, it explains how the paradox of the dual principles operates in a precise manner in any given situation. That is, any individual is a temporary answer to the paradox – indicating that it must be responded to but that it reappears in that response. This reappearance is not cause for despair – the response is not a choice because the point from which a further move must be made is part of the problem. It is not as if we stand independent of problems or that they are imposed on us from the outside. Deleuze's commitment to immanence with respect to problems or Ideas (*You, the situation, are the product of the paradox, as is the next move.*) militates against extreme feelings of guilt (*There was no ultimate solution.*) or resentment (*The problem came from within.*). Furthermore, it not as if we can grasp the problem as a whole in consciousness (*The future is open in ways you do not have access to.*). This is because he defines problem and Ideas as structures that always go beyond any given faculty.

So the chapter is called 'The ideal synthesis of difference' to point to the way in which Ideas must give determinacy to the chaos of pure differences but without rendering it finally determined in any way. Chapter 5 then points to the way in which this determinacy is completed by a relation to actual things through sensibility and through individuals that are both actual and virtual. The argument of chapter 4 remains incomplete until we reach the fifth chapter of *Difference and Repetition,* on the asymmetrical synthesis of the sensible, since it is only there that the role of a synthesis in individuals through a synthesis of virtual intensities is added to the ideal synthesis.

The important function of Ideas in the fourth chapter is lost somewhat in the Patton translation of the chapter title. The title is not given literally as 'The ideal synthesis of difference' but as 'Ideas and the synthesis of difference'. No account is given of the reasons for this departure. Perhaps it is to avoid crude misunderstandings, such as 'this chapter is on the best or the most perfect synthesis of difference'. The departure from the literal misses a second sense at play in Deleuze's title – that is, that his dialectical method depends on the generation of Ideas for its synthesis. So there is some sense in the altered chapter title but this panders to a fear of shallow interpretations at the expense of the more precise original sense – Ideas are a necessary synthesis of difference.

So far, the study of the validity of Deleuze's arguments has raised a series of critical points that make his work on ideal synthesis very delicate. Foremost is the objection that his deductions begin at hypothetical points or that he takes a contingent given as the starting point for his deductions. In view of this objection, he must deduce the determinacy of Ideas without depending on the determinacy of the given they are the condition for. There is no certainty in any actual thing that could allow us to determine Ideas or the form of Ideas directly. Instead, Ideas have been introduced through their relation to problems rather than to certainty. In terms of Deleuze's dialectics, Ideas are the condition for the problematic nature of actual things (*There is no certainty. Why is that?*). In turn, Deleuze will define Ideas as problems and insuperably problematical, in the sense that they do not allow for solutions once and for all but for partial solutions that pose the problem in a novel way. Again, this shows the impossibility of relying on the given for work on Ideas since any given will only be a partial solution to an ideal problem.

However, if we attempt to approach the determinacy of Ideas from the other direction – from pure difference or difference in itself – the difficulty seems even greater since Deleuze's work has defined pure difference as determined by actual repetitions but, by the end of chapter 3, he has failed to explain how in any satisfactory way. Any such explanation will have to counter the objection that it is impossible to approach something indeterminable – difference in itself – through something determined (*When an infinity is truly infinite, then it cannot be understood from a finite point of view.* or *God's infinity cannot be fully grasped by humans.*).

In the first section of the chapter on the ideal synthesis of difference, Deleuze introduces these difficulties in a Kantian context. He seeks to explain how an Idea can be, at the same time, undetermined, determinable and determined according to an ideal of infinite determination. For example, the idea of the perfect surgical intervention is undetermined in terms of the understanding since it can have no corresponding experience (*How many stitches? What convalescence is appropriate? What should the survival rate be?*). Its real object is not something we can experience. It is a problem – that is, something that can be expressed by an unstable set of contradictory questions and answers. The perfect intervention responds to the tension between damage and cure, between a high degree of toxicity in post-operatic drugs and a rapid return to a 'normal' life, for instance (*There's always going to be some degree of cellular damage and yet cellular damage is undesirable.*).

As an abstract that takes experience and knowledge beyond its bounds, the idea is undetermined. But it is determinable in terms of experiments that attempt to express the idea and temporarily resolve the problem in an actual operation (*With keyhole surgery, the risks of a long convalescence are diminished.*). What is more, the idea can be thought of in terms of determination through the ideal of an infinite determination, for example, in the development of our concept of the perfect intervention through an infinite set of experiments (*new sutures and the latest drugs and keyhole surgery and genetic screening and post-operative counselling and the addition of whatever the latest research shows up as a benefit...*) In this use of maximisation and perfectibility, the closeness of Deleuze's Ideas to Kantian Ideas of reason comes out very strongly, belying crude definitions of the French philosopher as 'anti-Kantian'.

So the challenge for Deleuze is to define his Ideas in such a way as to maintain a similar structure to the Kantian Idea: 'There is neither identification nor confusion within the Idea, but rather an internal problematic objective unity of the undetermined, the determinable and determination.' (DR, pp. 170, 220) By objective unity, Deleuze means that the object of the undetermined Idea (the problem), the objects through which it is determinable (actual objects) and the ideal of infinite determination (representation in a concept) complete one another, in the sense of responding to what the others must presuppose.

This unity is itself problematic insofar as the ideal problem is never finally resolvable in any actual object. The problem is determinable but never finally determined. It is also problematic insofar as the ideal of infinite determination cannot coincide with any actual object and, as such, leaves the problem indeterminate. The ideal of the perfect surgical intervention only gives a direction to the actual search for the perfect operation, through the concept of what constitutes a better procedure. It cannot provide us with a model for that procedure (*In theory, we can have an abstract concept of how interventions will keep on getting better but that concept does not tell us how to make them better in every case here and now and into the future.*). Any actual operation will always be an unsatisfactory solution to the problems contained in the idea of the perfect intervention (*excellent post-operative and 5-year survival rates but a worrying dip at ten years. The route we have always taken to perfect our techniques has finally led us to an impasse*).

However, Deleuze remains critical of the Kantian Idea for not going far enough in viewing the indeterminate-determinable-determination structure as a problematic unity. This is because Kant's account, at least in the way Deleuze has characterised it, associates the indeterminate with the Idea alone, completing it with well-determined entities external to the Idea – objects of experience and concepts of the understanding. So the problem lies wholly with the Idea – objects of experience and concepts can be detached from its problems and, indeed, can serve to determine the problem. Concepts remain unproblematic so long as they are not thought of in relation to the Idea (*We can know this surgical intervention perfectly well. We can also have a secure concept of the perfect intervention – total survival and return to 'normality'.*).

For instance, Deleuze claims that, for Kant, only the self is problematic and undetermined in its free openness to an infinite set of possibilities (*What will I choose to be?*). Whereas the world is determinable as an object of experience (*What is it now?*) and God is unproblematically the ideal of determination (*God is perfection.*). But Deleuze holds that we cannot separate the determinable and the ideal of determination from the indeterminate (*You cannot understand a given operative procedure in full without taking account of its relation to the problem that defines procedures – survival in as many cases as possible, with the least damage, for as many years as possible – and the same is true of the concept of the perfect procedure.*). Thus, for him, since the self is problematic, so is the world and so is God.

It is a mistake, therefore, to view the object of experience and the ideal of determination as external to the Idea. Instead, they form an indivisible whole with respect to problems. It is in this context that Deleuze returns to his critique of Kant and Aristotle from earlier in the book. What both thinkers miss is the way in which the object and the ideal are generated by the Idea and by the indeterminate:

It is here, perhaps, that we should seek the real reason for which, just as the post-Kantians objected, Kant held fast to the point of view of conditioning without attaining that of genesis. If the mistake of dogmatism is always to fill that which separates, that of empiricism is to leave external what is separated, and in this sense there is still too much empiricism in the Critique (and too much dogmatism among the post-Kantians).

(DR, pp. 170, 221)

For Deleuze, there is no object of experience, as an evolving thing, independent of Ideas. Furthermore, an ideal of determination is internal to Ideas as problems. The task of chapter 4 of *Difference and Repetition* is, then, to define the Idea as problem and as that which conditions and gives rise to actual objects of experience and to the ideal of determination.

IDEAS AS MULTIPLICITIES

Prior to giving his definition of Ideas, Deleuze sets out a lengthy discussion of differential equations and the role of the notion of the infinitely small, represented by the symbol dx in mathematics. This discussion does not imply that his theory depends on mathematics for its validity. Rather, Deleuze uses mathematics as an example that introduces two key elements of his approach to Ideas: an Idea can only ever be approximated through constructs that reveal aspects of its internal relations; the method of approximation is dialectical and must be thought of in terms of the indeterminate-determinable-determination structure outlined above. Broadly, Deleuze is interested in the property of equations as determinable through differential equations that reveal significant points of the first equation. Moreover, the equation and its differentials are in a relation of reciprocal determination – that is, in different ways, the equation determines the differential and the differential determines the equation. Finally, a principle of complete determination can be found in the determination of an equation through successive differentiations and integrations, as well as through the drawing up of groups of equations that allow for a 'more precise distinction of the roots of an equation', in Galois theory, for example. (DR, pp. 180, 234)

It is worth noting how this interest in mathematics reflects the important distinction drawn in Deleuze's work between facts and significance. I have discussed this distinction in the opening chapter above and it will return with greater force in Chapter 7. In the case of equations, it leads to an emphasis on the significant points of an equation, for example, where a change in curvature occurs, as opposed to a concern with solutions to the equation – that is, the different values taken by y for given values of x. It may be very straightforward to calculate the values of y for a given x but very difficult to approximate significant points or even to discover what significance is for a given equation in relation to other mathematical problems or to problems in science and engineering that require mathematical modelling.

This does not mean that all Ideas and problems must be thought of as mathematical. Rather, mathematics provides us with an exemplary model for Ideas in terms of reciprocal determination, the determination of significant points and a principle of complete determination. Like equations and their differentials, Ideas and problems, as expressed in actual things, reveal one another's significant points. They determine one another reciprocally. They must be thought of in terms of a principle of complete determination – that is, through ever more extensive relations of reciprocal determination and more complete calculation of significant points.

Ideas always have an element of quantitability, qualitability and potentiality; there are always processes of determinability, of reciprocal determination and complete determination; always distributions of distinctive and ordinary points; always adjunct fields which form the synthetic progression of a sufficient reason.

(DR, pp. 181, 235)

So it is misleading to read the example of mathematics as implying that Deleuze thinks that all problems allow for solutions according to mathematical calculations, as if a problem were resolved through the solutions to the equation that corresponded to it. Instead, each problem must be viewed like an equation that cannot be exhausted in terms of what can be known of its significant points. The problem is an endless challenge to view it in new ways to reveal different significant points and to view significant points in different ways:

> If Ideas are the differentials of thought, there is a differential calculus corresponding to each Idea, an alphabet of what it means to think. Differential calculus is not the unimaginative calculus of the utilitarian, the crude arithmetic calculus which subordinates thought to other things or to other ends, but the algebra of pure thought, the superior irony of problems themselves – the only calculus 'beyond good and evil'.
>
> (DR, pp. 182, 235)

However, if this calculation is not mathematical, what is it? Why are Ideas irresolvable? What is the sense of an 'algebra' defined in terms of irony? How can mathematical theory be used to define the progression of a sufficient reason? In the example on mathematics, Deleuze closes off the possibility of mathematical calculations but is it at the price of revealing a lack of precision in the use of mathematical terms?

These questions are answered through a definition of Ideas as multiplicities allied to the statement that everything is a multiplicity. But what is a multiplicity? Against his demand to define difference through affirmation rather than negation, Deleuze gives prominence to a negative definition. A multiplicity cannot be thought through the opposition of the one and the multiple – that is, a multiplicity is not an identifiable unity, nor is it a number of such unities, even infinite (*Twelve is not a multiplicity, nor is a structure of twelve electrical components, nor an infinity of identities such as the series of natural numbers.*). Instead, positively, a multiplicity is a variety, that is, something that captures a variation rather than a fixed number or structure (*the continuous infinity of shades of red between this dark red and that light red* or *the continuous degree of nausea in relation to a continuous variation of wave amplitude between X and Y*).

This positive definition certainly takes inspiration from mathematics, though Deleuze is rather cryptic as to exactly how. For him, a multiplicity is like a continuous function, that is, a function that contains no 'breaks, or jumps or wild oscillations' (Spivak, *Calculus*, p. 93). For example, the function 'all colours of red are either light or dark' has such a break at the point where we jump from light to dark colours of red. The same could be said for the function 'all colours red can be assigned to one of these ten degrees of red'. But this would not be the case for the function describing the continuous variation of red from light to dark according to the equation $y = \frac{1}{x}$, over the interval $\frac{1}{2}$ to 2 of values of x, where y stands for dark and x for light and where y and x are real numbers. The absence of breaks is significant because it allows Deleuze to think of ideas as multiplicities of continuous variations that are not fully captured if they are thought of in terms of significant breaks or approximated to fixed, identifiable values. Even if I identify an interval of the continuous function of reds as Red 0–1, I have not given a sufficient definition for Deleuze since that interval will imply limits at Red 0 and Red 1. However small an interval I choose, it must always be possible to segment it into smaller intervals and to include it into larger ones. The variation of reds cannot be identified by defining it in terms of well-defined sub-sets of something non-red.

Deleuze defines an Idea as an 'n-dimensional well-defined and continuous multiplicity' where the dimension is the number of variations and where the variations are continuous, that is, involve no discrete steps. However, the crucial move lies in Deleuze's move away from a mathematical definition of continuity to three properly philosophical, that is, metaphysical, conditions for the definition of a continuous multiplicity:

1. It must not be possible to fix the sensible form, the conceptual signification or the function of the elements of the multiplicity. In other words, the multiplicity is not one of identifiable forms, concepts or functions.
2. However, the elements must be determined but only through their reciprocal relations. In other words, you cannot identify A or B in a multiplicity except through the way in which a variation in A can be related to a variation in B.
3. A particular multiplicity or set of such reciprocal relations must become actual in diverse spatio-temporal relations. The elements of that multiplicity must be actually incarnated in varying terms and forms.

The multiplicity is, therefore, a structure of elements defined as: things in continuous variation resistant to identification; relations between those elements; relations between those relations and actual relations; and relations between the elements and actual forms and terms. This definition is critical for Deleuze's work since the definition of Ideas is a stage of the trail of arguments and definitions that leads back to the definition of pure differences and forward to his definitions of the virtual and the actual in terms of intensities. The elements of Ideas are pure differences. The virtual is the totality of Ideas and intensities. Actual things incarnate and presuppose Ideas and, therefore, pure differences but they do so through the mediation of intensities (exactly how this mediation operates is explained in Chapter 7, below, on the concept of the individual). So, given the definition of Ideas, what are pure differences?

Pure differences are continuous variations that cannot be fixed in terms of forms, concepts or functions. As such, pure differences cannot be named accurately, in the sense of identified with a concept, or shown, in the sense of identified with an ostensible thing, or demonstrated, in the sense of identified with an actual process. Becoming this red, becoming closer to this red, being turned from red to orange through the addition of yellow are not pure differences. So what can we say positively about pure differences?

Though identifying a pure difference will always be to miss something, we can identify them through their relation to one another as expressed in actual things. In other words, when actual things vary in an identifiable and significant way, where identifiable means that we can identify a change and where significant means that the change involves a correlation of at least two differences, we can deduce, at least, that two pure differences are related to form an Idea. We can also name those differences, though with the caveat that this naming must not be confused with a satisfactory identification of the pure difference. For instance, the relation of the intensities of love and hate changes according to which envelops the other (and, therefore, changes the relations of envelopment of all others). This change accompanies an actual expression of love and hate in a sensation that accompanies an actual identifiable situation. This is itself an expression of a variation of the relation of the Ideas of becoming love and becoming hate in terms of clarity and obscurity (and all other becomings). *He loves another (sensation). Love is expressed differently through me now – its intensity is dominated by that of hate (intensity). I cannot bear the idea of love anymore and prefer the invulnerability of hate but there can be no love without hate and no hate without love (Idea-problem).*

It is very important not to confuse this line of thought with a scientific empirical series of observations. Rather, Deleuze is implying that, when we experiment creatively, that is, when we sense signs by trying to innovate with them, we incarnate relations of pure differences. For example, when an artist associates a colour with a sensation in a style of painting or when a writer associates a style with an emotion, they are expressing the relation of the colour and sensation as pure differences (the Idea red-anger

147

presupposes an intensity of becoming red and an intensity be-coming angry enveloping one another in a different way, that is, covering and revealing one another in a different way). Unlike an hypothesis based on a series of observations, the inference from the actual to virtual relations and to pure differences is not a mat-ter of identifying universal laws or lasting properties of any kind. Rather, it is a matter of triggering the variations that are presup-posed in the creation with an actual local sensation, not in order to be able to make future predictions but in order to be able to criticise the denial of those relations and variations at that locality and in order to experiment with the way in which those relations can be expressed anew.

Ideas defined as multiplicities are critical and creative tools that are, themselves, expressed through critical and creative work allied to the reflection on the necessary conditions for actual signs. Ideas are not discovered through empirical sciences and their significance does not lie in scientific causal laws. Instead, they serve Deleuze's two principles of forgetting and connecting. The creative expression of Ideas is aided by the critical work on how Ideas have been expressed and how they have been hidden, in the sense where we have to try to forget those things that hide Ideas and try to connect to those Ideas that have been expressed. But that creative expression must go beyond these critical moves to an experimentation beyond the limits that have been discovered through critique. These principles and the Deleuzian dialectics related to them do not stand in opposition to science or to the arts, in the sense where Deleuze would be proposing a new science or art of Ideas. Rather, they may guide how we view the significance of scientific discoveries and innovations in the arts, in relation to Ideas defined as structures of pure differences.

The definition of Ideas as multiplicities and, hence, as struc-tures involving pure differences, relations of pure differences and the actualisation of the differences and relations in actual things explains the important references to structure from earlier in *Difference and Repetition*. In particular, the structure that emerges from Deleuze's study of the three passive syntheses of time in his chapter on repetition must be understood as such an Ideal structure. In the study of that work, in my Chapter 4, we found that Deleuze failed to give a full account of how such a structure fits together and what its components are. The definition of the multiplicity answers some of these questions but invites other crit-ical points:

148

1. The reference to three 'conditions' in the definition of Ideas
   as multiplicities is not in the sense of a transcendental condition but, rather, in the sense of tests for the proper definition
   of a thing (*If it quacks like a duck . . .*). Only in very unusual circumstances do these kinds of conditions lead us to conclude,
   albeit controversially, that the defined thing must exist (*I have
   an idea of a perfect God. A perfect being must not lack anything. So God
   cannot lack existence. Therefore, God exists.*). Deleuze still needs to
   prove that multiplicities exist and that, indeed, all things are
   multiplicities or are part of multiplicities.
2. Up to this stage of the book, Deleuze has spoken of actual things
   with very little precision. Now he has introduced a series of
   new expressions that themselves require clear definition. What
   spatio-temporal relations is he referring to? What does actual
   mean? What does he mean by term and form?

Prior to answering these questions, though, it is important to
note what he thinks is important for the study of structure in
his definition of multiplicities. It is that the definition allows us
to think of structures in terms of genesis and evolution because
the variations in a multiplicity must be thought of in relation to
the actual situations they are related to and transform. This is in
opposition to a synchronic view of structure, where it is defined as a
snapshot of relations at a particular time. Structure as multiplicity
is in movement and does not give priority to fixed structures when
thinking of evolution through time (*What happened between this
snapshot and this one?*).

In fact, Deleuze's structures have to be thought of as outside
historical linear time. This is because actual spatio-temporal things
are only actualisations of variations that persist and of the changing relations between them. The variations must be thought of as
outside the unfolding of spatio-temporal time – their persistence
is ahistorical. The relations change in a non-linear manner, de-
feating any attempt to think of them according to linear historical
time. Again, this refers back to Deleuze's work on the third passive
synthesis of time in his chapter on repetition and forward to his
work on the impossibility of reducing intensities to a measuring
system. Evolution, thought of in historical terms, must be referred
to genesis with respect to Ideas and intensities that cannot be
thought of in this way: 'This is genesis without dynamism, evolving necessarily in the element of a supra-historicity, a *static genesis* which may be understood as the correlate of the notion of a

149

passive synthesis, and which in turn illuminates that notion.' (DR, pp. 183, 239) Passive synthesis occurs when variations, or pure differences, and their relations become actualised in actual relations and incarnated in actual 'terms'.

THE NECESSITY OF IDEAS

After the definition of Ideas, Deleuze goes on to provide much of the detail lacking in his descriptions of difference in itself, Ideas and structures. I will outline key definitions, the critical questions they answer and how they contribute to the overall thesis regarding the foundation of actual things in difference in itself and repetition for itself. These definitions serve in nearly all of the work contemporaneous and subsequent to *Difference and Repetition.* Once again, this supports the view that the book is the keystone to his work.

In order to clarify the relation between Ideas and actual disciplines, Deleuze defines varieties of Ideas. He claims that Ideas can be distinguished according to their 'ordinal', 'characteristic' and 'axiomatic' variety. The forms of distinction are in no way determinant or essential – they have to be thought of as a way of relating everyday classifications to Deleuze's inseparable relations of Ideas. The ordinal variety differentiates Ideas according to their elements and the relations that hold between them. In other words, Ideas can be grouped and related according to the elements that they share and according to the relations that hold between those elements. These orders can be interpreted as corresponding to what is more commonly known as actual subject areas – for example, differences between sciences and between arts are reflected in the different orders of Ideas they come to express. This does not mean that elements only belong to one order. Rather, it means that elements enter into relations of greater and lesser clarity and obscurity that allow for an order to be defined (*Physics and chemistry imply different relations between expansion and division as pure variations.*).

The characteristic variety is not concerned with actual ways of thinking about elements or relations but with the way they include one another. Ideas can be distinguished according to the relations of envelopment within an order – that is, according to the relation of intensities in similar relations of Ideas (*The relations between moving, changing and building are given different stresses or relation of which intensity takes precedence over another in the nomadic*

Idea and the city-dweller Idea.). Whereas an axiomatic variety is a way of relating and distinguishing Ideas of different orders through a third that combines both of them. Thus, two Ideas may be of different orders, they may be expressed in very different subject areas (poetry and building, say), but it could be possible to relate them through a third that brings their elements together in a new structure (architecture and the concept of harmony, for example).

This definition of varieties is designed to respond to two related problems that have grown through *Difference and Repetition*: If things cannot be treated as belonging to essential categories, how can they be distinguished at all? If things can be distinguished, why can't this be the basis for the definition of fixed categories? Thus, Deleuze insists that all Ideas 'coexist' but that this coexistence is a differentiated one. He uses differentiated in a highly specialised manner. It does not mean different, in the sense of opposed in some way, but involving different degrees with respect to pure differences or variations. This explains why the varieties outlined above involve the elements of Ideas and their relations. However, this solution can only be seen as a moment in Deleuze's argument, designed to connect his work to more familiar forms of classification. Later in the book, he will make clear that such classifications are merely illusory when viewed from the point of view of individuals that cross such classifications and deny their priority.

The main metaphor here, perhaps the only important metaphor in *Difference and Repetition,* is that of clarity and obscurity or light and shadow. It is used to convey differences in degree in a whole that cannot be separated into distinct zones. Ideas are differentiated because they are differently lit versions of the whole of Ideas. Deleuze calls this interrelation of Ideas their perplication, which will, itself, be explained in terms of the way in which intensities envelop one another. Later in the book and in his work on Leibniz and the baroque, he will insist on the way in which this perplication reflects the different ways in which ideas are folded and unfolded into one another. This sense of folding avoids possible misinterpretations of the light and shadow metaphor. That which is left obscure in an Idea is neither unimportant nor intrinsically threatening – it is merely combined in a less intense way (*Clarity only appears because of obscurity.*).

The metaphor of clear and obscure, allied to the concept of a perplication or folding of all things in all others but to changing degrees, reinforces the opposition between Deleuze's philosophy and the Cartesian legacy. Deleuze does not accept that things can be distinct, only more or less clear and more or less obscure. According to his method, we never arrive at a truthful understanding of a thing since the more clearly it appears, the more things it is inextricably connected to fade back into obscurity. Yet that which is obscure matters and can itself be brought back into sharper focus. This allows us to explain further Deleuze's attachment to Spinoza's synthetic method of searching endlessly for causes as a way towards having a clear and distinct understanding of the thing. The obscurity of some things is the cause of the clarity of others, in the sense that some things have to fade into the background for others to come to the fore. Clarity does not make sense until we understand how obscurity has allowed it to come about.

The definition of perplication matters much more than the definition of the varieties of Ideas. Indeed, it shows how varieties must be taken as provisional, a convention for classifying Ideas that, in reality, resist classification through the way they are all folded into one another. It is important that Ideas should be differentiable but exactly how they are differentiated is secondary and variable. Moreover, each differentiation must be thought of in terms of variations and not identities. So, when Deleuze defines varieties of Ideas, he is relying on two senses of the word *variétés*: there are varieties of Ideas and these varieties are, themselves, varying and temporary. So the ways of differentiating Ideas given above are contingent and will change according to the actual cases that express Ideas. In that sense, they are necessary as a kind, (*We have to differentiate Ideas*), but not as particular ways, (*There is nothing necessary in this particular way of thinking about differentiation.*). This comes out more clearly in the French than in the Patton translation, where the sentence 'Let us distinguish three dimensions of variety' is rendered as 'We can distinguish three dimensions of variety'. The exact way in which we come to distinguish Ideas, based on a given state of actual knowledge and activity, matters less than other factors that follow on from the perplication of Ideas.

Against the accusation that Deleuze's definition of specific Ideas and varieties is contingent and dependent on a superficial grasp of the sciences, in particular, comes the reply that his interest in them is as examples of the relation, genesis and evolution of Ideas. The emergence of traditional academic subjects can be seen as a result of a perplication of Ideas but not as the basis for its deduction. Perplication is characterised by properties that

152

are beyond the scope of the sciences. On the other hand, though, Deleuze's philosophy of Ideas can only make modest claims with respect to the sciences. It cannot define°their individual fields or methods. Rather, it must map out those fields and methods after they have become defined.

The concept of the event is the most prominent property of perplication, taking it beyond the grasp of the sciences. *Difference and Repetition* shares this concept with *The Logic of Sense* and with much of Deleuze's later work, with Guattari and alone. Deleuze gives a definition of events that could not give rise to a science of events. Against the very general definition of an event as anything that occurs (*Something happened*) and against the most familiar definition of the occurrence of something essential (*These events came to define the revolution*), the Deleuzian event is something 'inessential'. By this, he means that events allow us to define Ideas despite the fact that, as multiplicities, they cannot be defined according to an essence since such a definition would cut Ideas off from one another and deny their necessary connection in perplication:

> Ideas are by no means essences. Insofar as they are the objects of Ideas, problems belong on the side of events, affections or accidents rather than that of theorematic essences . . . Consequently, the domain of Idea is that of the inessential. They proclaim their affinity with the inessential in a manner as deliberate and as fiercely obstinate as that in which rationalism proclaimed its possession and comprehension of essences.
>
> (DR, pp. 189, 243)

Ideas must be defined as differentiated from, but also connected to, other Ideas. In terms of the metaphor of clarity and obscurity, when we turn to the evolution of Ideas, what the Idea leaves obscure (its connection to other distant ideas) is more significant than what it makes clear (its well-determined difference from other Ideas). Ideas are set in motion by what lies at their furthest reaches and by what appears to be of little importance to them.

Ideas change when the obscure impinges on the clear and that is why events are a matter of the inessential. So events are occurrences that reveal interrelations against the tendency to identify Ideas with what belongs most clearly to them and against the tendency to classify actual things as if they bear nothing in common at the level of essences. For example, the emergence of seventeenth-century rationalism is not an event when defined as having the elevation of the reason of human subjects as its essential core. Rather, the emergence of thinkers defining themselves as rationalists is an event where it begins to appear, in an as yet un-theorised and hard to identify way, within in a different and well-defined system of actual identities – both thoughts and things.

The event is, therefore, always missed if it is thought of in terms of essential characteristics since it is about changing intensities in relation to sensations accompanied by a re-arrangement of the perplication of Ideas. Thus, the bubbling up of animal passions in a riot, in an apparently settled rational age, is an event for reason in that it is a sign, for some individuals, that the rational 'essence' of the human is part of a wider system of connections and that this actual time is coming to express that relation in a different way – more passion and less reason. Events are a matter not of the revelation of an essential truth or core but of relations between elements that appear to be impossible or unlikely from the point of view of such essences. For Deleuze, an event is more of the order of the uncanny connection than the essential internal truth.

The Deleuzian event is, therefore, also of the order of the anomaly associated with a scientific paradigm shift or an unexpected turn in evolution. These cannot be predicted from within settled normal science or, at least, cannot be given a high degree of probability. Instead, events, as anomalies or mutations, are distant and hard to digest occurrences requiring shifts in our established forms of knowledge or ways of thinking. But it is important to view paradigm shifts in science or evolutionary jumps as cases that reveal something about Deleuze's events rather than as the sole or main type of event. The event has to be individual, in the sense where a sensation within an individual is the sign of an ideal event. So the shift from one set of scientific laws to another is not the event, neither is the emergence of a new species. The event is the first sign of mutation or the first sensation that something anomalous is significant (in a scientist, a spectator, an actor, animal, plant or molecule).

Later, in *A Thousand Plateaus*, Deleuze and Guattari go on to investigate the relation between these individual events and paradigm shifts or 'large scale' alterations in science, biology or politics. One of their theses is that such shifts occur when individual events occur in many individuals and become expressed in many actual actors or things at the same time, thereby leading to actual shifts from one state to another. The French revolution would, therefore, be explained through the expression of an ideal shift through the sensations and actions of many activists, thereby triggering the actual events leading up to 1789 and beyond.

There could not be a science of this relation between actual and ideal events. If the sciences have the role of extending knowledge, then Deleuze's metaphysics of the event takes on the role of revealing what is significant about the events that mark the limits of knowledge. However, this difference with science poses the problem of how to reveal such significance. Events are signs of change but they are unexpected and unpredictable signs – they are irregularities and, therefore, not the subject of an established science. To reflect on how we should respond to this inessential aspect, Deleuze returns to the process of vice-diction inspired by Leibniz and treated first in his chapter on repetition for itself. Put simply, vice-diction can be understood as a way of working with the Ideal events that are creating an individual by replaying them. In the attempt to reveal the Ideal events determining and determined by actual events, vice-diction must accord with the two main aspects of Ideas – that is, their interrelation through clarity and obscurity as changed according to different envelopments of intensities and as signified by sensations. In order for a sensation to appear, there must be a disruption of settled identities and that disruption expresses a perplication of the whole of Ideas.

This returns us to the two practical principles of Deleuze's philosophy: connect with everything and forget everything (forget all identities). He describes vice-diction in terms of the contradictory demands to throw all Ideas into a single sublime occasion but also to uncover all the connections between Ideas. These demands have to be thought of in terms of the event. We have to find ways of expressing the connections between Ideas but also to express the way in which they are transforming one another through events. In line with his treatment of drama from earlier in the book, he links the latter with a dramatic anger and the former with love. Vice-diction is the creation of actual events that throw an Ideal problem into greatest clarity with respect to all its components (*You cannot understand this unless you come to accept that this and this and this are inevitably part of it, to be loved with it.*). But it is also the creation of actual events that expresses the way in which Ideas are constantly undoing one another through obscure connections (*This tears this apart and this and this.*).

Vice-diction is, therefore, a response to irresolvable problems in two ways. First, because problems come out of the tensions between Ideas, as method, vice-diction must seek to map those tensions as carefully as possible. Second, because the nature of that tension lies in Ideal events, where distant and obscure connections undo apparently clear Ideas, vice-diction must seek to obliterate the illusion of fixity in Ideas and actual things:

> Vice-diction has two procedures which intervene both in the determination of the conditions of the problem and in the correlative genesis of cases of solution: these are, in the first case, the specification of adjunct fields and, in the second, the condensation of singularities.
>
> (DR, pp. 191, 245)

The practice of vice-diction is, therefore, two procedures that are, themselves, split between the demand to connect and the demand to condense or forget. It is not as if there is a historical work that sets the problem out but with no difficulty in identifying the problem (*What's going on?*). This would then be followed by a creative search for solutions that was purely experimental and unhistorical (*We have not tried this before.*) Instead, there is already a creative selection at the level of the mapping out and a mapping out at the level of the creative 'solution'. Both are stuck with the paradox that, the more connections are emphasised or made clear, the less intensity remains in each element of the problem and 'solution'.

For example, at the level of individuals caught in a web of con-flicting feelings and demands, there are pressures to go for dra-matic one-track solutions both at the level of the diagnosis of a crisis and how to live it (*Got to get out of this place!*). But this can be a terrible error when the violent, all-consuming solution turns out to replicate what it is driven from and to betray what it is driven to (*It seemed so pure and now I have destroyed it.*). This is rendered even more difficult in that, in accordance with Deleuze's views on knowledge, the diagnosis and response cannot be direct and in the form 'I know this' and 'I choose that'. Rather, we have to act in such a way as to allow the problem, and how we shall follow on from it, to appear or to become expressed in us. This difficult web, explained by Deleuze's view of the Ideal event, feeds into his treatment of individuals learning to live with forces that are both the source of the intensity of their lives but also the means of its destruction (for example, in his discussion of intoxication and of events in *The Logic of Sense* and *A Thousand Plateaus*).

However, even at the relatively simple and artificial level of an individual life, Deleuze's injunctions seem woefully thin and, once again, abstract. What tools does he allow for this diagnosis and selection, having distanced himself from the sciences as unique source of learning? This returns us to the question asked earlier:

Can his metaphysical concepts of the virtual, of actual things, of Ideas, of multiplicities and, now, of vice-diction be expanded into valid and precise concepts with a view to their justified practical application?

HOW TO ACT

The concept of vice-diction is Deleuze's answer to the question of how to live with the way virtual Ideas and, therefore, pure differences condition our actions. This leads to answers to the question of how to act. The concept is, therefore, central to Deleuzian ethics and politics and to the question of how to live well. In chapter 4 of *Difference and Repetition*, he defines vice-diction in terms of the principles of connecting to all Ideas but, also, of throwing all those Ideas into turmoil by expressing the events that signal the way in which Ideas are transforming one-another in a distant and inessential way. He then goes on to refine what this practice must involve.

Put simply, an individual must learn to create in such a way as to express how it is a perspective on the whole of reality but, also, how its sensations express an intense and singular transformation of that reality. Elsewhere, for example, in *The Logic of Sense*, he describes vice-diction as a doubling of the event or its 'counter-actualisation', indicating thereby how individuals have to create with the Ideas and ideal events that create them. Expressing those Ideas and events in new ways, experimenting with new events and combinations of Ideas, is the only way to live with the virtual processes that condition our evolution.

In order to understand how these principles work in practice, it is worth looking at them in the context of Deleuze's philosophical method as defined under the term Deleuzian dialectics. The method has four branches that can be summed up under the principles of a critique of representation, of the search for conditions for any given thing, of the search for completeness in terms of conditions and of creative destruction – that is, the creation of the new that leaves the old behind. Each of the principles is also operative in the concept of vice-diction – that is, in any given practical situation, there has to be a critical engagement with representation of the situation that hides its real conditions as something that is in movement; there has to be a search for those conditions; the principle governing that search is one of completeness; the method has also to go beyond those conditions and representation in a process of creative destruction.

157

A translation of the practical method of vice-diction into a more familiar language of moral imperatives would give something like the following imperatives (these are put in the form of questions, since the imperative, for Deleuze, is not of the form that commands a direct action but of an unavoidable question – one that presses itself upon us like an imperative):

1. What are the mistaken representations at work here?
2. What conditions set this situation in movement?
3. What other conditions are at work?
4. How will the representations be overcome and the conditions affirmed?

So 'Know thyself' becomes 'Criticise what you know of yourself' *and* 'Learn about what sets you in movement' *and* 'Always seek to learn more' *and* 'Escape what you have learnt and what is known by expressing what sets you in movement'.

Whether we are dealing with Deleuzian dialectics or with vice-diction or with this Socratic caricature, it is essential to view the four strands as interdependent but not reducible to one another. Each strand is incomplete if it is viewed as self-sufficient, in the sense where critique requires the search for conditions and where the search for conditions requires vigilance with respect to representations. This is true of each of the relations between strands. However, critique is not simply the search for conditions, creative destruction is not the search for completeness and so on. It is possible that a case of the dialectics or of vice-diction may stress one strand over others very strongly, to the point of appearing free of them. But any such case will be readable in terms of its compliance with the other principles, if it is true to the principle it stresses over them. For example, there is only an illusion of creative destruction where there is an overriding dependence on representation.

Deleuze unpacks these rather brute characterisations of his method in the closing sections of chapter 4 of *Difference and Repetition*. He begins with a discussion of representation in relation to vice-diction:

In short, representation and knowledge are modelled entirely upon propositions of consciousness which designate cases of solution, but those propositions by themselves give a completely inaccurate notion of the instance which engenders them as cases, and which they resolve or conclude.

(DR, pp. 192, 248)

This claim rests on the study of concepts and of the image of thought from earlier in the book. The point is that a problem is not mapped accurately on the grounds of what is known about the situation in which it arises, where knowledge is based on concepts viewed in terms of propositions and predicates. Problems arise because that knowledge is inadequate in some radical way. They cannot be resolved by adding further predicates, or knowing more, but by escaping the constraints set by what is known: 'To what are we dedicated if not to those problems which demand the very transformation of our body and of our language.' (DR, pp.192, 248)

Rather than being a way of resolving problems, the critique of representation is a starting point for understanding why the problem has been hidden or approached in a mistaken way. It means that knowledge and propositions are important for Deleuzian practice but only as a way of setting the scene for action (*What are the obstacles to real responses to the problem?*). However, the critique of the insufficiency of knowledge sets the further practical moves off on a difficult and dubious path since it appears to force Deleuze into the claim that aspects of his practice cannot take knowledge as their basis. We would then ask what else is there to act upon? Bias or superstition?

Yet this objection only works if we restrict knowledge to his critical definition of it in terms of concepts and predicates as opposed to the definition he favours in terms of the conditions for a given situation. This distinction is rendered in the opposition between knowledge and an infinite learning. In the case of the latter, we learn to respond well to problems by experimenting with cases of solutions which, thereby, reveal the conditions of the problem. Learning is, therefore, indirect. We do not 'learn that', we 'learn by' which 'reveals that' without allowing us to 'know that'. In other words, a capacity to learn well grows as we learn, independently of what we come to know as a result of each act of learning (*If you know how to swim, you'll pick up this new stroke quickly but be sure to forget everything you know about the strokes you currently use.*).

Deleuze's doctrine of learning brings together the four strands of his method, insofar as learning requires critical work on knowledge, allied to an experimentation that reveals conditions of a problem, allied to the principle that this learning is endless. He goes on to characterise this further by responding to the question of how learning can reveal something, but without revealing it as at least an object of possible knowledge. In other words, he responds to the question 'Why can't Ideas be known?' His first move is to reject the answer that Ideas cannot be known because they are beyond the grasp of a single faculty dedicated to knowledge – the understanding, for instance. This move is rejected because it depends on the thought that another faculty gives us access to Ideas (*You cannot know Ideas but you can reason about them.*). This line of thought leaves spheres untouched by Ideas – the proper realm of the understanding, for example. It also ascribes Ideas to a faculty that we have in common, thereby going counter to his critique of common sense and recognition in his work on the image of thought. Yet, in excluding this first explanation, he makes his case all the harder to prove since he has extended the initial question to any possible faculty: *Why can't Ideas be known, reasoned about, felt, imagined?*

The answer is that Ideas are the conditions for the genesis and development of *all* faculties. They are not within the grasp of any given faculty because, at any given stage of development, faculties come about and move forward through relations with that which they later exclude (*You cannot grasp the full significance of science without understanding its relation to religion.*). Yet, when we consider such a claim with respect to conflicts between actual given faculties, it makes no sense: the realm of this actual understanding and the realm of this actual reason may indeed have nothing actual in common. Instead, they have to be seen as related through pure differences, things that belong to no faculty but that explain how unrelated faculties share the same roots. However, this does not mean that faculties share the same historical roots since these can be seen as contingent with respect to Deleuze's understanding of a necessary condition (*Science may have emerged out of a conflict with religion but it did not need to.*).

Deleuze draws an important conclusion from the statement on the independence of Ideas from faculties. Learning itself cannot be a matter of any given faculty but of either 'penetrating' into the Ideas underlying a given faculty (*Coming to embody a sense of what 'to resist' means whilst learning to swim – and having that in the background when thinking about politics*) or of pushing beyond the boundaries of a given faculty to apply it violently to another (*What if we think of science as a matter of faith or of faith as a matter of science?*). Neither of these approaches need be large-scale, as of a faculty need be utterly undermined or exploded. The view is rather that, whenever a faculty evolves, it does so through the influence of other faculties and of Ideas outside those it expresses most clearly (*What if we think of human agents as machines? What if we think of machines as human agents?*).

Both ways of learning show how far Deleuze has moved on from a definitions of faculties as immutable things that have to be thought of 'in principle', as in the statement 'in principle we all share the same faculty of the understanding'. In place of this definition, he maintains a sense of actual faculties present in this or that individual but where an individual is also a singular set of Ideas, a configuration of intensities, sensations. The actual faculties have to be understood in terms of that set, configuration and sensation. But what are the arguments to support this view that faculties presuppose this transcendental reality of Ideas and Ideal events?

DETERMINATION AND GROUNDLESSNESS

The contingent ground for his transcendental deductions is confirmed when Deleuze argues for the necessity of Ideas on the grounds of an actual thing, in chapter 4 of *Difference and Repetition*. In other words, we have to grant him a premise the necessity of which he refuses to prove – indeed, accepts cannot be proven. Moreover, in his argument for the necessity of Ideas, he is explicit in advocating a departure from apodictic foundations such as the Cartesian cogito or Kantian pure a priori intuition. Later, in chapter 5 of his book, the reasons for this contingency are set out in the definition of reality in terms of singular individuals. There can be no universal apodictic ground because all thought and all reality must begin with individuals that have nothing identifiable in common.

So Deleuze's philosophy begins with the singular, rather than the universal: there are individuals determined by questions that they cannot avoid – that is, imperative questions (*What can I be? What should I make? Where should I proceed? What should I live with?*). Such questions are driven by sensation rather than intellectual deductions (*I am drawn to this. This feels wrong.*). It is important to dissociate these questioning beginnings from conscious human subjects. On the contrary, they are more like a behaviour or process identified with a living thing that can be interpreted as existing according to such an imperative (*as if an animal line of descent was responding to the question of how to live with a changing environment*). Deleuze defines these questions according to three key points:

1. The questions cannot be eliminated through an empirical response (*I am x. I should make y. This is our path. These are our partners. This is the essential environment for these animals.*).
2. They 'put the questioner into question' – that is, they are about change or, to use Deleuze's favoured term, they are about becoming something different.
3. They unite that which is becoming with what it becomes with – that is, they are not only questions concerning how a thing should become but also how it should become in a world that is itself, essentially, questionable or problematical (DR, pp. 195–6, 252–3).

Two points should be stressed about this definition. First, Deleuze does not seek to show that these questions are necessary or universal. He cannot do so because, by definition, they find no ground in either the questioner or that which is questioned (unlike Cartesian doubt, for example). Questions have no ground in the object nor in the subject – they arise with and for contingent individuals. Second, this definition of questions reflects the starting points chosen for deductions earlier in the book – for example, the different sensations of expectation, passing into stock and of creating the new in his three deductions of the passive syntheses of time. Each of these sensations must be understood as a question in Deleuze's terms (*What is coming? What am I passing into? What should I select?*). The sense of expectation arises because we do not know what to expect. The same is true of the senses of passing away and deciding of the future. But how do we know that such questions whatever they may be, really arise for individuals?

In answering these questions, Deleuze resists phenomenological or scientific approaches to an experience. This refusal to take on the challenge of describing the experience or fact of being gripped by a question, as he defines it, can seem a serious flaw in his philosophy from the point of view of the search for valid grounds. His strategy, in the chapter on the ideal synthesis of difference, is to discuss the role of the question in the works of other philosophers, notably Heidegger, or in works of literature, in Joyce and Blanchot, for example. These moves are cursory and lacking in arguments and justifications. At this stage of his book, he is seeking to dramatise his point rather than give the full arguments based on his definition of the individual in terms of Ideas, intensities and sensations.

Until those arguments are put, Deleuze uses philosophical and literary references to give a sense of the importance of questions, as opposed to certain foundations, but he gives no accurate description of what it would be to experience such an experience or why such experiences occur and will continue to occur. Neither are we given objective criteria in order to verify that such questions are at work behind forms of behaviour or evolution. Deleuze can claim that his definition does not allow for a phenomenological or objective test since it is about a becoming beyond any given form of intentionality or objective form. But the objection remains that this indicates that what he has defined does not exist or is not reflected in our experience or lacks objective evidence to verify it. Without a clear ground, his philosophy runs the risk of appearing to be a fanciful way of thinking about the world.

Deleuze nods towards these objections in admitting to the unsatisfactory nature of his responses: 'But how disappointing this answer seems to be' [translation slightly modified to avoid Patton's addition of an exclamation mark] (DR, pp. 200, 258). His admission concerns the lack of a firm foundation for his philosophy, where all finally comes down to 'an aleatory point at which everything becomes ungrounded, instead of a solid ground'. (DR, pp. 200, 258) But the objection is stronger than that. It is not so much that Deleuze does not provide us with a ground for his philosophy but that the form of his arguments depends on a highly specified lack of ground that is not presented in such a way that it can be verified or discussed in terms of its existence. His philosophy depends on the construction of complex structures where relations between the elements of the structures are deduced in terms of the way in which they presuppose one another. Yet the point at which the structure begins in the actual, the point at which any deduction should begin, is not defined in such way as to allow for a discussion of its reality – we have to believe that there are imperative questions but there can be no final universal rational grounds offered for such belief.

However, the lack of a ground for the philosophy does not imply that Deleuze's work on the ideal synthesis of difference fails to provide the determinacy called for at the start of the chapter. The exact form of that determinacy, concerning the processes relating the actual and the virtual in individuals will be discussed in detail in the next chapter on the asymmetrical synthesis of the sensible. Yet, there are some general points that can be made here, though a full critical engagement with their validity will only take place in the next chapter.

First, Deleuze insists that the virtual must not be opposed to the real. This is because Ideas play a full part in the genesis and evolution of actual things. The real must be seen in terms of the structure of virtual and actual and their reciprocal determination. Ideas become determined as clear and obscure when they are expressed in actual things, through a process that Deleuze calls differen*c*iation – that is, when changes in the relations of intensi-ties accompany a shift in the clarity and obscurity of Ideas as the intensities are expressed in actual individuals through their sen-sations. It is because actual things become identifiable that Ideas become determined. But actual things are set in motion as they express Ideas, through a parallel process of differen*t*iation – that is, when intensities bring about shifts within individuals beyond their actual identities as their sensations express the intensities that accompany a shift in the clarity and obscurity of Ideas. It is because Ideas are at work in actual things that the identity of those things is illusory from the point of view of the connection of actual things to the whole of Ideas and, thereby, to the whole of all other actual things.

Second, the virtual must not be confused with the possible. Virtual Ideas are not things that actual things might express but do not, and Ideas do not correspond to different possible but not actual outcomes for a given actual thing. This is because the whole of Ideas is only differentiated in terms of relations of clarity and obscurity and not existence and non-existence. Distant and very obscure Ideas have a real – rather than a possible – role to play in the Ideas that are expressed with greatest clarity by an actual thing. That other life is not simply possible for you. The intensities and Ideas that made it live for you once still exist, though the intensities do not envelop others and the Ideas are not clear in the current actualisation (*I have always been haunted by what I could have been – you are what you could have been, what you will be and what you have been, but at different degrees of intensity . . .*).

7

What is Reality?

Despite its contingent foundations, Deleuze's metaphysical structure of virtual Ideas that stand in a reciprocal relation to actual
things may still have great philosophical merit, in particular, if it
can be shown that other philosophical positions have to make similar leaps. If it is the case that there can be no well-founded philosophy, based on universal and apodictic beginnings, then Deleuze's
assumptions concerning given actual forms that presuppose his
virtual Ideas may be the best way of coping with this necessarily
uncertain situation. However, for such a line of argument to be
valid, the apparent contradictions and lacks of his structure must
be addressed – as must the necessity of Deleuze's line for a thought
based on the absence of foundations. It may be the case that there
are no apodictic foundations for philosophy but, in itself, that
does not justify his complex structure of actual things and virtual
conditions.

In earlier chapters of this book, I have raised certain objections
and I list these below. Deleuze develops answers to most of these
objections in Chapter 5 of *Difference and Repetition*. The point of
the present chapter is to assess how successfully he deals with the
questions and problems.

1. When Deleuze appeals to 'the given', he does not always follow
   the latest science. At times, he refers to the given as if this can
   be done without having to depend on scientific studies – for
   example, in his appeal to sensations with respect to time or
   in his frequent references to creation in art-works. Shouldn't

any philosophical approach to the actual respond to scientific theories, accepting that philosophy can only play a critical and analytical role with respect to scientific methods and discoveries?

2. In order to observe actual things and reflect upon them, science must identify them conceptually and as objects of empirical verification or falsification, even if this is only indirectly. Identification, verification and falsification are essential aspects of scientific discovery and Deleuze's philosophy of pure becomings is mistaken in denying the importance of this for a philosophy of the given.

3. What grounds are there for an to appeal to transcendental Ideas and to the virtual in relation to the actual, since everything we can know about the actual depends on observations and theories about the actual and not on the virtual?

4. What is the precise relation between actual things, as defined by Deleuze, and virtual Ideas? Can Deleuze explain his assertion that there is a relation between actual things and virtual Ideas without falling back on a law of cause and effect, thereby contradicting his claims on their causal independence?

Deleuze introduces the chapter where he engages most closely with science and with objections to the transcendental nature of his philosophy in an allusive and dense style. It is prone to statements rather than arguments. It mixes genres and topics, passing rapidly from science to philosophy, to strange quasi-mystical statements. However, true to his sense that Ideas must be dramatised, this apparently dogmatic and mystifying approach is designed to introduce us to the two main concepts of his chapter, with their distant connections and signals, but without fixing them prior to their appearance in more precise guises and contexts. The two concepts are disparity and intensity. His strategy will be to show how these philosophical concepts are essential for an understanding of reality even where it is subject to scientific theories and to a philosophy of science. Thus, the work on disparity and intensity completes the statements on reality and possibility that closed the previous chapter.

Put simply, Deleuze's answers to the questions set out above are that scientific theories can only give an incomplete account of reality unless they are seen in conjunction with philosophical work on transcendental conditions. This work reveals aspects of reality that are not open to scientific approaches – barring the tactic of incorrectly naming the transcendental and creative aspects of the philosophy a 'new science'. Reality, for Deleuze, is more than that which can be treated and discovered by empirical science because reality is a structure that involves disparities between its orders, between the universe as object of enquiry for the sciences and the transcendental conditions for that universe. We have to work with both sides of this disparity because the empirical universe of identifiable measurable differences presupposes the order of immeasurable differences that allows us to explain how the former differences come about and change in terms of their significance. There is only significant measurable diversity because there are differences that cannot be measured: 'Diversity is given, but difference is that by which the given is given, that by which the given is given as diverse.' (DR, pp. 222, 286)

So a first sketch of Deleuze's argument is that actual identifiable diversity presupposes a history and context of significance. This significance cannot be understood as mere identified diversity because it is a new and incomparable change in degrees of significance. Here, 'new' must be understood in the radical sense where it is a change beyond all established measures. Intensity is the concept for that change that cannot be measured or captured in terms of a final identity. So Deleuze denies that there are ever pure givens, such as sense-data. It matters little how pure they may appear to us as any purity conceals varying intensities of significance (*Yes, it is this degree of temperature but that matters little until we experiment with what that degree means for these individuals.*). Even the most neutral data are related to those that shock us out of an established pattern of thought and prompt us into others. This means that all phenomena are related to intensities beyond measure: 'Every phenomenon is composite because not only are the two series which bound it heterogeneous but each is itself composed of heterogeneous terms, subtended by heterogeneous series which form so many sub-theories.' (DR, pp. 222, 286–7)

The first heterogeneity is that of actual and virtual – the physical cause of a phenomenon and theories about causes or the nature of phenomena are not of the same order of the virtual 'causes' of the phenomenon that explain its significance for us ('Every phenomenon flashes in a signal sign system' (DR, pp. 222, 286)). The second heterogeneity concerns the elements of each order. Neither contains elements that can be related to a common measure or identifiable essence. We never fully grasp a phenomenon or an intensity in relation to all other elements. This echoes the claim from earlier in *Difference and Repetition* that we can never grasp the elements of an Idea defined as a multiplicity. But why can significance not be thought of in physical or chemical causal terms (*I can cure your despair with this drug.*)? Why is significance an essential component of the given? Could there not be scientific theories of great explanatory power that make no reference whatsoever to meaning? Why can intensity not be captured by a science? If it cannot, why must we refer to it?

EXPLANATION

It is important to avoid confusing Deleuze's arguments against the dominance in philosophy of empirical verification or falsification with an anti-scientific position. As part of his dialectics, his critical work on science is not concerned with an attack on any particular science or science in general. Instead, like his critical work on philosophy in chapter 3 of *Difference and Repetition*, where he seeks to separate philosophy from an image of thought that it presupposes and supports, Deleuze's work on science criticises certain habits of thought that follow from a scientific approach to the world. This criticism is in no way a general attack on scientific theories or on the approach to the data that they are based on. It is an attempt to undermine the dominance of habits of thought that follow from an attitude to science – that may, indeed, be dominant in science but not necessarily so. In fact, when Deleuze distinguishes different scientists, it is not on the basis of their specific scientific discoveries and theories but on the way in which their meta-scientific accounts of their work exhibit or resist these habits. So, though he resists enslaving his philosophy to the latest science, he is careful to engage with science both as a source of inspiration and as an important topic for critique. Scientific discoveries and theories are a very important 'given' for Deleuze but they are not the sole arbiters of significance in the actual. Neither can they stand alone, free of critical and creative work with respect to their transcendental conditions – science has to be made to matter.

Deleuze focuses on the habits that emerge when attitudes to scientific explanation and prediction become part of our assumptions about the nature of reality in relation to understanding. In particular, he aims to criticise the way in which those habits imply

168

mistaken views on time, difference and the value of difference in relation to understanding. Put simply, he argues that, when we become used to thinking of explanation as going from difference as something lacking identity to diversity as well-ordered, we come to view time as a direction from a 'bad' state of chaotic difference to a 'good' state of order. Similarly, thanks to explanation and understanding, we move from an unpredictable and negative state of differences to a predictable state of diversity. Explanation and prediction are the ways in which time is given a positive direction from chaos to order. Through this process, habits of thought associated with science become part of good sense, itself defined as our faculty of distinctions and distributions. Deleuze criticises this faculty and the habits of thought that follow from it throughout *Difference and Repetition (There are these categories. This fits here. The more we can attribute things to categories the better.).*

He refers to the alliance of thermodynamics and philosophy at the end of the nineteenth century and to the division of energy into an intensity and an extensity to show how science can be co-opted by good sense. According to Deleuze, even scientists such as Carnot and Curie, who come close to a concept of pure difference in their concept of energy, end up thinking of difference in terms of identity. This is because they divide energy into intensive and extensive components. The extensive component allows the intensive component to be identified and compared – it acquires a quality. So energy has a non-spatial, intensive side that must be completed by a spatial side where the energy is extended over a particular surface or in a particular volume. For example, the energy associated with a particular weight is only fully understood in terms of the size of the surface over which it is exercised as pressure. More importantly, intensity is destined to cancel itself out in the surface where it is exercised – for example, where a difference in temperature is annulled due to entropy.

The issue here is not so much whether Deleuze has fully understood the nineteenth century science and even less whether that science can be considered true. Rather, it is in the way that science supports a view of reality where energy or intensity has to be cancelled out and distributed spatially in order to be understood and in order to have an effect. The habit that is supported is that, although intensity or energy are the reason something happens, that reason must disappear in favour of a rational good sense that determines the order:

Good sense does not negate difference: on the contrary, it recognises difference just enough to affirm that it negates itself, given sufficient extensity and time. Between mad difference and difference cancelled . . . good sense necessarily lives itself as a universal rule of distribution, and therefore as universally distributed.

(DR, pp. 225, 290)

This habit is to be criticised because it turns us away from the significance of difference – that it generates change. It also turns us away from the positive role of that change as the production of diversity. Instead, change is devalued in favour of distribution and the production of change is supplanted by the good sense associated with distribution.

Thus, once we fall into the habit of viewing difference as that which is cancelled out to our benefit through distribution, we miss the productive role of difference and the value of the production of difference. Furthermore, we begin to think of reality in terms of objects that have become identified. Whereas, if the productive and active role of difference is retained, instead of well-identified objects, we have to work with individuals – that is, individual fields constituted by varying degrees of change (later in this chapter, we shall see that these fields are to include Deleuze's Ideas, intensities and actual things). In the same way that difference is cancelled out by good sense, individuals are cancelled out as multiplicities of varying elements when they are identified as objects belonging to a particular class. This is also true of those individuals identified as selves. Through this cancelling out we are able to think of the universal object, defined as that which can be recognised, and of the universal self, defined according to its faculty of recognition.

In this way, Deleuze connects his critique of the habits acquired with science with his critique of the image of thought based on recognition from his critique of Kant. Furthermore, he is able to connect the emphasis on creativity and the new from his work on difference and on repetition – in particular, in terms of the future – with the elimination of that creativity in a good sense and common sense, bolstered this time by concepts of explanation and predictability loosely adopted from science:

Good sense and common sense each refer to the other, each reflect the other and constitute one half of the orthodoxy. In view of this reciprocity and double reflection we can define common sense by the process of recognition and good sense by the process of prediction.

(DR, pp. 226, 292)

170

Yet these broad links across Deleuze's book carry through earlier weaknesses. The remarks on habits, good sense and common sense appear to be sociological or cultural with no empirical evidence given to back them up. The allusions to pure difference still need to be defended against the view that it is right for science to think of intensity as that which must be cancelled out in extension.

The response to the first objection is that Deleuze is not so much concerned to prove uncontrovertibly that good sense and common sense exist but to guard against them and to ward them off should they be used against a different view of the role of thought – one that goes beyond recognition and prediction. His point is that thinking is a creative response to irresolvable problems that demand to be renewed rather than solved as well classified and predictable:

> Subjectively, paradox breaks up the common exercise of the faculties and places each before its own limit, before its incomparable: thought before the unthinkable which it alone is nevertheless capable of thinking; memory before the forgotten which is also its immemorial; sensibility before the imperceptible which is indistinguishable from its intensive . . .
>
> (DR, pp. 227, 293)

This point, though, depends on showing that intensity, the imperceptible, does not have to be thought of as something that must be identifiable and recognised, only sensed by that which has no final identity – the individual.

DEPTH AND SPACE

Deleuze avoids a mystical approach to intensity, in his answer to the problem of how to explain that which is cancelled out in explanation, by making use of a transcendental deduction. Intensity is the condition for significance in a well-ordered space. Explanations based on an undifferentiated ordered space cannot account for the role played by individuals partially but necessarily encountered within that space, for whom that space involves radically different sensations of significance. There must, therefore, be something expressed within the space that is the condition for this significance. In other words, if space is viewed as something extended and uniform, how come certain positions and things within that space acquire greater significance than others? There can be causal chains within an extended space that allow us to explain certain effects but these chains do not allow us to explain the significance of variations within individuals. For example, though we can measure distances and compare them, these do not allow us to explain why a particular distance is important for a given individual, why a particular distance and orientation is significant for that individual as a thing caught in a process of change. *Why is this walk a sign of that which is individual to you but not for me? Why does this feature begin to appear in this individual bird or rock face and not on another? What is the 'cause' of that individuality and significance?*

The answer to the question is that this cause is an intensity and that intensity cannot be the same kind of cause as that which operates in terms of physical cause and effect, in a measured space, because intensity cancels itself out in that space or is resistant to being thought of as an internal property of the space defined as a measurable extension. Thus, Deleuze believes that we cannot explain why a particular cause is significant without referring the order of physical causes to the order of intensities:

Whence the double aspect of the quality as a sign: it refers to an implicated order of constitutive differences, and tends to cancel out those differences in the extended order in which they are explicated. This is also why causality finds in signalling at once both an origin and an orientation or destination, where the destination in a sense denies the origin.

(DR, pp. 228, 294)

Deleuze uses the French *expliquer* both as the opposite of implicate (to explicate or unfold spatially) and in the sense of 'to explain'. It is sensible, in translation, to use explicate rather than explain, where the emphasis is on the explication–implication opposition that indicates a more technical use of *expliquer*. His point is that explanation is viewed in terms of the habit of thought of valuing a distribution of difference according to an order, according to good sense. Yet this ordering can never be a full explanation. It is not capable of giving a satisfactory answer to questions such as 'Why does this matter?' and 'Why does this sign set this individual off?'

This argument about the presuppositions of significance is reenforced by a study of the opposition of depth and extension. Deleuze seeks both to convince us that signs and signification exist in extended space – that they are actual – and to convince us that, in order to explain signs, we have to refer to intensity as 'cause'. He begins with the remark that the sensation of a depth in space is different from its length – that is, though any sensed or expressed depth is measurable as a length, that measure does not fully account for the significance of depth. This point is developed further through the introduction of the Leibnizian question of the reason for the original depth – What is the sufficient reason for that which distinguishes depth from distance? Or, from the point of view of individuals in a space – What explains the power of depth and its difference for different individuals? For example, distance alone cannot explain the presence of vertigo in one case and not in another or the adaptation to depth in one case and flight to a more shallow depth in another.

The argument is then extended from particular sensations or expressions of depth to a conclusion about all extensions. No extension makes sense with respect to its distances without reference to individuals. Individuals only provide that sense due to depth as resistant to distance. The intensity of depth makes it a sign for individuals. Extension comes out of and relies upon depth: 'Extension as a whole comes from the depths. Depth as the (ultimate and original) heterogeneous dimension is the matrix of all extensity, including its third dimension considered to be homogenous with the other two.' (DR, pp. 229 [slightly modified], 298) So distance in any space depends on sensations or expressions of depth that, themselves, must be intensities. The use of both sensation and expression is important since Deleuze's argument does not rely on a phenomenology or psychology of sensation but on sensation viewed as a sign, as defined according to his distinction of actual and virtual, where the virtual is the realm of intensity and the actual the realm of depths and distances. His argument relies on changes that cannot be explained through reference to distance and that, therefore, express depth. But these need not be a matter of consciousness or intentionality – a behaviour or an adaptation are also signs of depth.

Deleuze goes on to describe depth with greater precision through a series of important remarks that show the difference between his dialectical method, dependent on a search for conditions, and phenomenology or strict materialist scientific accounts. First, the form-ground or figure-ground distinction makes no sense without depth because the ground is not made up of distant objects but of the expression of depth. (For example, the sensation of a ground in an art-work does not only depend on objects or perspective but on the way in which colour shading, brightness and darkness capture sensations of depth.) Thus, figures presuppose a ground that is itself non-figural and the ground itself depends on figures to appear as ground. Deleuze goes on to develop this short remark in studying Francis Bacon's use of figure and ground in *Francis Bacon, Logique de la Sensation*.

Second, depth relies on passive syntheses in the same way as time, as treated in Deleuze's chapter on repetition for itself. Depth depends on the passive synthesis of habit for its explication. We are able to move from depth to distance through habit (for example, after successive long jumps we come to know how far we can jump, as opposed to seeing far marks as perhaps frightening depths). Depth depends on the passive synthesis of memory for its intensive aspect – that is, distances become depths and remain depths through the passive synthesis of all earlier depths in memory (it is because we have passive memories of depth on land that we are able to experience depth for the first time at sea). Depth also depends on the passive synthesis of time with respect to the future. In order to create the new we presuppose that all earlier depth and, therefore, all distances could be expressed differently (for example, in the way in which our search for speed has altered depth and distance through motorised transport and presupposed that change, without our being conscious of it).

Third, the difference in orders of extension and depth and the status of explanation of the former with regard the latter and signification regarding the latter to the former means that depth must be defined independently of extension. It also means that extension comes out of depth. That is, we do not have a full understanding of any extension until we relate it to the intensities that give rise to it – that make it matter – and to the intensities that are transforming it – that make it matter now and into the future. This means that all the intensities that are at play with regard an extension must be taken into account – where all means all past intensities and future intensities, irrespective of any individual extension.

The extensity whose genesis we are attempting to establish is extensive magnitude, the *extensum* or term of reference of all the *extensio*. The original depth, by contrast, is indeed space as a whole, but space as an intensive quality: the pure *spatium*.

(DR, pp. 230, 296)

This reference to the wholes of extended space and space as intensive depth returns us to Deleuze's insistence on the connection of everything to everything else, actual and virtual, and to his principle of connecting with everything outlined at the beginning of this book.

174

This frightening and apparently wild metaphysical claim rests on the second point raised above and on Deleuze's work on the passive syntheses of time, in particular in terms of Bergson, as developed in the chapter on repetition for itself. There is no reason to separate any given extension from all past sensations of depth because the intensities that are most clearly at work in any given extension are related, albeit obscurely, to all other intensities (*Is there ever love without even the glimmer of jealousy? Is there ever the sensation of distance without the sensation of movement as walking, running, falling...?*). Moreover, even the most distant and most obscure sensation of depth is related to future changes in the significance of any given extension. Thus, it is not only a metaphor at work when we 'surf' something. We really experience un-sea-like mediums through the sensation of depth associated with surfing. Those same mediums cannot be excluded completely from other sensations. However, what arguments are there for this difference of extension and depth? Why are extension and depth fundamentally different? If they are fundamentally different, how are they related? If they are related, what reasons are there for believing that depth plays a role in the 'genesis' of extension?

Deleuze's answers turn on a close, if very short, study of the sensation of depth and the perception of extension. First, he claims that neither judgements of depth nor of distance depend on the size of objects but on the depth that surrounds them. For example, without a sense of perspective that allows us to judge closeness, we cannot judge the relative size of different objects. Second, this depth is a matter of intensities of sensation. For example, in the way gradations of different shades allow us to sense distance in a landscape. This explains Deleuze's frequent references to the works and writings of Paul Klee and to Klee's fascination with the relation between colour and perspective (allowing him to achieve an 'architecture of the plane' through colour rather than lines of perspective) – see, for instance, chapter 7 of Deleuze and Guattari's *What is Philosophy?*.

We perceive distance because we have sensed depth, because we continue to sense depth and because we create depth. To the objection that depth need not be a matter of intensity in the case of lines of perspective towards a vanishing point, Deleuze would argue that these lines cannot be judged in terms of whether the vanishing point is the closest or furthest point of the representation without the introduction of either familiar objects – thereby begging the question – or differently shaded ones – thereby accepting

his argument. Escher's puzzles can be explained through this am-
bivalence of pure perspective and its dependence on objects and
shades.

But, equally, depth could not be sensed without referring to
the objects in extended space that Deleuze's arguments started
with. Even in Klee's experiments with colour and perspective, the
sensations of intensity are allied to coloured areas that have to be
divisible, if only in terms of a direction of lightening and dark-
ening. Again, the concept of a reciprocal determination between
heterogeneous fields (extension and intension) comes out as essential for Deleuze's account. This explains why his statement that
'Intensity is both the imperceptible and that which can only be
sensed' is not the paradox that it seems (DR, pp. 230, 297; translation slightly modified to avoid the addition of a reference to time
in the addition of the concept of simultaneity). As the condition
for depth, intensity cannot be sensed fully in an object or extension. But it must be perceived in some way in order to be deduced
at all.

Thus, intensity can be perceived as qualities in extension (this
shade of red), but we never sense the intensity that allows us to
perceive that shade since it varies in what it can make us sense
with the quality according to the contexts in which it is expressed.
That is, the sensations associated with that quality vary according
to the other qualities that are present, according to the actual objects they appear with and according to the individual they appear
in. This shade of red may appear at different depths depending
on what other shades it accompanies – it may arouse different
passions depending on the shapes in which it appears and the
other colours and words associated with it. These different contexts 'have an effect' on the intensities expressed through them
because they bring different intensities into relations of greater
and lesser clarity and obscurity. This it what Deleuze means by the
title of the chapter 'The asymmetrical synthesis of the sensible' –
different actual relations of qualities imply different syntheses of
intensities (and, therefore, of pure differences or of elements of
Ideas defined as multiplicities of pure variations). This reciprocal
quasi-causal relation between the condition and the conditioned
is perhaps Deleuze's greatest metaphysical innovation and the key
to understanding the power of his philosophy.

So here is the first version of the crucial thesis of the fifth chapter of *Difference and Repetition*: the sensations that allow us to order
actual things imply syntheses of virtual intensities that cannot be

fully rendered as actual and these syntheses are the reason sensations and orders are significant. Significance is the result of the asymmetrical synthesis of the sensible, where asymmetrical means that the causal relations between actual things and sensations is not the same, is not mirrored, in the re-arrangement of relations between intensities.

This completes and explains Deleuze's account of the structure of virtual and actual in his work on difference in itself and repetition for itself. But, even if we accept that it is not possible to account for sense by reference to the actual alone, why should we assume that sensation relies on something resembling intensities? Does Deleuze only allow us to deduce that there is something that is the condition for sensation or is he correct that this something can be characterised as intensities that enter into syntheses? Even granted this, can he show us that we have anything to learn from these syntheses since we appear to know nothing of the logic or laws that govern the 'causal' reciprocal relations of actual to virtual?

We have already seen Deleuze respond to similar questions in the chapter on the ideal synthesis of difference. However, the answers put forward there, regarding the deduction of Ideas defined as multiplicities, required further work in terms of the relation of that synthesis to actual things and to the practical consequences of the relation between the actual and the virtual. It is this lack that Deleuze aims to remedy thanks to the arguments developed in the following section. The link between the ideal synthesis of difference and the asymmetrical synthesis is emphasised by a quick remark on Kant, where Deleuze returns to a point made earlier in the book. According to Deleuze, Kant's error is to retain the primacy of extension over intensity by insisting that intensity occurs in a pre-defined space as opposed to allowing that space to be defined by individuals and their intensities.

For example, in terms of altitude, different intensities of sensation should not be referred to different heights. Rather, heights only make sense and change in their sense due to the intensities that occur. Intensity makes space and only depends on it as a necessary condition for its expression rather than as a necessary condition for its measure. Heights mean radically different things for the sufferer of vertigo and the insouciant mountain climber. They inhabit different spaces and the measured relation between those spaces cannot account for that difference or for the relations that hold between the differing senses of height and other wider structures and sensations. The world of the sufferer of vertigo is ordered differently and makes sense differently from the world of the mountain climber. But those worlds are related through the intensities they express in different ways and through the relations between different significances of depth (*My vertigo has bequeathed a love of tightly defined spaces. Her insouciance at altitude has bred a contempt for constrained lives.*). Finally, because these worlds are related through the transcendental space of intensities, they cannot communicate with one another except by creating new sensations that synthesise intensities anew (*I can only give you signs of my love, of my addictions.*).

INTENSITY

The critical points set out above can be summed up in the crude statements that, although Deleuze may be able to deduce that there must be something more than actual things, he cannot deduce anything more than that. Or that he need not even have to deduce that there must be something more than the actual – for example, by falling back on strict materialist explanations of phenomena (*The sense of depth is a property of our psycho-sensory apparatus.*).

His response is to show that it is possible to demonstrate that intensity has three key characteristics and that these characteristics imply a necessary relation to the actual and condition for the actual but also a resistance to being fully thought in terms of the actual. These arguments are abstract and the demonstrations rely on at least some knowledge of mathematics but, from these austere characteristics, Deleuze will reconstruct a subtle and powerful account of the reciprocal determination of virtual and actual encompassed in individuals. He also gives us original arguments for bridging the gap between a 'known' realm and a real but 'unknowable' one, on which the former depends. However, the resources used in these arguments are not in themselves original. The originality lies in the use Deleuze put them to.

The first characteristic of intensity is that it 'includes the unequal in itself'. Deleuze goes on to explain this rather strange statement by saying that intensity is that which cannot be annulled in quantity. This statement makes sense when we refer back to his work on depth and distance. It is important because it goes beyond the particular example of depth, open to objections regarding Deleuze's avoidance of psychological, psychoanalytical, phenomenological or psychological theories of depth. His point is that, in mathematical accounts of quantity, there is something, like depth, that escapes measure, that 'cannot be annulled' or related to other measures.

So intensity, as that which cannot be annulled, is a necessary aspect of any quantity. But quantity, as that which seeks to annul the unequal, is the essence of measuring. Deleuze claims that a system of numbers, used for measuring space or things in space, generates numbers that cannot be annulled in that system. Yet these numbers are significant in some way – as if it ought to be possible to fit them into a system where they can be annulled. The sensation that such numbers are significant, even though they cannot be annulled, must be put down to intensity. However, new number systems, that allow recalcitrant numbers to be annulled, do not account fully for the problem such numbers caused in lower systems. What is more, a new system generates its own recalcitrant numbers. Number systems seem to be unable to escape intensities related to numbers they generate but cannot annul.

Deleuze supports these arguments by referring to number theory and to the way in which different systems of numbers – natural, real, imaginary – respond to the challenge of measuring numbers that can be generated in a simpler system but not measured. For example, the fraction $\frac{4}{3}$ has no place in the series of natural numbers, even though 4 and 3 are natural numbers, so a further series must be thought of that accounts for this fraction that we deem significant but we cannot account for it in the series of natural numbers. However, Deleuze's point is not so much that it is possible to generate problematic numbers but, rather, that any number understood as a measure must also be understood in terms of the problems it partially resolves and partially hides from different number series. In other words, it is false to say that a higher system of numbers fully accounts for a lower one in terms of the significance of the measures set out in the first. For example, 2 in the series of natural numbers has a different significance from 2 in the series of real numbers.

He shows this point by referring to the difference between ordinal numbers (where the number indicates a place in an order, first, second . . .) and cardinal ones (where the number indicates a quantity of things, one, two . . .) It can seem that, since ordinal and cardinal numbers are 'the same', the cardinal series is deduced from and includes the ordinal one – that is, that, in addition to allowing us to number things according to a series (1 or first,

2 or second...), cardinal numbers also allow us to explain relations between quantities ($4 = 2 + 2$). But, according to Deleuze, this is a mistake since a number must be thought of as either ordinal or cardinal. For example, the fact that something comes second does not mean that it is two times the first: 'We should not, therefore, believe that cardinal number results analytically from ordinal, or from the final terms or finite ordinal series...' (DR, pp. 233, 300) So a space measured according to cardinal numbers only 'includes' ordinal properties thanks to intensity – the sensation of order rather than its measure. Conversely, the sensation of order can only be expressed in a space measured thanks to cardinal numbers – that is, a spatially represented order implies distances (first by this much).

This argument concerning numbers is developed further in a long remark on Plato's reflection on the divisible and the indivisible. Let A be indivisible, except by itself, and B be divisible, where divisible means divisible only into two unequal parts (x times A and $\frac{B}{2}$). Can we show how B be can divided to give us a system that can be thought of fully from A alone? Each time we attempt to do so by dividing B, we obtain new indivisible numbers when they are added to A ($A + \frac{B}{2}$). (Note that Deleuze is very ambiguous at this point since, when he writes $\frac{B}{2}$, he means the unequal part of B when A or a factor of A is taken away from B. He really should have used the notation $B = x$ times $A + C$, where C is not divisible by A. His explanation of Plato's point is, therefore, far from clear – perhaps even unnecessarily complicated or, if we are feeling ungenerous, simply wrong.)

Additions of A with the unequal part of B lead to series (multiples of A and multiples of $A + C$) that have gaps between their members that can be filled by new recalcitrant numbers (for example, 2, 4, 6 and 3, 9, 27 lead us to 5). Thus new prime numbers, or indivisibles in Plato and Deleuze's terminology, keep appearing however hard we try to bring all numbers to a finite set of indivisibles. The perfection of the indivisible A or even a set of As cannot be made to cover the imperfection of the divisible into two unequal parts: 'The labour of God [in Plato's account] is always threatened by the third hypothesis of the Parmenides, that of the differential or intensive instant.' (DR, pp. 234, 301) The importance of this work on number and the unequal is that it means that intensity is not simply unknowable but unknowable in a specific way – it cannot be measured according to a single principle, such as generating all numbers from known indivisibles. It is not that we do not know whether it can be measured or not, it is that we must think of intensity as that which can never be annulled.

But what kind of argument has Deleuze given to support his statement on the inclusion of inequality? It cannot be based simply on the rather superficial and unclear observation of different number theories since the statement is meant to hold for all intensities in any extension, whereas the observation covers only a limited number of theories with no claim to the possibility of inductive move from that limited number to all. Neither is Deleuze's argument of a similar type to philosophical conclusions drawn from Gödel's proof or from set-theory, where the necessary incompleteness of formal systems is deduced.

Deleuze's statement does not regard propositions that cannot be proven but that are consistent with the proven propositions of a given formalisation. It regards a system of propositions on which formal systems must depend but where the two systems are heterogeneous in some way. Perhaps this explains why he avoids the resources of logic and set-theory despite their apparent closeness to his own intuitions. Instead, the appeal to mathematical cases is, once again, as exemplars of a philosophical argument. The mathematical cases are a further example of the way in which a well-ordered extension or numbering presupposes something that resists that order and yet is important for it. We sense that a new abnormal number, such as $3/4$ or the square root of -1, is significant even though we cannot account for that significance without generating a new number series. Moreover, that new number series still fails to fully explain the earlier significance. In that sense, the mathematical reference is to further examples of another given, rather than to a source for a universally valid argument on intensity.

It could seem, from the nature of this argument, that Deleuze can answer the problem of contingency raised throughout this book but, in particular, in the previous chapter. However, sensation has to be presupposed for the argument to work. We are never given space without sensation in Deleuze but this does not mean that we cannot be given space without sensation – just that, in the cases considered, we cannot. Every time Deleuze has to answer the possibility of a space without sensation, he has to tackle it in a case by case manner because his argument depends on convincing us of the presence of signs of an intensity that cannot be accounted for, as opposed to having a general and well-founded argument for the presence of such signs in any measurable space.

181

It is tempting to read Deleuze's statements on the relation between the virtual and actual as apodictic but they can only be speculative, based on contingent foundations. This is shown most clearly in the way depth itself is a particular expression of intensity and not a general one in his account. By definition, it cannot be general or universal. This confirms that his appeal to mathematics in *Difference and Repetition* cannot be as the foundation for his philosophy and its validity. Deleuze does not have knock-down a priori arguments against any of the following possibilities:

1. that space – or life – can be fully theorised in such a way as to explain all events according to a common measure (a form of extreme rationalism);
2. that space – or life – is a matter of probability – that it is chance-driven but where chance is governed by the laws of probability and statistics – and that, hence, our only proper response is a statistical and theoretical survey of the results of those changes;
3. that space – or life – should, indeed, be thought of in relation to intensity or energy but that this relation can be modelled mathematically (Deleuze's use of the word matrix for virtual intensities should not be taken mathematically but in the more poetic sense of a formative place).

He only provides us with the materials for a critical and transcendental survey of the foundations of these claims and of specific accounts of space based on them.

I will not go into the detail of the arguments for the last two characteristics of intensity since this would be to rehearse some of the points made above. The second characteristic gives a more formal account of the importance of imperceptible changes in Deleuze's theory of events. The characteristic is that intensity 'affirms difference'. This claim has to be understood in the sense that all intensities understood as changes, however 'small', are affirmed in themselves, thereby making a nonsense of statements regarding the relative magnitude of an intensity or change. There is no sense of scale, of a negative or of a zero point with respect to intensities – these only appear when intensities are explicated in terms of distances. Intensities are the conditions for sensation and for significance such as depth, as such, it is a mistake to abstract from the sensation to a grid that allows for comparisons, including ones that involve opposed values (higher/lower), or that allows for a zero point. Instead, if there is sensation, if there is significance, then there must be a change and that change matters in itself.

182

The third characteristic brings the first and second together. Since intensities cannot be grasped in terms of mathematical measures – for example, in terms of distance – it is a mistake to think of intensities as primarily implicated in distances, in the sense of 'Here is a distance. What intensity does it imply?'. It is not the case that, for each distance, there is an intensity that gives the sense to that distance and that behaves like the distance with respect to operations (half-distance, half-intensity). Neither is it the case that, because intensity is that which is singular or incomparable in a distance, then intensities have to be thought of as unique, unchanging and indivisible. Rather, intensities have to be thought of as indivisible, with respect to measure, but divisible, with respect to the configurations they take on with respect to other intensities. The whole configuration of intensities changes while they remain the same pure differing. Deleuze calls this whole the spatium of all intensities. It is the transcendental condition for measurable actual space but cannot be approached through the empirical sciences, as shown by the three characteristics outlined above.

He explains these changes in configuration in terms of the concept of envelopment. In relation to a change in actual things, that itself forms a sign involving a change in the configuration of intensities, the latter change must be thought of in terms of different intensities enveloping one another in different ways. This has to be the case since, according to the points given above, singular intensities do not divide or diminish – instead, they include one another in different ways. For example, in an actual shift from love to hate, the intensity of hate 'covers' or envelops the intensity of love. The significance of the concept of envelopment lies in avoiding the possibility of a measuring proper to intensities. It also lies in allowing us to understand that, in the relation of whole of actual things to the whole of intensities and to the whole of Ideas, there is no logic of negation in the sense where an intensity negates another. Rather, they temporarily cover one another and there is not overarching logic of envelopment.

These remarks on the connectivity of the whole must be related back to Deleuze's remarks on clarity and obscurity and on the connection of all Ideas. Ideas are multiplicities of pure varying elements. They are interconnected and form relations of clarity, where the connectivity is greatest, and of obscurity, where it is less so. These changes are in relation to but also condition changes in terms of actual things. The intensity of vertigo or love you experience out of the blue, throwing your life into turmoil as the expression of an Idea, was always there as a virtual intensity. But, in parallel to the actual sensation and change in actual relations, the intensity has been reconfigured in terms of its relation to others. Through the intermediary of an intensity, an Idea has come clearer and the others have become more obscure.

Deleuze returns to this dialectic of virtual intensities and actual sensations, and to the structure of signals and signs (sensations are signals of a reconfiguring of intensities) in a further remark on Nietzschean eternal return. Since it is intensities that return, in the sense of being reconfigured with sensation, eternal return must be the eternal return of pure differences – defined according to the three characteristics of intensity outlined above – not of the same. Eternal return and intensities are then linked to his study of thought and to his opposition of an image of thought to a thought of difference. We only think with difference when a sensation associated with an intensity sets that thought in motion, putting actual thought in touch with an Idea. Thought, for Deleuze, must be open to sensations that cannot be recognised or measured.

This is a further sense of the experimental and creative facet of Deleuzian dialectics – a part of thought is about troubling set measures, values and distinctions by opening our senses to the intensities that they presuppose and that make and unmake them: 'Along the broken chain of the tortuous ring we are violently led from the limit of sense to the limit of thought, from what can only be sensed to what can only be thought.' (DR, pp. 243, 313) So, if we accept that there is a sensation that presupposes the transcendental spatium of intensities, then Deleuze argues that we must also accept that sensation is a necessary aspect of thought, whereby thought renews itself. This realm is barred when thought is defined as pure intellectual identification and conceptualisation.

Deleuze's work on intensities allows him to begin to answer the questions of practical action raised through this book. The principles of connection and forgetting and the method of a dialectic combining critique, the search for transcendental conditions, completeness and creation are given focus by the statement that only difference, only intensities and Ideas return to give life new impetus. It can seem that the paradox of the principles and the four-fold structure of the dialectic with no dominant element leads Deleuze into a situation where either all acts or no acts are consistent with his principles and methods. But that is a mistake. Connection *and* forgetting are only possible through sensation as the expression of intensities. The creative aspect of the dialectic is only possible through the expression of intensities and, if that is disallowed in following any other part of the dialectic, then it is not Deleuzian dialectics.

However, these answers are at the price of great complications regarding the structure that Deleuze ascribes to reality. Reality is a structure of virtual Ideas, virtual intensities and actual things. How exactly does this structure function? How does it allow us to understand actions and determine values? Does this structure allow Deleuze to counter the accusations regarding the contingency of his thought and its apparent relativism (*If you do not sense movement, then the thought will not strike you as true; the movements you sense are yours and yours alone.*)?

THE INDIVIDUAL

With the concept of the individual, Deleuze brings together Ideas, intensities, actual things and his resistance to generalisation and universality, including those at the foundation of philosophical arguments. The real individual is set in motion by sensation, expresses Ideas, falls into actual identity. It is a take on the whole of Ideas, bringing some into greater clarity, throwing others into obscurity. The real individual is driven by sensations that signify a reconfiguration of intensities, a change in which intensities envelop others and which are enveloped. It is the site of creation, movement in Ideas and a reconfiguration of intensities expressed in the destruction of the identity of an actual thing and the formation of new identities.

This connection of all the main concepts of Deleuze's philosophy is made in the penultimate section of the last main chapter of *Difference and Repetition*: 'The aesthetic of intensities thus develops each of its moments in correspondence with the dialectic of Ideas: the power of intensity (depth) is grounded in the potentiality of the Idea.' (DR, pp. 245, 315) It is a mistake to think of Deleuze's principles of connecting with everything and forgetting all identities as a choice between disconnection and connection, identity and pure difference. As an individual, nothing has that choice – the individual is always an expression of the whole of Ideas. It is rather that, in denying connection and seeking identity, individuals turn away from their reality. To do so is to decrease the intensity of expression and not to escape it. Deleuze's argument and his dialectics are, therefore, a matter of reality and illusion rather than truth and falsehood. The illusions of identity and of

185

difference defined as opposition or disconnection turn identities away from their reality and, in so doing, weaken them:

> Already the illusion we encountered on the level of the aesthetic repeats that of the dialectic, and the form of the negative is the shadow projected by problems and their elements before it is the inverted image of intensive differences.
>
> (DR, pp. 244, 315)

For Deleuze, then, the individual is a series of processes that relate Ideas, intensities and actual identities. In his dialectics, it makes no sense to separate these relations or their terms, since Ideas and intensities are related to all others but in differing relations of clarity and obscurity or envelopment. Neither does it make any sense to give priority to a single process or even a subset – they are all interlinked and interdependent. The envelopment of intensities expresses changes in the clarity and obscurity of Ideas. Actual sensations emerge because they express the envelopment of intensities. An individual, then, is like the Leibnizian monad that he will study in greater depth in his *The Fold: Leibniz and the Baroque*. It is the whole world but only under a singular perspective. Unlike Leibniz, Deleuze defines this singularity through the processes that make the individual – its sensations and how they express Ideas and intensities and transform actual identities.

The processes are easy to list but much harder to understand in terms of their function and in terms of the arguments that focus them on the individual. We have already followed through his arguments for the reality of Ideas, intensities and for their relation to identities. What is lacking is the all-important argument of why the individual is the site for their relation. Why aren't intensities general phenomena? Why aren't Ideas universal? Why aren't the processes that relate Ideas, intensities and identities the same for all or the same within species or the same for all things that share the same concept?

The relation of Idea to actual identity involves a pair of related processes, from Idea to actual thing (differenciation) and from actual thing to Idea (differentiation). The necessity of reciprocal determination of Idea and actual thing means that an actual thing only acquires determinacy in terms of genesis and evolution by expressing an Idea. Conversely, an Idea only acquires the determinacy of clarity and obscurity by being actually expressed. So we must think of the two processes as irrevocably connected – hence, the notation of different/ciation used in *Difference and Repetition*. However, this treatment of Ideas in terms of determinacy must remain incomplete until Deleuze can explain why particular Ideas come to be related through particular actual things. We know that Ideas and actual things must be related but we do not know what causes that relation to take on particular forms. This, in turn, is a version of the critical question that continues to afflict *Difference and Repetition* – Given the structure described, how should we act? Until he can explain the relation between particular situations and the structure, that question cannot be answered.

The answer lies in sensation and intensity. Where there is sensation, there is an expression in the actual of a particular configuration of intensities. Where there is a particular configuration of intensities in the virtual, there is a coming into clarity and obscurity of Ideas:

> Intensity is the determinant in the process of actualisation. It is intensity which dramatises. It is intensity which is immediately expressed in the basic spatio-temporal dynamisms and determines an 'indistinct' differential relation in the Idea to incarnate itself in a distinct quality and a distinguished extensity.
>
> (DR, pp. 245, 316)

Put simply, a sensation (*this love, this rage*) is related to a given situation, to identities in the actual (*my love for this, my rage against that*). Thereby, the configuration of intensities is reconfigured (*love enveloping rage*) accompanied by the Idea where love and rage are in clarity, given greater intensity, and other elements move back into obscurity (away from the more connected centre of a nexus of varying Ideas). Sensation moves identity and reconfigures intensity. Intensity creates sensation and lights up Ideas. Ideas give sense to sensation and sensations express Ideas.

This necessary role for sensations and intensity within his whole structure explains Deleuze's perplexing concern with drama and irony in earlier parts of *Difference and Repetition* and his concern to use drama and irony in the more overtly aesthetic passages of the book. An Idea must be dramatised in particular sensations for it to be expressed in actual situations. Without such sensations, there is no creative movement in the actual – sensation is the sign that something has changed, both at the level of Ideas and at the level of actual things. But Deleuze's reflection on sensation goes much further than dramatisation. He argues that sensation is only a matter for individuals or, more precisely, individuation, the process through which individuals emerge with sensation.

He has shown that intensity cannot be reduced to measure and, hence, to identity. That is why intensity can only be a matter of sensation or of the transformation of an identity beyond its known boundaries in an event. Intensity could not be a matter of a well-defined perception for, then, it would enter the realm of the measurable and comparable. This restriction on identification also applies to the comparison of sensations between individuals. If they are to be compared and identified as the same sensations in different individuals, then they cannot express intensities since this would again allow intensities to be identified and measured. An individual is singular because it has singular sensations that express its individual take on the whole of Ideas. Individuals cannot be compared through their sensations but only related through their different dramatisations of the whole of Ideas (*It moves me to do this. How does it move you?*).

So Deleuze distinguishes the process of individuation from the process of differenciation where an Idea is expressed in actual identities. His point is that, where an Idea is expressed in a given actual situation (*Poverty is wrong.*), that expression is incomplete and cannot be seen as way of thinking through the tensions in the Idea, the Idea as problem, until it is given an intensity in the sensations of an individual (*her nausea in the face of poverty*). The Idea and an objective situation have to be articulated through the individuation of a thing for which the Idea is a problem and for which the situation is a spatio-temporal given:

Individuation is what responds to the question 'Who?', just as the Idea responds to the questions 'How much?' and 'How?'. 'Who?' is always an intensity... Individuation is the act of intensity, determining differential relations to be actualised, according to lines of differenciation, within the qualities and extensions that it creates.

(DR, pp. 246 [modified], 317)

In the process of individuation, the individual is put in touch with a reconfiguration of all intensities, with a differentiation of all Ideas and with a transformation of an actual situation. Once again, as individuals, we are connected to the whole of Ideas and to the whole of intensities. It is, therefore, wrong to associate sensation and individuation with a particular sensation as if it stands alone. It is, rather, that a sensation gives determinacy to the widest possible set of Ideas and intensities (*Love is a side of hate too and a side of*

188

the Idea of injustice and of the Idea complete fusion.). So it is a mistake to think of individuals as identifiable particulars – they cannot be separated from the wholes they connect and from the way in which they are a dramatisation of that connection.

You are not an individual and nor is this bird. The way in which you express Ideas and intensities through sensation and through thought as sensation – and the way in which Ideas tear you asunder through them – is as an individual. The way in which this bird begins to vary its song, distinguishing itself from the rest and giving rise to a new sub-species in contact with the whole world and all Ideas, is an individual. So individuals must not be thought of as members of a species. They cross species and are a condition for the emergence of species through a process that Deleuze calls indi-drama-different/ciation, thereby, bringing together all the processes that connect Ideas, intensities and actual things. Categories of actual things only emerge because individuals vary with their sensations.

This priority of individuals over species owes much to the work of the French biologist Gilbert Simondon. Deleuze reviewed his book, *L'Individu et sa genèse physico-biologique* in 1966. This work is used again in *Difference and Repetition* in two important ways. First, Deleuze draws on Simondon for the complex definition of individuals in terms of relations of virtual Ideas and intensities and their expression in actual characteristics. Second, he draws on biology when he begins to respond to critical arguments that insist that individuals must be secondary to species because we cannot know whether we are dealing with an individual until we know which species it belongs to. Again, these arguments cannot be seen to depend on empirical biology. They are prompted by them: 'a philosopher can take his inspiration from what is contemporary in science and nevertheless rejoin the great classical problems by renewing them.' (Gilles Deleuze, review of Gilbert Simondon's *L'Individu et sa genèse physico-biologique*, Pli, Volume 12 (2001), p. 49) But how exactly was Deleuze inspired to respond to the classical priority of species over individuals? Did that inspiration give rise to valid philosophical arguments? Are there mere individuals rather than individual birds and individual humans?

INDIVIDUALS AND SPECIES

The question regarding the priority of the definition of species over individuals returns us to an important arguments from

Deleuze's work on difference in itself. He has already countered the Aristotelian ontological argument for the priority of species and genres and for the definition of being as multivocal as opposed to univocal. The argument depended on what he called a nomadic distribution whereby a space was said to be defined by the individuals that distributed themselves in it, as opposed to a sedentary distribution where the individuals could only be identified by a prior definition of the space in which they have to be distributed. So, instead of the question 'Where does this go?', Deleuze advocates the priority of the questions 'What spaces does this draw up?' and 'How is space continuing to be transformed by individuals?'.

In the chapter on difference in itself, Deleuze's arguments were ontological and, in the chapter on the asymmetrical synthesis of the sensible, they become transcendental. He claims that the individual is the condition for the emergence of species. There are two arguments – the latter is the more important. Put simply, the first is that the significant aspects of species, how they are organised, presupposes individuals and their openness to change through sensations and intensity. The second is that species are only species of individuals. They are illusory and temporary restrictions of what individuals are, in order to fit them into well-defined categories. Therefore, species are not a ground for judging where individuals vary in terms of intensity and where they do not. The transformative and signifying power of individuals is present in all their aspects even as defined as members of species. In other words, we cannot respond to the significance of how species come about and change without referring to individuals and we cannot limit where individuals go through such change by appealing to limits set by species.

The treatment in terms of limits allows us to understand the stakes of Deleuze's argument and its detail better. His concern is that the scientific objections to his philosophy and the scientific legacy of explanation defined by identity returns to quash his definition of individuals. The first objection he counters is: Even though individuals are where species change, aren't the points at which individuals change defined by species? (*Birds evolve in song or beak – humans evolve in brain or limb.*). Thus, species define the limits for individuation. The answer is that the definition of parts in terms of species doubly presupposes individuals. First, judgements regarding the importance of parts for the evolution of species must be understood in terms of significance for individuals (species evolve through individuals and the importance of different parts for species depends on their importance for the evolution of individuals). Second, the importance of parts in the evolution of individuals cannot be fully accounted for by reference to the species (the definition of the importance of parts according to species is not the same as the definition of the importance of parts for individuals).

So it is a mistake to think that individuation and evolution are limited in principle in terms of species and the way in which they allow for an organisation of individuals into parts and of parts into those where evolution can and cannot happen and to what degree. Deleuze's view on the connection of all things and intensities is at stake here. If such a limitation is possible, then his argument on the univocity of being – that it is said in the same way for all things – collapses. By the end of *Difference and Repetition*, we can define how being is said in the same way: all things are individuals or incomplete parts of individuals defined as reciprocal relations between Ideas, intensities, sensations and actual identities. Any individual is an expression of all Ideas, though more or less clearly and obscurely. It is an expression of all intensities, though in different configurations of envelopment. Through the Ideas it expresses and the intensities that envelop it, an individual's actual side is connected to all other actual things.

Deleuze illustrates this point by referring to biology and to Darwinian evolution. He claims that an egg or embryo can be seen as the point at which intensities are expressed in actual parts and species. In the embryo, a sensation relates the emergence of an actual change in parts and hence species to the intensity that gives rise to it: 'We think that difference of intensity, as this is implicated in the egg, expresses first the differential relations or virtual matter to be organised.' (DR, pp. 251, 323) In other words, there is a point at which the evolution of the egg is separate from the characteristics or qualities of its species.

As such, an embryo or egg is open to transcendental 'causes', intensities, that define it as an individual undergoing sensations in the process of dramatisation. Actual parts and, hence, actual species emerge after this process of dramatisation and do not determine it. On the contrary, dramatisation in the egg allows species and parts to be determined:

191

This intensive field of individuation determines the relations that it expresses to be incarnated in spatio-temporal dynamisms (dramatisation), in species which correspond to these relations (specific differenciation), and in organic parts which correspond to the distinctive points in these relations (organic differenciation).

(DR, pp. 251, 323)

However, in no way should the example of the egg be seen as a necessary part of Deleuze's argument, either for the necessary role of individuals or against purely causal accounts of the emergence of species. If that were the case, then Deleuze would be open to refutation through changes in the scientific view. He would also be open to the accusation that he is merely a well-informed layman stumbling through a topic that he does not fully understand. As we can see from his work on intensities and Ideas, Deleuze's point is, rather, that scientific accounts of the egg, or of anything else, can only provide inspiration for thinking about intensities and Ideas and knowledge of the actual aspect of the individual.

That knowledge can be more or less open to a deduction of the virtual side of the individual, to the extent that it resists the scientific tendency to move from difference in itself to disparity. This is true even for sciences that allow for undetermined actual events that resemble intensities, such as the egg, because those events are still set within identifiable boundaries (the egg) and in terms of identifiable, if undecided, outcomes (different actual adult members of the species). Such a treatment overlooks the way in which intensities relate Ideas to actual identities.

As in the earlier discussions of mathematics, or of physics and energy, the appeal to biology must be seen as Deleuze's way of illustrating the contingent grounds for his deductions. It is not that the biology is seen as an absolutely certain ground, it is rather that it is a good way of thinking about Deleuze's sensations and their relation to intensity, and about the scope of his philosophical claims. The sensations in the egg as studied in biology, or the treatment of energy in physics, must themselves be seen as dramatisations – ways of expressing sensations rather than true representations of them.

This weakens Deleuze's argument, from the point of view of a claim that he is devising a philosophy supported by the latest science, but it defends it against two criticisms. The first is that his philosophy fails to take account of the falsifiable and falsified nature of scientific discovery (*It's only the latest paradigm not the last one.*). The second is that intensities or unpredictable variation in biology or physics are nothing like sensations in individuals. The former are well defined with respect to relative locations – to the egg or embryo or to specific unstable thresholds. But there can be no such limitations on the expression of intensities, they are not a matter of probability or special cases.

Deleuze develops his argument to take account of both criticisms. He points out that, so long as intensities and Ideas are associated with a particular space and time, such as the egg, they will be thought of in terms of general characteristics shared between species (*Every species evolves through its embryos.*). This will render intensities secondary to species in the sense where differences between species, with respect to that general characteristic, will allow us to define difference in Ideas and intensities (*This egg is capable of greater changes faster than this one. This egg carries more information that cannot change.*).

This cannot be the case, he argues, because any individual is connected to all Ideas, expressing some more clearly and obscurely in function of the way in which the intensities it expresses are configured or envelop one another. This explains the strange statement in the treatment of biology in the chapter on the ideal synthesis of difference: 'The entire world is an egg'. (DR, pp. 216, 279) Every part of the world is evolving through a openness to intensities and Ideas. But the dramatisation of that evolution depends on individuals, their sensations and what they create in order to express a change in the envelopment of intensities and in the clarity and obscurity of Ideas.

The impact of this view is summed up in the extension of the concept of the individual beyond the egg. There must be no privileged field of individuals:

> The form of the field must be necessarily and in itself filled with individual differences. This plenitude must be immediate, thoroughly precocious and not delayed in the egg, to such a degree that the principle of individuals would indeed have the formula given to it by Lucretius: no two eggs or grains of wheat are identical.
>
> (DR, pp. 252, 324)

But the statement 'all things are individuals' seems absurd. Is it not the case some things do not change at all? Or at least that, when they change, it has very little significance? Or that change only comes from some individuals and only matters through them?

Deleuze's answer to these objections lies in the necessary relation between significance and the concepts of Ideas, intensities and sensations. Significance, change and cause must be thought of in terms of the relation of the whole of Ideas to a change in intensities and to a sensation in an individual. Put simply, anything can be significant and can be thought of as an important cause, so long as it is accompanied by a sensation expressing a change in intensities and Ideas, independent of what change occurs. This claim follows from the incomparability between the Ideas an individual brings into clarity and obscurity and those that other individuals express. There is no scale of sensations, intensities or Deleuzian events.

From the point of view of a dominant set of Ideas or actual categories of species and things, a particular grain of wheat – a particular human – may seem of little significance, as if it were replaceable by any other. But, in terms of the sensations of different individuals, that particular grain may be of great significance to the expression of the whole of Ideas. There can be no limit in principle on where sensations occur – they may even occur in a grain. Neither can there by a hierarchy of sensations. To be part of a sensation and of the expression of intensity and Ideas is enough and no external measurement of value can stand as a more important determinant of significance (*It's this grain that makes this individual world.*).

So science must be thought of in relation to individuals. The sciences can help to define the actual oppositions and identities that sensations go beyond. Knowledge has an important role to play in Deleuze's dialectics, in terms of allowing us to determine the space disrupted by sensations and by helping us to unmask false sensations (*Look, there's nothing new in this.*). The sciences can also dramatise Ideas and intensities, triggering sensations and opening up the actual to new movements. Biology plays this role for Deleuze in *Difference and Repetition*, where it inspires a stronger sense of the concept of intensity and of the role of sensation in the individual. But no science can finally prove Deleuze's claims on sensations and their virtual conditions because these are not a matter for identification or even for the identification of the boundaries within which they may occur.

In a further distancing of his philosophy from a grounding in any particular science, Deleuze links the processes around each individual, the way in which they express Ideas through intensities, to his earlier definition of Ideas as problems. Each individual determines a different series of problems in terms of the Ideas it brings into clarity and obscurity. As I will show in the final section of this book, the significance of those problems and the sensations associated with them has an expressive power on other individuals and their problems but no direct causal relation. It is like the way in which a death defines different worlds and plays different roles depending on the perspective from which it is viewed. *A fighter falls – mere statistic from the point of view of a commander dealing in masses, the end of a world for a lover or a child, trigger of a new sense of injustice for a witness, cause for rejoicing for an enemy defined by hatred.* But, according to Deleuze, the death and what it expresses are really disconnected from no individual.

Yet, if we identify that death, if we identify any individual, we detach it from its intensities and Ideas. That is why any individual is only carried without destructive illusions when it becomes part of the Ideas we express through our own creations, sensations and identities (connect by forgetting identity). This explains why Deleuze ends the chapter on the asymmetrical synthesis of the sensible with two points that then become touchstones for his philosophy from then on. Everything thinks and is thought – there is no hierarchy of sensation and expression and there are no limits in principle to their occurrence. The individual thinker is charged with stones, diamonds, plants and animals: it is inescapably connected to all things actual and virtual and its life is connected to the same intensities and Ideas, but in its own singular way. (The original translation of *chargé* as 'burdened' misses the positive sense that Deleuze is giving to the term. He is moving beyond the sense of burdened to a sense where humans, plants, rocks and animals share a common charge in intensities and Ideas and, hence, a common responsibility – not in the sense of a burden but in the sense of a common destiny.)

It would be wrong, though, to assume that the importance of the individual and the impossibility of devising hierarchies and probabilities for sensations commit Deleuze to an individualism or to an extreme relativism. Sensations can occur in many individuals in the same actual states. A science can define those states. Philosophy can determine and dramatise the Ideas that those sensations express. A practical and collective Deleuzian politics can be constructed on those grounds. But it must not settle into the illusion of taking the actual science as the last arbiter of reality and possibility. Neither must it move from any particular dramatisation of a relation of clear and obscure Ideas to the thought that it is the only relation or even the most likely one. Individuals are primary and the creative destruction of emerging identities must not be subsumed under a dominant view of actual differences or of the settlement of individual sensations into general perceptions.

When we sense, through creative acts that free us from fixed identities, or, when a plant evolves with its environment, the sensations that are involved change all Ideas. When individuals open their thought to sensations and, hence, to Ideas and intensities, they connect to all things and allow a common charge to run through all of them, lighting them in different ways. That opening of thought can only take place through experimentation and through moves beyond the boundaries of what is known or deemed proper to a given faculty, since to remain within such limits is to remain with actual identities and to strengthen the illusion that thought takes place through identification as opposed to transformation.

8

Conclusion: Beyond the Self

REALITY

The dominant principles of Gilles Deleuze's philosophy are that we should seek the most complete expression of reality as possible but that this requires creation rather than discovery. For him, creative expression must also be destruction, in the sense of going beyond what we are and what we can identify through understanding. Reality is not the sum of all we know – more complete views of reality can only be expressed through acts of creative experimentation (*How rich and intense is reality if we do this?*). This is because Deleuze thinks that actual identifiable things presuppose virtual unidentifiable ones. What is more, the virtual can only be approached through experimentation because it cannot be identified as an object of knowledge.

This search for a complete view of reality, one that includes a virtual realm in a relation of reciprocal determination to an actual one, makes his philosophy particularly hard to accept from a realist standpoint. *Difference and Repetition* is a carefully argued response to the realist and common-sense belief that reality is only the actual, where everything else is but unnecessary and damaging fantasy. The philosophy responds to the restriction of reality to actual identifiable things that can be pointed to, or at least deduced according to causal laws (*We cannot point to it and we cannot even point to its effects.*).

This response depends on the deduction of conditions for actual things that aren't themselves actual, that cannot be shown. These conditions do not cause actual things, in the sense of a physical cause, they provide different angles for responding to their

197

significance and for responding to the way in which actual things evolve and can be created. Significance must be understood as a combination of thought and sensations, where thought accompanies sensation as its creative pair (*As the pigment was stirred in, the colours capturing the smell of blood and terror emerged, turning the callousness of the firing squad into an inescapable fact.*).

According to Deleuze, sensation and creation cannot be accounted for through a simple appeal to the actual. Explanations that capture the physical causes of sensation and creation, and classifications that order them according to ranks of importance or centrality, necessarily miss the real ground of the intensity of sensation and the power of creative thought. This is because there is something incomparable in each sensation and its accompanying creative thought. Each sensation alters the ways in which its intensity relates to those that accompany other sensations (*In love, her senses of touch and hearing heightened, while the visible became indistinct and unimportant.*). Each thought in relation to such a sensation brings some ideas into clarity, whilst others become distant and obscure (*Killing became impossible after witnessing the field hospital – and victory irrelevant.*).

But why does Deleuze think that the virtual realm exists? His arguments can be separated according to the four strands of his dialectics, as described through this book: critique; the search for transcendental conditions; the search for completeness; destructive creation. He attempts to show that philosophies based purely on the actual or purely on identification miss and suppress virtual pre-conditions for their own arguments. He studies actual sensations in order to deduce these transcendental conditions and he argues that a failure to account for such conditions gives an incomplete view of any actual thing.

Deleuze claims that the virtual and the actual are related to one another and entail changes in one another. So virtual conditions must be turned back on to the actual to investigate their effects on the actual and these must then be turned back on to the virtual in an endless process towards a more complete view of both. Deleuze searches for the conditions for each new transcendental condition in order to determine the virtual as fully as possible. In order to convey the sensual aspect of this relation between the virtual and the actual, he dramatises the role played by the virtual in real thought through an artistic form and through examples from aesthetics. This dramatisation is the creative and destructive aspect of his method; it is destructive due to the necessary selectiveness of the form and examples; some sensations come to the fore while others are relegated into the background.

The result of these arguments is a description of reality as a structure of relations that hold between the virtual and actual. The virtual is made up of Ideas and intensities. The actual consists of actual things or actualities. The only things that can be considered to be real are both actual and virtual, made up of relations of Ideas, intensities and actual things; these are individuals and signs, where signs prompt the evolution of individuals. The relation between Ideas is one of clarity and obscurity – that is, Ideas can be differentiated according to the different clarity and obscurity of their elements, where clarity comes from being at the centre, in the sense of greatest number of connections, of a nexus of relations and obscurity from a peripheral position. The relation between intensities is envelopment, intensities envelop or cover one another – that is, intensities can be differentiated according to the way in which some take the foreground whilst others move into the background, but without in themselves changing in intensity (*like viewing the world through a green lens, then through a red one*). Actual things cause one another to change but that causal explanation is not sufficient for understanding reality or evolution.

These relations between the same things (between Ideas, between intensities or between actual things) are not as important as the relations that hold between different things that belong to different realms. This is because the clarity or obscurity of Ideas, the relation of envelopment of intensities and the sensual significance of actual causal events must be understood as emerging out of their interrelation. Ideas become determined when they are expressed in actual things, in a sensation that accompanies an actual event, and when that sensation is accompanied by a change in the relation of envelopment of intensities. This is the process of differenciation where actual differences allow for Ideas to become determined in terms of clarity and obscurity. A virtual Idea only becomes clear when it is incarnated sensually and, hence, there is a necessary role for actual identities in Deleuze's account of reality.

The process of differentiation, on the other hand, shows how actual events go beyond actual identities when intensities and Ideas are expressed in the actual. Any actual event is significant because it is the expression of a change in the envelopment of intensities and in the clarity and obscurity of Ideas. Crucially, for Deleuze, there is no differentiation without differenciation – they are two sides of the relation of Ideas and actual things (which is, therefore, described as a reciprocal determination). But this relation must be mediated through the expression of intensities in actual sensations. He calls this mediating process dramatisation. The role of sensation in dramatisation, and its association with a singular relation of envelopment among intensities and clarity and obscurity among Ideas, focuses his philosophy on individuals. They are a singular relation of Ideas, intensities and sensations, set in motion by signs or changes in the relations through an interaction with other individuals.

Due to the turn away from realism and to this complicated structure of virtual and actual, Deleuze is open to persistent and difficult philosophical objections. Their most precise form centres on the difficulty of defining his key terms of Ideas, intensities, individuals, signs and sensation. This is because, having stated that intensities and Ideas cannot be identified or shown as actual, Deleuze is in danger of having to fall back on to a mystical and paradoxical communication of these terms (*It's there and it's not there – Ideas are felt but never shown.*). No doubt there will always be mystical interpretations of Deleuze's work but they could not be more mistaken. His deductions from sensations to virtual intensities and Ideas never appeal to mystical forces, intuitions or sources.

This explains his interest in the concept of expression. Actual things express Ideas but are not caused by them. There is nothing imprecise and unexplained in this shift from cause to expression. Rather, Deleuze wants to explain the asymmetrical relation of actual to virtual, in a series of ways. First, as opposed to cause, expression is not regular, each expression is one off and cannot be repeated or guaranteed to behave in the same way at another time. This is because any expression changes the relations of envelopment of intensities and of clarity and obscurity of Ideas, in such a way as to make each new relation of actual to virtual different from the former. So we can only have signs as to how to express anew and never knowledge. Second, expression relates radically different entities. Actual things have an identity, but virtual ones do not, they are pure variations. An actual thing must change – become something different – in order to express something. Whereas, the expressed virtual thing does not change – only its relation to other virtual things, other intensities and Ideas changes. This explains the conceptual innovations of *Difference and Repetition*. Deleuze has to introduce the concepts of multiplicities of pure differences and of envelopments of intensities in order to escape ways of thinking of change in terms of causal changes in parts that effect a whole.

He introduces these new concepts through the dramatisation of Ideas and intensities and through the critique of positions based on identity. Dramatisation depends on triggering sensations. These may or may not be sensations we share with many others or positions we think are important, but this does not imply that they are inaccessible by definition (*This does not make you laugh? You do not think that modernity begins with Descartes?*). So his philosophy has contingent rather than universal beginnings, but these are not arcane. This means that the philosophy cannot make claims to universality – it is a gamble that other individuals have similar sensations and views of the way in which the world is ordered by science and philosophy. But it is also a critique of the view that philosophy can have universal grounds.

In opposition to mystical or deliberately obscurantist philosophies, Deleuze does not argue that, since there cannot be universal grounds, there cannot be valid arguments. Quite the contrary. Once the gamble in the form of a dramatisation 'hooks' another individual (*Yes, I feel it too. Yes, the problem lies in the Cartesian method.*), he deploys a series of careful arguments designed to show the necessity of his structure of virtual and actual. These arguments have been traced through this study of *Difference and Repetition*. They include ontological arguments, developed in response to Aristotle and picking up on arguments from Scotus, Spinoza and Nietzsche. There are also arguments on conceptuality and its role in an understanding of repetition, as well as arguments in epistemology and the philosophy of science, designed to show that there is always more to an object than its identifiable properties and to show that any scientific classification is always rendered obsolete when viewed from the point of view of evolution.

Yet, the questions, 'What is an Idea?' 'What is an intensity?' and 'What is an individual?', retain some of their force despite Deleuze's many arguments for their necessity and for their well-determined form and relations. This is because they are necessary and well-determined only as relations. An Idea is a multiplicity of relations between pure variations (*The pure variation 'to become love' is becoming clearer, as 'to become hate' is falling back into obscurity because their relation to 'to become fear' has changed.*). Intensities are determined by relations of envelopment with other intensities (*The intensity associated with 'to love' envelops 'to hate' as the Idea*

201

and problem love-hate-fear is dramatised in the actual sensation of love for an outsider.). The actual description of those pure variations is, therefore, either open to the accusation that it has identified something unidentifiable (for example, in my use of 'to become love' and of the 'intensity associated with the sensation of love') or it is open to the accusation that, because there is always this risk of misattribution, the philosophy is, in fact, wilfully imprecise and hence useless or liable to generate contradictions.

When we attempt to apply the philosophy or to think about it in concrete situations or to set it the challenge of working in specific political, ethical and existential situations, the dependence on relations between things that cannot be identified can seem a great weakness. With the refusal to view identities, whether values (the good) or things (humans, animals) or concepts (freedom, truth) as fundamental to a philosophy, come great practical difficulties due to the lack of hierarchies, directions and actual differences on which to act and on which to base action. Yet, this need not be the case. In the closing sections of chapter 5 of *Difference and Repetition*, Deleuze gives three precise practical contexts to his philosophy in a reflection of the self, on death and on the relation of self to others. The work on death has already been covered here in the introduction. The thought on the self and others will be covered below.

THE SELF AND THE SUBJECT

Deleuze is concerned to separate his concept of the individual from the philosophical concepts of the self and of the subject. More precisely, he situates the self and the subject as moments in the processes associated with the individual. Two important points follow from this situation. First, neither the self nor the subject can be seen as foundations for thought since they presuppose other processes that undermine them. These primary processes allow us to explain the evolution of the self and the subject. So, for Deleuze, the subject is not free – it is the product of virtual events that it can shape but never control fully. As described in earlier chapters of this book, we can counter-actualise or vice-dict events – that is, play them in different ways – but we can never be the absolute instigators of events – virtual or actual. The assumption of an actual freedom may be an important aspect of this counter-actualisation but, from the point of view of the virtual, it is but one contingent form of the necessary reciprocal determination of the virtual and the actual. Freedom is an illusion, though a strong and alternately dangerous and productive one. As such, freedom cannot be a foundation or source of certainty. It is a fiction to be deployed with care and to be resisted where it gains too great a hold on thought.

Second, in Deleuze's complex terminology, the self and the subject emerge out of processes of differenciation and explanation. That is, they are part of the necessary identification of Ideas and explanation of intensities rather than part of the dissolution and vivification of identities in the name of creative thought. Though there are no absolute values in Deleuze, due to connection of all things (expressed best in terms of the reciprocal determination of the virtual and the actual), his philosophy allows us to distinguish things according to which processes they are associated with. In turn, this allows for different choices to be made with respect to how to act according to the mapping of a given situation in terms of those processes.

Thus, the subject belongs to a method, according to which individuals are seen as thinking but where that thinking is given a specific unique form – the 'I' or thinking subject. On the other hand, the method identifies the self with the partitioning and organisation of that thinking. Deleuze attacks this philosophical method because the combination of subject and self is defined as fully encapsulating the individual as thinker. He takes Descartes as the paradigm of such philosophies, arguing that Descartes refused to take the subject as a sub-species of a genre of thinkers – of thinking animals, for example – because this would break the identity of the thinking subject with any determinable thought. For Descartes, thought can only be the thought of a subject. For Deleuze, thought is much more than the thoughts of a subject.

He goes on to argue that, for Descartes, the self is the thinking organism. It is all the different faculties that belong to thought, such as imagination, memory, will and understanding. These must all be accessible to the subject, as summed up by Deleuze in what he defines as the fundamental formula: 'I think Myself'. His opposition to this formula takes two forms. First, it allows for no thought outside itself (*If an animal thinks, it must be as a subject and as a self.*). Second, it reduces differences, for example, the differences between faculties, to sameness – the comprehension of all faculties under a subject: 'In the end, the I appears therefore as the universal form of psychic life, and the self appears as the universal matter of that form.' (DR, pp. 257, 331) But why is this a mistaken way of thinking about psychic life?

The answer is that the subject – defined as the necessary form for thought – and the self – defined as the necessary organisation into which any thought must fit – cannot account for what makes thoughts individual. What differentiates my thoughts from yours? If there is a relation of identity between you and me as subjects (*As pure 'I', we are the same.*) and, if relations of resemblance hold between my faculties and yours (*My imagination and my will is like yours and both can be recognised as faculties by a subject.*), why do we not think the same thing? In this question we see Deleuze's fundamental assumption and challenge – we sense, rather than think, that there are different and irreconcilable thoughts. Given this difference, we deduce that there must be something beyond the self and the subject at work in thinking. What is it?

If we follow Deleuze in accepting that we sense such things (*I'll never fully understand how Euler first thought of this theorem. I'll never under fully understand how Picasso came to paint Guernica. I'll never understand why she left.*), then we have to explain why there can be radically different thoughts. That explanation cannot itself depend on arguments that allow for full comparisons between thoughts or thinkers. This is one way of thinking about the whole project of *Difference and Repetition.* The book explains how thought is individual, it defines the individual as a structure of relations holding between the virtual and the actual, it affirms that individuality and it gives principles for working with rather than against the creative power of that individuality. But the project depends on a dramatisation that attempts to trigger certain sensations – these stand as the assumptions necessary to get the project off the ground.

If we say that two radically different thoughts are different in this identifiable way (*It's because Euler was born at exactly the right time in history that he was able to be the first to formulate the theorems. It's because Picasso was trained in Barcelona and Paris. It's because you are a man and I am a woman.*), then we will have returned the difference to an identity in the thoughts that are able to reflect upon the difference. That's why Deleuze deduces the unidentifiable virtual intensities and Ideas that are the conditions for given sensations that accompany thoughts. The occurrence of an identifiable thought 'We are different.' is accompanied by a sensation or set of sensations that give the thought its power (*awe, despair, love, jealousy*). Those sensations presuppose different envelopments of intensities associated with different sensations (*Despair-intensity covers jealousy-intensity, covers love-intensity, covers awe-intensity.*). This change in the envelopment of intensities brings different Ideas into greater and lesser clarity (*To become painter fades as to become collector comes into greater clarity*).

Thinkers – that is, individuals – must be taken with their virtual side of ever-changing relations of intensities and Ideas with no fixed limits or finally identifiable components. It is wrong, therefore, to think of the individual as identifiable. Rather, the individual is a process of individuation, of actual and virtual relations that work against a necessary identification: 'Individuation is mobile, strangely supple, fortuitous and endowed with fringes and margins; all because the intensities that contribute to it communicate with each other, envelop other intensities and are in turn enveloped.' (DR, pp. 257, 331) Deleuze calls these margins the 'dark precursor' working away behind the scenes of a well-determined subject and self. Both apparent identities are fractured by their virtual side. This makes them individual, but it undermines any claims to full self-knowledge or to absolute freedom as a subject.

Deleuze is keen to stress the positive aspects of individuation above the subject and self. His main points are interesting because they stand as a defence against a series of criticisms that extend to his philosophy as a whole:

1. The stress on processes can be criticised for giving his philosophy an incomplete ground. In the context of the individual, this would imply that the unfinished and open-ended quality of individuation means that nothing can be known about it, as opposed to the certainties available to a philosophy based on the subject and the self. However, in response, Deleuze replaces the values of completion and certainty with the values of openness and indeterminacy. Completion is a damaging illusion that turns us away from deeper processes. The certainties associated with the self and with the subject are illusory and close us off from the range of sensations, intensities and Ideas. Some of these may be obscure and distant from us but, nonetheless, we are connected to them and we can bring them into play in life-affirming ways (*It's not what you are but the relation between what makes you and unmakes you – what you create and how you become.*). This relative indeterminacy and openness are only negative when the illusion of the possibility of absolute certainty is kept;

2. Deleuze's appeal to the virtual could be read as an appeal to a universal indeterminate ground, since his concept of Ideas and intensities seems to preclude precise definitions yet is

205

presupposed by all actual things. So, against his claim that the subject and the self do not allow for real differences because they are universal forms and organisations, comes the retort that his own philosophy rests on such universal forms, with the added flaw that these forms cannot be determined. His answer is that the processes associated with an individual are neither universal nor indeterminate. Ideas, intensities and their relations to actual things vary from individual to individual. But each individual, each one of 'us', can be determined according to its singular sensations, the envelopment of intensities expressed in those sensations and the relation of clarity and obscurity of Ideas lit up by that envelopment (*We all have an actual and a virtual side but these are different, singular sides for each one of us. What you can be is not what I can be.*).

For Deleuze, individuality is universal, whereas subjectivity is a damaging illusion of universality. However, individuality is only universal as a structure and not as the content of that structure. As individuals, we are the same because our difference fits into the same structure whereas, as subjects, we are the same abstract subject that only acquires a difference according to the content of the organisation of the self. According to the structure, individuality is determined as an ongoing dynamic process that relates actual ideas, events and sensations to virtual intensities and Ideas. The process is singular to each one of us. Yet, this singularity raises a criticism that has also been put to the Cartesian philosophy of the subject. How can we relate individuals, given their singularity? Is it the case that, like Cartesian subjects, individuals can only know themselves, only to have a secondary and lesser knowledge of others? If the philosophy of individuals is caught in a problem of solipsism, doesn't this raise serious problems for an ethics derived from *Difference and Repetition*? Are other individuals to be lesser ethical beings?

OTHERS

Deleuze gives a two-fold response to the criticisms that his philosophy of individuals is solipsistic and, therefore, cannot give a full ethical role to other individuals. First, he distinguishes the relation of individual to other individual from the relations of subject to subject or subject to object. Second, he claims that the other has a crucial role to play in the dynamic processes that define individuals. In other words, the structure that defines individuals is such that the other is an important aspect of the individual. More precisely, the individual is determined in relation to virtual intensities and Ideas through a relation to other individuals. This is not the case for the Cartesian subject – at least as it is defined by Deleuze.

The philosophy of the subject is criticised for having to oscillate between a definition of the other as either another subject or as an object. The problem with this oscillation is that it never settles to a relation between subjects – either you are an object, in relation to which I am a subject, or you are a subject, in relation to which I am an object. Returning to his earliest work in philosophy, Deleuze gives the example of Sartre's attempts to break with this dissymmetry. According to Deleuze, the attempt must fail because we cannot simultaneously be subject and object. This can be can be seen in Sartre's analysis of the necessity of bad faith in human relations – for instance, in his study of the oscillation between considering oneself as the passive object of a sexual advance and as the subject of a sexual seduction but never both at the same time (see *Being and Nothingness*, Section II, Chapter 2). When I am free to act, I cannot be an object (*I choose you.*). But, when the other is free to act on me, I am reduced to the rank of object (*Will you choose me?*).

In order to avoid this problem, Deleuze fits the other into two systems – the other for myself and myself for the other. Neither pole of these systems is a subject or an object, rather, they are both expressive individuals. The other expresses intensities that are hidden from me and Ideas that are obscure for me – the same is true in return. In other words, the relation of individual to other individual is not about the freedom to act and not about the restraints of being acted upon – it is about what another individual can trigger in me or allow me to express when intensities are expressed as part of its world and, therefore, potentially, as part of mine: 'In every psychic system there is a swarm of possibilities around reality, but our possibles are always Others. The Other cannot be separated from the expressivity which constitutes it.' (DR, pp. 260, 334)

However, this relation between individuals can seem puzzling given Deleuze's definition of the individual as an expression of the whole of Ideas and intensities. If each individual is a singular expression of the whole, how can they relate to one another? Each individual is a singular perspective on the whole, determined by

sensations and, hence, by intensities and Ideas. This determination is beyond comparisons since, otherwise, the intensities would
themselves be open to common measurement. So how can individuals communicate their individuality to other individuals? The
solution to this return of the problem of solipsism can be found in
Deleuze's later work on Leibniz. In chapter 1 of *The Fold: Leibniz
and the Baroque,* Deleuze explains how Leibnizian souls or monads
have no windows on to the world and how that does not mean
that souls have no relation to other souls – it only means that such
relations are indirect and result from different immersions in a
common series of folds of matter and ideas. Souls and individuals
resonate with another but cannot know each other.

In the language of *Difference and Repetition,* this means that,
because individuals are determined by expressions that imply
changes at the levels of Ideas and intensities, individuals are related through the way they perceive the changes brought about by
the sensations and acts of other individuals, albeit indirectly and
without any final clarity or certain knowledge. It is worth noting
that this reference to *The Fold* can be carried through many of the
most difficult metaphysical difficulties of *Difference and Repetition.*
The Leibniz book comes twenty years after Deleuze's masterwork
but it replays, deepens and strengthens the metaphysical structure of the earlier one better than any other of Deleuze's post-'68
works. It is as if he felt that the difficult concept of expression
from *Difference and Repetition* and *Spinoza and the Problem of
Expression* would benefit from a reworking in the context of the
concept of the baroque fold.

Deleuze gives a lot of weight to a single example of the expressive relation between individuals. This is the look of one individual
into the terrified face of another, as it gazes off into a world that
cannot be seen. This set-up is designed to emphasise a series of
important points about the relation:

1. The relation of an individual to another depends on sensations
   on both sides (the terror and my reaction to the terror);
2. The other individual does not show or reveal an actual world to
   me. Instead, it shows a different relation of sensations, intensities and Ideas (the possible world is outside the frame and only
   expressed through the other's dramatisation of that world);
3. No particular sensation or sensing organ is to be privileged with
   respect to the expression of other possibilities for me – it just
   depends on what happens to connect my sensations to those

of the other (It need not even be the face of the other. Hands, bulging veins, sobs, a pig's squeal, a dying tree could all stand at the nexus of a transfer of intense sensations and possible worlds);

4. It is a mistake to think of this relation as if it is a relation between subjects and objects because this works against the sensual power of the other's expressivity – it loses the capacity to trigger intensities and change the clarity of Ideas (It is because there is something that is not identified that sensations draw us towards intensities and Ideas).

So the relation between individuals is neither one of a shared experience of a shared world, nor is it a shared understanding, nor an empathy. Instead, it is an interference between different dynamic processes that neither pole fully grasps. The encounter with the other makes my world more strange and, hence, more intense, not more comfortable or communal or better known (*Stop trying to know me – you'll destroy everything.*).

The final pages of the last main chapter of *Difference and Repetition* point to a possible Deleuzian ethics. This ethics of the individual can be given a caricature that follows the four aspects of the Deleuzian dialectics. Criticise what you think you know of the other, to undermine the illusion of the identity of the other individual – *It is inevitable that you will identify the other but you must seek to show how that identification is illusory.* Search for the transcendental conditions for the sensations and identity of the other individual – *What do the other's sensations express? What Ideas and intensities does my knowledge of its identity hide and suppress?* This search for conditions and the undermining of identities is endless and must be extended ceaselessly – *Seek the conditions of the conditions and undermine identity wherever it returns.* There must be a creative destruction that rekindles intensity in the other individual and in the relation between individuals: *Experiment with the other's sensations through creative destruction.*

Deleuze's ethical pronouncements are more sparse than this interpretation of the ethical scope of his method and of his concept of expression according to the dialectics. At the close of the main body of *Difference and Repetition*, he repeats the following rule from earlier in the book: 'not to explicate oneself too much with the other, not to explicate the other too much'(DR, pp. 261, 335). This 'rule' must be understood as an ethical principle, or a principle for an intense life, rather than as a law. Through the qualification of the 'not too much', it requires the interpretation and individual aspect of the operation of a principle. It invites an individual to allow others to sense through it but to do so without fixing their identity or any identity.

Do not impose identity on the other. Do not impose an identity on yourself for the other. But, by expressing your singularity, by replaying the events that make and unmake you, prompt the other individual to express what sets it in motion and makes it significant. This modest principle must not be seen as a tentative sketch in the face of the profound difficulties carried by any essay at ethics, as the shadow of the twentieth century is thrown over the twenty-first. Deleuze's ethical reserve condenses an extended and complex work of critique, deduction and creation. The work sets out arguments against the dream of a foundational role for settled truths and identities in ethics. Instead, there is the practical counsel to intensify life as a relation between individuals but with the guidance of one of the most subtle and powerful philosophical creations – a structural account of reality as virtual and actual, where the repetition of intense differences escapes the choking demands of identification.

Bibliography

WORKS BY GILLES DELEUZE

Note: The excellent research source, webdeleuze.com, has a comprehensive and carefully prepared Deleuze bibliography by Timothy S. Murphy. See: http://www.webdeleuze.com/TXT/ENG/GDBIB2.htm

Empirisme et subjectivité: Essai sur la Nature humaine selon Hume (Paris: Press Universitaires de France, 1953). Trans. Boundas, C. *Empiricism and Subjectivity: An Essay on Hume's Theory of Human Nature* (New York: Columbia University Press, 1991).

Nietzsche et la philosophie (Paris: Presses universitaires de France, 1962). Trans. Tomlinson, H. *Nietzsche and Philosophy* (New York: Columbia University Press, 1983).

La Philosophie critique de Kant: Doctrine des facultés (Paris: Presses universitaires de France, 1963). Trans. Tomlinson, H. and Habberjam, B. *Kant's Critical Philosophy: The Doctrine of the Faculties* (Minneapolis: University of Minnesota Press, 1984).

Le Bergsonisme (Paris: Presses universitaires de France, 1966). Trans. Tomlinson, H. and Habberjam, B. *Bergsonism* (New York: Zone Books, 1990).

'Gilbert Simondon – *L'Individu et sa genèse physico-biologique*' (book review) in *Revue philosophique de la France et de l'étranger* CLVI:1–3 (janvier–mars 1966), pp. 115–18. Trans. Ramirez, I. 'Review of Gilbert Simondon's *L'Individu et sa genèse physico-biologique* (1966)' *Pli, The Warwick Journal of Philosophy*, Vol. 12, 2001, pp. 43–9.

Présentation de Sacher-Masoch (Paris: Éditions de Minuit, 1967). Trans. McNeil, J. *Masochism* (New York: Zone Books, 1989).

Différence et répétition (Paris: Presses Universitaires de France, 1968). Trans. Patton, P. *Difference and Repetition* (New York: Columbia University Press, 1994).

Spinoza et le problème de l'expression (Paris: Éditions de Minuit, 1968). Trans. Joughin, M. *Expressionism in Philosophy: Spinoza* (New York: Zone Books, 1990).

Logique du sens (Paris: Éditions de Minuit, 1969). Trans. Lester, M. and Stivale, C. *The Logic of Sense* (New York: Columbia University Press, 1990).

Proust et les signes (Paris: Presses universitaires de France, 1970). Trans. Howard, R. *Proust and Signs* (New York: George Braziller, 1972).

and Félix Guattari *Capitalisme et schizophrénie tome 1: l'Anti-Oedipe* (Paris: Éditions de Minuit, 1972). Trans. Hurley, R., Seem, M. and Lane, H. *Anti-Oedipus: Capitalism and Schizophrenia* (New York: Viking Press, 1977).

and Félix Guattari *Kafka: Pour une litterature mineure* (Paris: Éditions de Minuit, 1975). Trans. Polan, D. *Kafka: Toward a Minor Literature* (Minneapolis: University of Minnesota Press, 1986).

and Claire Parnet *Dialogues* (Paris: Flammarion, 1977). Trans. Tomlinson, H. and Habberjam, B. *Dialogues* (New York: Columbia University Press, 1987).

and Félix Guattari *Capitalisme et schizophrenie tome 2: Mille plateaux* (Paris: Éditions de Minuit, 1980). Trans. Massumi, B. *A Thousand Plateaus: Capitalism and Schizophrenia* (Minneapolis: University of Minnesota Press, 1987).

Spinoza: Philosophie pratique (Paris: Éditions de Minuit, 1981). Trans. Hurley, R. *Spinoza: Practical Philosophy* (San Francisco: City Lights, 1988).

Francis Bacon, Logique de la Sensation (Paris: Éditions de la Différence, 1981).

Cinéma-1: L'Image-mouvement (Paris: Éditions de Minuit, 1983). Trans. Tomlinson, H. and Habberjam, B. *Cinema 1: The Movement-Image* (Minneapolis: University of Minnesota Press, 1986).

Cinéma-2: L'Image-temps (Paris: Éditions de Minuit, 1985). Trans. Tomlinson, H. and Galeta, R. *Cinema 2: The Time-Image* (Minneapolis: University of Minnesota Press, 1989).

Foucault (Paris: Éditions de Minuit, 1986). Trans. Hand, S. *Foucault* (Minneapolis: University of Minnesota Press, 1988).

Le Pli: Leibniz et le Baroque (Paris: Éditions de Minuit, 1988). Trans. Conley, T. *The Fold: Leibniz and the Baroque* (Minneapolis: University of Minnesota Press, 1993).

Pourparlers 1972–1990 (Paris: Éditions de Minuit, 1990). Trans. Joughin, M. *Negotiations 1972–1990* (New York: Columbia University Press, 1995).

and Félix Guattari *Qu'est-ce que la philosophie?* (Paris: Éditions de Minuit, 1991). Trans. Tomlinson, H. and Burchell, G. *What is Philosophy?* (New York: Columbia University Press, 1994).

Constantin V. Boundas (ed.) *The Deleuze Reader* (New York: Columbia University Press, 1993).

Critique et clinique (Paris: Éditions de Minuit, 1993). Trans. Smith, D. and Greco, A. *Essays Critical and Clinical* (Minneapolis: University of Minnesota Press, 1997).

Gilles Deleuze (et al.) 'Gilles Deleuze' Philosophie, numero 47, 1995 (includes the important last essay by Deleuze 'L'Immanence: une vie . . . ')

SELECTED WORKS ON GILLES DELEUZE

Alliez, Eric (ed.) *Gilles Deleuze: une vie philosophique* (Paris: PUF, 1998).

Ansell Pearson, Keith (ed.) *Deleuze and Philosophy: the Difference Engineer* (London: Routledge, 1979).

Ansell Pearson, Keith *Germinal Life: The Difference and Repetition of Gilles Deleuze* (London: Routledge, 1999).

Badiou, Alain *Deleuze: La Clameur de l'Etre* (Paris: Hachette, 1997). Trans. Burchill, L. *Deleuze: the Clamour of Being* (Minneapolis: University of Minnesota Press, 2000).

Bogue, Ronald *Deleuze and Guattari* (London: Routledge, 1989).

Buchanan, Ian *Deleuzism: a Metacommentary* (Durham· Duke University Press).

Buchanan, Ian and Colebrook, Claire *Deleuze and Feminist Theory* (Edinburgh: Edinburgh University Press, 2000).

Buchanan, I. and Marks, J. *Deleuze and Literature* (Edinburgh: Edinburgh University Press, 2001).

Boundas, C. and Olkowski, D. (eds) *Deleuze and the Theatre of Philosophy* (London: Routledge, 1994).

Colebrook, Claire *Gilles Deleuze* (London: Routledge, 2002).

DeLanda, Manuel *Intensive Science and Virtual Philosophy* (London: Continuum, 2002).

Goodchild, Philip *Gilles Deleuze and the Question of Philosophy* (London: Associated University Press, 1994).

Goodchild, Philip *Deleuze and Guattari: an Introduction to the Politics of Desire* (London: Sage, 1996).

Hardt, Michael *Gilles Deleuze: an Apprenticeship in Philosophy* (London: University College London, 1993).

Holland, Eugene *Deleuze and Guattari's 'Anti-Oedipus': Introduction to Schizo-analysis* (London: Routledge, 1999).

Howie, Gillian *Deleuze and Spinoza* (Basingstoke: Palgrave, 2002).

Kennedy, Barbara *Deleuze and Cinema* (Edinburgh: Edinburgh University Press, 2001).

Marks, John *Gilles Deleuze: Vitalism and Multiplicity* (London: Pluto Press, 1998).

Massumi, Brian *A User's guide to Capitalism and Schizophrenia* (Cambridge, MA: MIT, 1992).

Patton, Paul (ed.) *Deleuze: a Critical Reader* (Oxford: Blackwell, 1996).

Patton, Paul *Deleuze and the Political* (London: Routledge, 2000).

Protevi, John *Political Physics: Deleuze, Derrida and the Body Politic* (London: Continuum, 2002).

Rajchman, John *The Deleuze Connections* (Cambridge, MA: MIT, 2000).

Zourabichvili, François *Gilles Deleuze: une philosophie de l'événement* (Paris: PUF, 1996).

OTHER WORKS CITED

For a full bibliography of the books that influenced Deleuze in writing *Différence et répétition*, see DR, pp. 334–43, 391–403.

Aristotle *Metaphysics* (New York: Penguin, 1998).

Benjamin, Walter *Selected Writing 1935–8* (Harvard: Belknap, 2002).

Bergson, Henri *Matter and Memory* (New York: Zone, 1990).

Derrida, Jacques *Writing and Difference* (Chicago, IL: University of Chicago Press, 1980).

Derrida, Jacques *Margins of Philosophy* (Chicago, IL: University of Chicago Press, 1984).

Derrida, Jacques *Of Grammatology* (Baltimore: Johns Hopkins University Press, 1998).

Duns Scotus, John *Philosophical Writings: a Selection* (Indianapolis, IN: 1989).

Freud, Sigmund *Beyond the Pleasure Principle* (London: Hogarth Press, 1971).

Goya, Francisco *The Complete Etchings and Lithographs* (New York: Prestel, 1997).

Kant, Immanuel *Prolegomena to any Future Metaphysics* (Manchester: Manchester University Press, 1953).

Kant, Immanuel *Critique of Pure Reason* (Cambridge: Cambridge University Press, 1999).

Leibniz, Gottfried W. *Philosophical Texts* (Oxford: Oxford University Press, 1998).

Lucretius *On the Nature of the Universe* (Oxford: Oxford University Press, 1999).

Nagel, Ernest *Godel's Proof* (New York: New York University Press, 2002).

Nietzsche, Friedrich *Thus Spoke Zarathustra* (Harmondsworth: Penguin, 1964).

Nietzsche, Friedrich *The Genealogy of Morality* (Cambridge: Cambridge University Press, 1994).

Proust, Marcel *In Search of Lost Time* (6 volumes) (New York: Modern Library, 1998).

Redon, Odilon *Les Estampes – The Graphic Work: Catalogue Raisonné* (San Francisco: Alan Wofsy Fine Arts, 2001).

Rotman, Joseph *Galois Theory* (New York: Springer Verlag, 1998).

Sartre, Jean-Paul *Being and Nothingness* (New York: Washington Square Press, 1993).

Simondon, Gilbert *L'Individu et sa genèse physico-biologique* (Paris: PUF, 1964).

Spinoza, Baruch *The Ethics and Other Works* (Princeton, NJ: Princeton University Press, 1994).

Spivak, Michael *Calculus* (London: W. A. Benjamin, 1967).

Index

Action *see* vice-diction
actual, 7–11, 17, 94, 131, 138, 165–7, 185–6, 197–202
affirmation, 78–9
analytic philosophy, 38–9, 64–5, 126–9
Aristotle, 22, 55, 59–63, 69–70, 75, 79, 97, 143, 190
Artaud, 123

beautiful soul, 29–30
Benjamin, 52
Bergson, 87–8, 94, 175
biology, 189, 191–4
Blanchot, 162

Carnot, 169
causality, 14, 200–2
cinema, 43, 97
clarity and obscurity, 151–2, 186–7, 191, 193–6, 199
common sense, 112, 118, 122, 171
completeness, 19, 21–3, 29, 50, 86, 157, 198
concept, 32, 39–44, 60–3, 142–3
condition, 18–20, 85, 157–9, 168, 171, 177, 198, 209
connecting and forgetting, 5, 13, 19, 105, 139, 148, 184
counter-effectuation *see* vice-diction
creative destruction, 19–20, 74–5, 98, 157
critique, 19–20, 112, 159
Curie, 169

death, 9–11, 47, 195
depth, 171–8
Derrida, 25–6, 86
Descartes, 50–1, 63, 98–9, 114–17, 119, 124, 202, 206
determinacy, 57–9, 101, 138–43
dialectics, 17–22, 85–6, 100, 113, 131–5, 139, 143, 148, 157–8, 173, 184–5
difference, 11–13, 18, 27–9, 42–3, 55–84, 138–9, 147, 169–70, 184

differenciation, 21, 186–9, 199, 203
differentiation, 21, 72–3, 143, 152, 186–9, 194, 199
disparity, 166
dramatisation, 44–6, 162, 187, 189, 191–6, 198–201, 208
Duns Scotus, 66–7

empiricism, 30
envelopment, 183–4, 186, 201, 204–5
error, 124–6
Escher, 176
eternal return, 77–9, 103–4, 184
ethics, 209–10
event, 9, 73–5, 85, 153–7, 202
experimentation, 30, 75–9, 122, 136–7, 159, 196, 197
explanation, 168–71, 202
expression, 20, 185, 191–6, 200, 207–10

faculty, 117, 122, 136–7, 160
Foucault, 3, 58
Frege, 39, 65, 126
Freud, 43, 46–9, 106–10

Gödel, 181
good sense, 112, 118, 169–71
Goya, 58–9
Guattari, 48, 76

habit, 12, 18
Hegel, 22, 26, 45, 55, 69–75, 77, 79
Heidegger, 25, 162
Hume, 86–8
humour, 20, 36–7, 43

Idea, 112, 131–5, 138–56, 160–1, 164, 183–9, 191–6, 199–202, 208
identity, 55, 60–3, 69–75, 77, 92, 204–10
illusion, 112–13, 119, 124–6, 185
individual, 5–7, 30–1, 37, 53–4, 154, 156, 161–2, 170, 172–3, 185–96, 204–10
individuation, 191, 205

215

intensities, 8, 149–50, 161–2, 166, 172–6, 178–85, 186–9, 191–6, 199–201, 208
intensity *see* intensities
irony, 36–7, 43

Joyce, 162

Kant, 18, 34–6, 41–2, 98–101, 107, 117–19, 123, 141–3, 161, 177
Kierkegaard, 37, 44–6
Klee, 175
Kripke, 40

Learning, 53–4, 60, 135–7, 160–1
Leibniz, 18, 39, 50, 55, 69–75, 77, 79, 173, 186, 208
limits, 69–75, 77, 122, 124
Locke, 75

Marx, 105
mathematics, 143–6, 178–81, 192
Meinong, 65
memory, 12, 18, 43, 88, 93–4
method, 4, 19, 49–51, 80–2, 85–6, 100, 152, 157–8
moral law, 34–7, 90
multiplicity, 145–9, 170, 183–4, 200–1

Nietzsche, 36–7, 44–6, 66, 68, 77–9, 103, 184
nihilism, 102
nomadic distribution, 65, 190

ontology, 56, 62–9, 190
other individuals, 206–10

passive synthesis *see* synthesis
Patton, 76, 163
perplication, 151–3
Plato, 39, 55, 79–83, 180
postulate, 111, 115, 118, 125–6, 129, 137
principle of reason, 17
problem, 57, 130–5, 139–40, 142, 144, 159
propositions, 64, 126–30, 133
Proust, 98
pure past, 94, 102

Quine, 65, 127

reality, 5, 11, 113, 163–4, 165–8, 185, 197–202
reciprocal determination, 11, 22, 144, 186, 202
recognition, 118–20
Redon, 58–9
repetition, 11–13, 15–16, 22–3, 27–9, 31–9, 48–54, 84–110, 138–9, 170
representation, 55, 60–2, 70–1, 78–9, 120–4, 157–8, 192
Rivière, 123
Russell, 39, 75

Sartre, 206
science, 24, 38, 50–1, 147–8, 155, 165–71, 190–6
self, 93, 202–6
sensation, 121, 123, 161–2, 177–8, 181, 186–96, 198, 204, 208
sign, 50–4, 90, 121, 136–7, 154–5, 167, 200
Simondon, 189
simulacrum, 27–9, 37
space, 65, 171–85, 190
species, 59–63, 189–96
Spinoza, 3, 18, 50–2, 63, 66–7, 84, 114, 152
structure, 80–2, 149–50, 163, 185, 204, 206
subject, 98–100, 114–17, 202–6, 207
suicide, 10–11
synthesis, 13–17, 18, 50–3, 63, 86–106, 139–40, 174–8

teaching *see* learning
time (three syntheses of), 86–106, 162, 175
tragedy, 44–6
transcendental deduction, 17, 86, 100–1, 123–4, 161–4, 171, 198, 209
truth, 2, 16, 133–5, 185

univocity, 62–9, 191

validity, 2, 16
vice-diction, 45, 85, 155–8, 202
virtual, 7–11, 17, 94, 112, 131, 138, 164–7, 185, 197–202

Wittgenstein, 39, 127